WHERE TO WA
IN ETHIOPIA

Claire Spottiswoode,
Merid Nega Gabremichael
and Julian Francis

CHRISTOPHER HELM
LONDON

Published in 2010 by Christopher Helm, an imprint of A&C Black Publishers Ltd,
36 Soho Square, London WID 3QY

www.acblack.com

Photographs by Hadoram Shirihai are contributed from the forthcoming projects: *The Birds of East Africa: A Photographic Guide* by Hadoram Shirihai, and *Birds of the World: A Photographic Handbook* by Hans Jornvall and Hadoram Shirihai (A&C Black, London).

ISBN 978-1408-1-3075-9

A CIP catalogue record for this book is available from the British Library.

This book is produced using paper that is made from wood grown in managed sustainable forests. It is natural, renewable and recyclable. The logging and manufacturing processes conform to the environmental regulations of the country of origin.

Commissioning Editor: Nigel Redman
Designed by Julie Dando, Fluke Art, Cornwall

Printed by Zrinsksi, Croatia.

10 9 8 7 6 5 4 3 2 1

Front cover, top: Ethiopian Bush-crow by Hadoram Shirihai
Front cover, bottom: Sanetti Plateau by Richard Saunders
Back cover, left to right: Abyssinian Woodpecker by Jacques Erard, Prince Ruspoli's Turaco by Jacques Erard, Northern Carmine Bee-eaters on Kori Bustard by Richard Saunders

CONTENTS

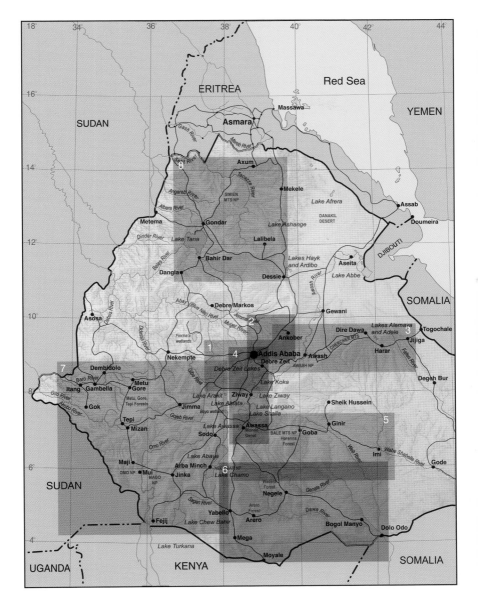

1. Addis Ababa Region
2. The North-Central Highlands
3. The Awash Region
4. The Central Rift Valley
5. The Bale Mountains and Beyond
6. The Southern Lowlands
7. The South-West
8. The North

Map of Ethiopia showing the eight regions used in the book (adapted from *Birds of Ethiopia and Eritrea*, Ash & Atkins 2009).

ACKNOWLEDGEMENTS

This book is a product of decades of Ethiopian birding and ornithology by many people from all over the world. Our first thanks are to all those who have shared their expertise and experience, from the authors of checklists, handbooks and conservation reports, to our many fellow birdwatchers and biologists. Our own journeys in Ethiopia would have been very much the poorer without them.

Callan Cohen, Nigel Collar, Tony Hickey, Steve Rooke, Cagan Sekercioglu and Mengistu Wondafrash heroically read and helpfully commented on the whole manuscript; we owe them much thanks. Additionally, we are grateful to Kristin Davis, Réné Dekker, Anssi Kullberg, Frank Lambert, John Miskell, Nigel Redman and Roger Safford for their very helpful comments on particular sections of this book, or for field-testing earlier versions. Any errors within it remain, of course, our own.

In addition, CS would like warmly to thank Michael Mills, and Duan Biggs, Callan Cohen, Nigel Collar, Abiy Dagne, Yilma Dellelegn Abebe, Paul Dolman, Lincoln Fishpool, Tasso Leventis, Gus Mills, Kiragu Mwangi, Debbie Pain, Greg Poole, Stephen Rumsey, Deirdre Vrancken and Mengistu Wondafrash (all companions on birding and research trips in Ethiopia over the years); Ethiopian Quadrants (and their many brilliant and patient drivers); and Tim Dee (who watched Lammergeiers over Gondar long before this book was thought of).

MNG wishes to thank his family (Addis, Israel, Robera and Adonay) and particularly Addis for her understanding and putting up with his frequent absences. He also thanks Tony Hickey, his first employer who has also become a good friend, and Alem Birhan Kiros for showing him much of Ethiopia.

JF would like to thank his family (Philippa, Celia, Guy and Hope) for putting up with his time away from home on birding trips. Thanks also to MNG and Alem Birhan Kiros for introducing him to Ethiopia and its fascinating birds in 1997, and to Tom Gullick and Hadoram Shirihai for inspiring him to start birding again in the 1980s and for many great trips together.

We would also like to thank the numerous contributing photographers: Nik Borrow, Callan Cohen, Greg Davies, Paul Donald, Jacques Erard, Dick Forsman, Mike Haley, Richard McManus, Michael Mills, John Miskell, Lajos Neméth, János Oláh, Richard Saunders, Andy Swash, Warwick Tarboton, and particularly Hadoram Shirihai and Tasso Leventis. The completion of this book was greatly helped by John Ash and John Atkins's marvellous new atlas of the birds of Ethiopia and Eritrea, and we are much indebted to them. We are grateful too to Nigel Redman at A & C Black for his editorial guidance, and to Julie Dando for her excellent design.

FOREWORD

Ethiopia is not like other countries. It will not take long for you to discover this for yourself. This year, the year 2010 in Gregorian calendar, is our year 2002, at least until our New Year's Day, which falls on 11 September. Christmas Day is not until 7 January. Our year has 13 months, and we time our days on a 24-hour clock that starts at 6:00 in the morning. Doubtless, we retain these seeming curiosities because we are the only country in Africa never to have been colonised. Perhaps for the same reason, we have no fewer than 82 living indigenous languages.

Probably the decisive factor that has allowed us to keep our independence and our traditions is the topography of the country. Our old name, Abyssinia, gives you an accidental clue: it is actually a corruption of Al-Habashah, the land of the Habesha people, but most people think it means 'the country of abysses', and indeed at the centre of Ethiopia are great mountains fissured with deep valleys, often with soaring cliffs. Such land is difficult to traverse and still more difficult to conquer. Our languages spring from the geographic isolation of our many tribes and cultures. Our independence has the same source.

Of course, it is also our varied topography that has produced so much biodiversity in the country and so many wonders for the ornithologist. The Horn of Africa contains 61 endemic bird species, and 39 of them occur in Ethiopia, with 15 of them *only* in Ethiopia. On the tops of the mountains, you find unique birds like the Blue-winged Goose and the Spot-breasted Plover. In the higher valleys, there are Abyssinian Longclaws and Rouget's Rails. On the lower-lying landscapes, we have wonders like the Ethiopian Bush-crow and Prince Ruspoli's Turaco. Besides, Ethiopia offers so much more: between finding all the endemics you have a multiplicity of birds to enjoy, many striking and remarkable, many representing real identification challenges.

For me, however, the greatest challenge is how to keep all these birds for future generations of birdwatchers and naturalists to experience and enjoy. Many of Ethiopia's endemic species have tiny ranges, and within these ranges, their habitats are being transformed by human activities. Our lakes and other wetlands are being put to new uses. Cattle, the prized possession of many millions of farmers, have reached every part of the country, from the montane parks to the driest regions. The threats to our birds are many; the resources to tackle them are scarce.

I am happy to think that many people will experience our ornithological riches by reading and using this invaluable book. I hope you will enjoy every minute of your time in my country. I hope, too, that you will remember us with affection, and lend us your support in our struggle to ensure that our birds stay with us forever. I am also optimistic that this book will be widely circulated within Ethiopia to prompt the interests of domestic tourists who will ultimately end up advocating for the conservation of the country's natural heritages.

Mengistu Wondafrash
Director, Ethiopian Wildlife and Natural History Society

INTRODUCTION

The Horn of Africa is an astonishing corner of the continent. There is nowhere like it on earth. The landscape is immensely varied and always dramatic. Ethiopia is much the easiest part of the Horn to visit and, ornithologically, it is also the most diverse. Birding within its rich and unique ecosystems is truly outstanding: birders on a two- to three-week visit can confidently expect to see 400–500 bird species, including up to 37 endemics and near-endemics. Ethiopia is also a relatively safe place to see many bird species that are hard to see anywhere else owing to the difficulty of access to neighbouring countries.

A still-common misconception is that Ethiopia is a ravaged and hungry land. This is mistaken. It has a spectacular range of habitats including the savannas of Awash and the dry south, the gorges and lakes of the Rift Valley, and the alpine moorland of the Bale Mountains. A fascinating endemic flora and fauna, besides birds, is found throughout the country: birding trips will be enhanced by Gelada Baboons, Ethiopian Wolves and Giant Lobelias. In recent years, Ethiopia's infrastructure has improved considerably. While some remote areas are still challenging, it is now possible to visit the country with relative comfort and efficiency.

Ethiopia is a welcoming country, and its culture has a beguiling mix of African and Arabian influences. Birding trips should make time for cultural activities: the history of the region and the Ethiopian Orthodox churches and monasteries of the north are fascinating, while the animist tribes of the south-west look intriguingly towards equatorial Africa.

It is not all good news. Economic progress and a steeply increasing human population have resulted in much habitat destruction, with consequent human suffering and the likelihood of imminent species extinctions. The conservation challenges faced by Ethiopia are daunting. A visit can and should support Ethiopian conservation, and contribute to its still incompletely-known ornithology. There are still new species to discover in Ethiopia (several are rumoured). This book will help you follow some routes and suggest others off the beaten track. There are great rewards to be had.

The dazzling Prince Ruspoli's Turaco is among the six Ethiopian endemics that are confined to the country's dry south; all are threatened. (Richard Saunders)

HABITATS AND ENDEMISM

Ethiopia is a country of extraordinarily diverse landscapes. This section aims to provide a broad overview of Ethiopia's main habitats (following no formal classification) in relation particularly to the region's endemic birds. For an excellent scholarly introduction to Ethiopia's vegetation types, as well as its climate, geology, and history of ornithological exploration, we strongly recommend the thorough opening chapters of Ash & Atkins's *The Birds of Ethiopia and Eritrea*.

From the Palearctic autumn to spring (September–April), Ethiopia's avifauna is vastly supplemented by migrants, many of them guided by the Great Rift Valley that bisects the country diagonally. Although migrants are a large and very enjoyable part of Ethiopian winter birding, the main focus of this book is on the region's endemic or range-restricted species.

Deserts and semi-deserts

Ethiopia's true deserts (e.g. the Danakil) lie in the far north and east, in areas not covered by this book; most of the desert species are shared with parts of North Africa and the Middle East. Semi-deserts, by contrast, are accessible in the Awash, Mega and Bogol Manyo regions, and are characterised by open stony or grassy plains, intersected by bushy watercourses and rocky hills. Although true endemism in Ethiopia's semi-deserts is also relatively low (represented only by **Sombre Rock Chat**), many of the species have relatively small or largely inaccessible ranges in north-eastern Africa. These include **Somali Ostrich**, **Heuglin's Bustard**, **Somali Courser**, **Black-faced Sandgrouse** and **Short-tailed Lark**. Certain more characteristically Somali desert species, such as **Little Brown Bustard** and **Somali Wheatear**, are widespread in Ethiopia's eastern Ogaden region; sadly, however, this area is prohibitively dangerous at present. Fortunately some of these birds do penetrate as far west as Bogol Manyo in Ethiopia's extreme south-east, which is more accessible.

Dry thornbush and savanna

Acacia and *Commiphora*-dominated scrub, bushy grasslands and sparse savannas exist over broad areas of Ethiopia's eastern and southern arid margins. Key sites representing this habitat are Yabello, Dawa-Wachile, Negele, Bogol Manyo and the Awash National Park. Several of Ethiopia's endemic birds occur exclusively in this habitat (in southern Ethiopia in particular), including **Liben Lark**, **White-tailed Swallow** and **Salvadori's Seedeater**. A good many more species have restricted distributions in north-eastern Africa, and are often inaccessible to birders in Somalia or far northern Kenya. A whole community of interesting species of the arid south much favour thornbush dominated by *Commiphora*, a genus of distinctively fat-stemmed and often thorny shrubs or trees with flaky bark, much referred to in this book. These include **Scaly Chatterer**, **Somali Crombec**, **Pringle's Puffback**, **Red-naped Bush-shrike** and **Northern Grosbeak-canary**. In addition, two species endemic to riparian bush

Some of Ethiopia's most accessible semi-desert habitat exists in the Awash region, only a few hours from Addis Ababa; here, the dormant volcano of Mount Fantale looms in the background. (Nik Borrow)

Commiphora bushes are a distinctive element of southern Ethiopia's dry bushlands, here in the Bogol Manyo region. (Claire Spottiswoode)

along Ethiopia and Somalia's Wabe Shebelle and Jubba (known in Ethiopia as Genale) River drainages are readily seen: these are **African White-winged Dove** and **Juba Weaver,** as well as the very restricted **Black-bellied Sunbird.** Overall, the birds of Ethiopia's dry bushlands are tremendously diverse; they are listed in detail in the Yabello section.

Woodland

Open, mixed woodlands of taller trees, dominated by thorny acacia but often mingled with broadleaved genera, are characteristic of Ethiopia's Rift Valley and associated areas. Like so many of Ethiopia's habitats, they are being rapidly decimated by human activities, particularly cultivation and charcoal-burning. Sites with good acacia woodland birding include Lake Langano, Lake Shalla, parts of the Yabello area and Awash National Park. Although acacia woodland has very high bird diversity, rather few species are endemic, and many have broader distributions particularly in East Africa. Characteristic species include **Abyssinian Ground Hornbill, Black-billed Woodhoopoe, Bearded**

Open acacia woodland near Yabello, prime habitat of the Ethiopian Bush-crow. (Claire Spottiswoode)

Woodpecker, **Buff-bellied Warbler** and **Rüppell's Starling**. Large parts of north-western, western and south-western Ethiopia are covered in broad-leaved woodland dominated by deciduous *Combretum* and *Terminalia* trees, and with fewer thorntrees. This habitat also has relatively low bird endemism, and most species have wider distributions in (especially) central and western Africa; both the habitat and the bird community are mainly represented here by Gambella and the Mago National Park, and its characteristic 'western' bird community is also quite well represented at the Gibe Gorge, Jemma Valley and Lake Tana. Typical species include **Vinaceous Dove**, **Green-backed Eremomela**, **Gambaga Flycatcher** and **Bush Petronia**.

Forest
Evergreen montane forests in Ethiopia range from relatively dry (e.g. Menagesha Forest) to drenchingly wet (e.g. Harenna Forest). Ethiopia's forests are comparatively low in species diversity relative to those in other parts of Africa, but harbour about a quarter of the country's endemic and near-endemic birds. *Hagenia abyssinica* (African redwood or kosso), often referred to in this book, is a tall Afromontane forest tree with flaky bark, compound leaves and an open canopy, and much favoured by **Abyssinian Catbird**. It often occurs alongside junipers *Juniperus procera* and yellowwood *Podocarpus (Afrocarpus) gracilior*, which together make up some of the most distinctive and dominant trees of Ethiopian highland forests above about 2,000 m. A beautiful example of all the altitudinal bands of forest types can be driven through at the Harenna Forest; other good forest sites are at Debre Libanos, Wondo Genet, Dinsho, Wadera-Kebre Mengist and Agere Maryam. Typical species include **White-cheeked Turaco, Abyssinian Woodpecker, Grey Cuckooshrike, Abyssinian Ground Thrush, Brown Woodland Warbler, Abyssinian Oriole**, and the difficult-to-see **Abyssinian Owl**. Aside from montane forests, Ethiopia's lowland and riverine forests also have an interesting bird community, albeit with reduced endemism compared to higher altitudes. Typical species include **Bruce's Green Pigeon, Red-shouldered Cuckooshrike, Double-toothed Barbet** and **Brown-throated Wattle-eye**.

Tall, dry forest at Menagesha, near Addis Ababa. (Claire Spottiswoode)

Hagenia trees growing near Dinsho in the Bale Mountains. (Claire Spottiswoode)

A typical marshy stream in the heavily-cultivated highlands around Debre Birhan, north-east of Addis Ababa. (Claire Spottiswoode)

Montane grassland and escarpments

A large proportion of Ethiopia's 80 million people makes their living in the grassy highlands, between about 1,800 and 3,000 m; so does a large proportion of Ethiopia's endemic birds. This habitat has been heavily transformed by agriculture, grazing and afforestation with exotic trees (especially eucalyptus), but productive and accessible sites are on the Sululta Plains and the Bale Mountains. Some characteristic species are **Wattled Ibis, Blue-winged Goose, Erlanger's Lark, Red-breasted Wheatear, Moorland Chat** and **Abyssinian Longclaw**. The highlands are incised by many precipitously steep gorges, where typical species (especially in the highlands north of Addis Ababa, to which a number of these species are confined) include **White-collared Pigeon, Nyanza Swift, Thick-billed** and **Fan-tailed Ravens, Rüppell's Black Chat, Abyssinian Black Wheatear, White-winged Cliff Chat** and **White-billed Starling**. Good places to see this species assemblage are (for example) Ankober, Debre Libanos and the Jemma Valley. **Northern Bald Ibis**, satellite-tagged in Syria, was rediscovered in 2006 to be wintering in this habitat, but this location is inaccessible.

High-altitude cultivations and plantations near Ankober. (Claire Spottiswoode)

Farmland, plantations and gardens

It is worth treating these as habitats in themselves, not least because large parts of the highlands have been thus transformed, and a number of Ethiopia's characteristic highland species thrive in them. These include (endemic) **Black-winged Lovebird** and **Abyssinian Slaty Flycatcher**, (endemic to Horn of Africa) **Brown-rumped Seedeater** and (widespread in eastern Africa) **Dusky Turtle Dove, Baglafecht Weaver, Tacazze Sunbird** and **Yellow-crowned Canary**. Coffee is an understorey plant indigenous to and first discovered in Ethiopia, and coffee plantations with native trees like figs can be excellent places for birdwatching, especially when the trees are in fruit.

Afro-alpine moorlands

Afro-alpine moorlands occur only at Ethiopia's highest altitudes (3,200–4,200 m) and are typically cold and windy, and often shrouded in mist. They are dominated by small shrubs, grassy tussocks and giant herbs (such as Giant Lobelias), and are intersected by marshes and permanent streams. At lower altitudes, as this habitat intergrades into forest, dense stands of giant heath (*Erica arborea* and *E. trimera*) occur. Afro-alpine moorland in Ethiopia has a high level of endemism: characteristic species (endemic and non-endemic) include **Blue-winged Goose, Lammergeier, Golden Eagle, Moorland Francolin, Spot-breasted Plover, Rouget's Rail** (at lower altitudes), **Red-billed Chough, Black-headed Siskin** and **Ankober Serin**. Some of these are confined to the highlands north of Addis Ababa (e.g. at Ankober and in the Simien Mountains), and others to the south (e.g. in the Bale Mountains); some occur throughout.

Giant lobelias in the alpine moorlands of the Sanetti Plateau in the Bale Mountains. (Lajos Németh)

Wetlands

Ethiopia's wetlands, particularly the string of lakes distributed down the Rift Valley, are of tremendous international importance, not least for migrants from both the Palearctic and the Afrotropics. Aside from those species of montane wetlands (for which please see preceding sections), most of Ethiopia's waterbird species have wide geographical distributions, although these habitats are extremely diverse in terms of species numbers. Excellent sites in Ethiopia for waterbirds include Lake Awassa, Lake Ziway, Lake Tana and the Debre Zeit lakes, and some of their more interesting species include **Eastern White Pelican, Saddle-billed Stork, Black Crowned Crane** and **Lesser Jacana**. Typical species of running streams at medium altitudes include **African Black Duck** and **Half-collared Kingfisher**.

Ethiopia's Rift Valley wetlands are critically important for migrant waterbirds; here, Palearctic Black-tailed Godwits mingle with Afrotropical White-faced Whistling Ducks. (Lajos Németh)

PLANNING A BIRDING TRIP TO ETHIOPIA

This section provides information specific to birding travel in Ethiopia, which often involves visiting remote areas. For general information on Ethiopian travel, please refer to the excellent Bradt and Lonely Planet guides (see Recommended books, maps and CDs on page 18).

Time to visit

An important advantage of visiting Ethiopia during the Palearctic winter (November to March) is that large numbers of migrants are present, including species that can be hard to see on their breeding grounds, and the majority of bird tourism in the country indeed takes place between October and January. However, winter is far from being the only time to go. Most birding sites are accessible all year round, and there are several advantages to visiting during the rainy seasons (which are complex and vary geographically): wildflowers in the Bale Mountains and elsewhere are wonderful from June to July, many birds are nesting or feeding fledged young during April to July, and species such as weavers and bishops are in breeding plumage (and remain so until at least September). Temperatures are much milder then too, which can be particularly welcome when only cold showers are available for washing. One area that may become temporarily inaccessible during the rains is the Omo valley, which is too wet to visit until the last week of June, and parts of it may remain inaccessible even later into the year.

Transport

The best way to go birding independently in Ethiopia is to hire a 4WD vehicle (typically a Toyota Landcruiser or similar) and driver. Self-drive is not an option, and in the absence of a guide, a driver is anyway essential to help with directions and interpreting. Hiring a 4WD is expensive (about US$160–180 per day at the time of writing), but the charge usually includes fuel and the driver's expenses, and other expenses (food, accommodation, etc.) will usually be relatively small. A Land Cruiser can take four passengers, five at a pinch. 2WD vehicles suitable for larger groups (e.g. Toyota Coaster minibuses) can also be hired, but many parts of (particularly) the south are not readily accessible without 4WD. Public transport is only an option for a very few of

Hiring a private four-wheel-drive and driver is much the most efficient way of seeing the best of Ethiopia.
(Claire Spottiswoode)

the sites mentioned in this book, and is not recommended unless time is not a limitation. Moreover, an English-speaking driver (and possibly an additional guide) can be invaluable companions for help with (e.g.) directions, translation, permissions and advice on accommodation.

Food and drink

Bottled water is now widely available throughout Ethiopia, even in relatively remote areas, so water purification equipment is not essential. Lager beer is also widely available and good, as is sweet, spiced tea (*shai*), and coffee (*bhuna*) often served from beautiful old Italian espresso machines. In larger towns, thick fruit juices made of pineapple, mango, papaya or avocado provide otherwise scarce vitamin C. However, they are sometimes made with tap water, so drinking them can be a gamble.

Excellent fruit juices are widely available in Ethiopia; here, avocado juice being drunk by two of the authors in Negele. (Nigel Collar)

In many remoter birding areas, away from the main tourist hotels, only traditional Ethiopian food is available. This usually consists of *injera*: an enormous, slightly sour pancake made of the indigenous and nutritious grain (*tef: Eragrostris tef*) served with *wat*, a usually meaty stew (such as *tibs* or *kitfo*). It is a useful investment to acquire a taste for injera as soon as possible! Vegetarians will eat a lot of spaghetti with tomato sauce, scrambled eggs usually cooked with onion and chilli (widely available), and traditional 'fasting' food (eaten by orthodox Christians on Wednesdays and Fridays), which can be excellent: *injera* served either with a selection of small blobs of various bean and vegetable stews or, in reduced form, simply a spicy chickpea paste (*shiro*). Most of these dishes are eaten without utensils, so a packet of antiseptic wet wipes or hand sanitiser is useful to carry. Portable food for birding during the day can be picked up at small stalls such as around bus-stops or at cafes, including excellent bread rolls, deep-fried dough balls (*kokorr*), roasted barley seeds (*kolo*), and lentil and chilli samoosas (*sambosas*).

Communications

Some internationally roaming phones do not have Ethiopian counterparts; if yours does not, or to save on extortionate roaming charges, a local SIM card for pre-paid calls can be bought in Addis Ababa 'telecentres' (but note that you will need to register it with your passport), and recharge vouchers are widely available. Most towns now have mobile phone coverage through ETC, and it

Hotel accommodation in remoter parts of Ethiopia can be rustic. (Claire Spottiswoode)

is possible to make calls from even the remotest parts of the country. Internet is now relatively widespread, and reasonably easily accessible (although slow) in larger towns such as Shashemene and Negele.

Suggested equipment

A telescope is strongly recommended for birding in Ethiopia, given that most habitats are open so using a scope is easy and helpful. A GPS (global positioning system) or compass can be useful for finding your way back to the vehicle after birding walks into the bush; GPS coordinates are provided for most of the birding sites in this book (see p.20). Ethiopia uses European (two-prong round) plugs and a 220 volt power supply. Electricity supplies are erratic so an LED head torch and spare batteries are essential. Alkaline batteries are not widely available, so bring an adequate supply; if using rechargeables, some spares could be useful in case of power failures.

If planning to stay in cheap hotels in remoter areas, a sleeping bag liner can reduce insect attack, as can pitching a dome tent (without the flysheet) on top of the bed. Plastic flip-flops, a towel, pliers for missing tap heads, and an extra toilet roll or two are also all useful in such places. It is not essential to camp in most of Ethiopia, since even in small and remote towns some sort of basic accommodation is usually available. However, camping (when it is safe to do so) can be much more pleasant and hygienic, and put you on the spot for an early morning start. Some vehicle hire companies can also provide tents and camping equipment; remember that the highlands are cold at night for much of the year.

Medicines and medical advice are not necessarily easily available outside of Addis Ababa (see travel guides for general medical information). Useful basic medical provisions to bring with you when travelling in remoter parts of the country might include oral rehydration solution (ORS) powder and a broad-spectrum antibiotic (particularly Ciprofloxacin) in case of severe diarrhoea. Bring your own sunscreen, anti-malarial pills, and insect repellent (for ticks as well as mosquitoes). Anti-histamine tablets or cream are useful against itchy insect bites.

Also be aware that drawing cash or using credit cards is unlikely to be possible outside of Addis Ababa, so take enough cash. Ethiopian birr is usually the best currency to carry as foreign exchange is little used in practice, although Euros and US Dollars can usually be exchanged in larger towns.

Safety and security

Much of Ethiopia can be visited in safety. Travel guides such as the excellent Bradt guide to Ethiopia provide much useful information on this subject, as well as comprehensive health advice. However, birders tend to consider it normal to visit more perilous places than most tourists. The security situation at many of the sites mentioned in this book is in constant flux, and we highly recommend making enquiries with your travel/vehicle hire company and their drivers and guides. Note that some general-interest tour companies in Ethiopia may try to discourage you from relatively safe destinations regularly visited by bird tour companies; ideally, arrange a vehicle and driver from a company accustomed to dealing with birders. They will be best placed to advise you on the current safety of your proposed itinerary, and should also be able to assist in arranging any necessary permits, since a number of the sites in this book require permission from local authorities (typically police) to visit.

Camping under riparian fig trees in the Awash National Park. (Claire Spottiswoode)

Sites in the Ogaden and surrounding areas close to the Somali border (e.g. Dolo Odo) can be dangerous, and it is absolutely necessary to enquire about the security situation in advance, be accompanied by a knowledgeable Ethiopian translator and guide, and (if it is possible to visit at all) check in with local authorities every step of the way. Note that it is not permitted to photograph bridges, dams, army posts, police stations or any other government infrastructure anywhere in Ethiopia. It is also a good idea to avoid photographing livestock, especially camels, as this may offend their owners.

All national parks now require that you are accompanied by a game scout, but this can always be arranged on the spot so no advance planning is required. At many sites other than national parks, visitors are increasingly expected to take a local guide for a small fee, which is an important job creation measure in places where local people often do not see many benefits from tourism. These guides can be extremely sharp-eyed, and are sometimes very knowledgeable about birds.

A driver or guide can be very helpful in requesting permission from local people, here Borana pastoralists on the Liben Plain. (Claire Spottiswoode)

Suggested itineraries

The following suggested itineraries are only intended to provide a starting point around which to plan a trip, and focus on the Horn of Africa endemics. Asterisks (*) indicate legs that ideally require a 4WD vehicle (all can be avoided by taking longer routes). Please be aware that these are intensive itineraries requiring non-stop travel on often rough roads, and may be gruelling for casual birders and non-birders! After the itineraries is a list of possible day trips that might suit those finding themselves in Addis Ababa for a short stopover or business visit.

Two weeks
Day 1 Addis Ababa to Wondo Genet via Rift Valley lakes
Day 2 Wondo Genet to Dinsho (Bale Mountains)
Day 3 Dinsho to Goba (Bale Mountains)
Day 4 *Goba to Negele via the Sanetti Plateau
Day 5 *Negele to Yabello via Melka Ghuba
Day 6 Yabello–Mega region
Day 7 Yabello to Lake Langano
Day 8 Lake Langano to Addis Ababa
Day 9 Addis Ababa to Jemma Valley via Debre Libanos
Day 10 Jemma Valley to Ankober
Day 11 *Ankober to Awash National Park
Day 12 Awash National Park
Day 13 Awash National Park to Bilen Lodge
Day 14 Bilen Lodge to Addis Ababa

Three weeks
Day 1 Addis Ababa to Wondo Genet via Rift Valley lakes
Day 2 Wondo Genet to Goba via Dinsho
Day 3 *Goba to the Harenna Forest via the Sanetti Plateau
Day 4 Harenna Forest to Negele
Day 5 Negele to Boyol Manyo
Day 6 Bogol Manyo area
Day 7 Bogol Manyo to Negele

Day 8 *Negele to Yabello via Melka Ghuba
Day 9 Yabello–Mega region
Day 10 Yabello–Mega region
Day 11 Yabello to Lake Langano
Day 12 Lake Langano to Addis Ababa
Day 13 Addis Ababa to Jemma Valley via Debre Libanos
Day 14 Jemma Valley to Debre Birhan
Day 15 Debre Birhan to Ankober
Day 16 *Ankober to Awash
Day 17 Bilen Lodge
Day 18 Awash National Park
Day 19 Awash to Addis via Debre Zeit

Possible day trips out of Addis Ababa
Menagesha Forest via the Meta Brewery
Gibe Gorge
Debre Libanos via the Sululta Plains
Muger Gorge via the Sululta Plains
Gefersa Reservoir
Debre Zeit lakes

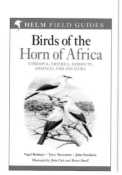

Recommended books, maps and CDs

This is not a comprehensive bibliography (for which please consult Ash & Atkins's excellent bibliography in *The Birds of Ethiopia and Eritrea*), but a list of suggested books to take with you to Ethiopia (or consult beforehand).

Key field guides

Kingdon, J. 2003. **The Kingdon Field Guide to African Mammals**. London: Christopher Helm. *Comprehensive field guide to all of Africa's mammals. Also available in a pocket guide version with only cursory treatment of more obscure groups such as bats and rodents.*

Puff, C. & Nemomissa, S. 2005. **Plants of the Simen**. Meise: National Botanic Garden of Belgium. *The only accessible field guide to Ethiopia's plants; many species are widespread throughout Ethiopia's highland regions.*

Redman, N., Stevenson, T. & Fanshawe, J. 2009. **Birds of the Horn of Africa.** London: Christopher Helm. *The only field guide to focus on the Horn of Africa and by far the best bird book to take to Ethiopia. Contains good text and illustrations with accurate maps.*

Sinclair, I. & Ryan, P. 2003. **Birds of Africa south of the Sahara**. Cape Town: Struik. *Covers all of Africa's birds, including Ethiopia, with generally good text and illustrations, but bulky.*

Spawls, S, Howell, K. & Drewes, R.C. 2006. **Pocket Guide to the Reptiles and Amphibians of East Africa.** London: Christopher Helm. *The closest field guide to Ethiopia's herps; many species are shared with Kenya but the Ethiopian coverage is of course far from complete. Also available in a comprehensive version excluding amphibians (2004). A guide to the amphibians and reptiles of Ethiopia and Eritrea by Largen and Spawls is in preparation.*

Ornithological references

Ash, J. & Atkins, J. 2009. *The Birds of Ethiopia and Eritrea*. London: Christopher Helm. *A complete atlas with maps, breeding data, comprehensive bibliography and scholarly general introduction the biology of the region; excellent.*

EWNHS. 2001. Ethiopia. In: *Important Bird Areas in Africa and Associated Islands: Priority Sites for Conservation* (eds L.D.C. Fishpool & M.I. Evans). Newbury & Cambridge, U.K.: Pisces Publications & BirdLife International. *Concise information on threatened species and conservation in Ethiopia's 69 designated Important Bird Areas.*

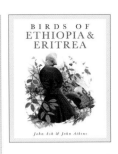

Maps, CDs and travel guides

Probably the best widely available map of Ethiopia is the 'Reise Know How' map for Ethiopia, Eritrea, Somali and Djibouti (Fernwald, Germany). The ITMB (International Travel Maps and Books, Vancouver, Canada) map is also reasonable.

At present there is no CD of Ethiopian bird sounds available, although MNG is currently preparing one. An increasing number of species are freely available from the Xeno-canto website (http://www.xeno-canto.org/africa). If you make any recordings on your trip, please consider depositing them with Xeno-canto.

We highly recommend carrying a general travel guide with you to Ethiopia. The Lonely Planet guide is good but we prefer: Briggs, P. 2009. *Ethiopia*. 5th Edition. London: Bradt Guides.

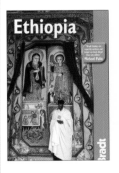

Useful contacts

For international calls, omit the leading 0 and insert the +251 country code.

Ankober Palace Lodge, Ankober 0112 23 00 12
Awash Falls (Fuafuate) Lodge, Awash National Park 0221 19 11 82/3
Bekele Molla Hotel, Lake Langano 0461 49 12 50/1
Bilen Lodge, Awash – book via Village Ethiopia
Bishangari Lodge, Lake Langano 0461 19 12 76/7
Ethio-German Park Hotel, Debre Libanos 0116 56 32 13
Ethiopian Quadrants (recommended for vehicle hire) 0115 15 79 90 /54 46 36
Ethiopian Wildlife and Natural History Society 0116 63 67 92
Genet Hotel, Awash 0222 24 00 08
Ghion Hotel, Addis Ababa 0115 51 32 22
Green Hotel, Negele 0464 45 03 74
Kuriftu Resort and Spa, Lake Tana 0582 26 48 48
Midroc Hotel, Awassa 0462 20 53 97
Nile Hotel, Negele 0464 45 15 82
Tana Hotel, Bahir Dar 0582 20 05 54
Wabe Shabelle Hotel, Goba 0226 61 00 41
Wabe Shabelle Hotel, Lake Langano 0981 19 01 31
Wabe Shabelle Hotel, Wondo Genet 0461 19 07 05
Wenney Lodge, Lake Langano 0911 40 59 66
United Africa Hotel, Awassa 0462 20 00 04
Village Ethiopia 0115 50 88 69
Yabello Motel, Yabello 0464 46 07 85

Useful updates on accommodation options are available on the Bradt guide's website, http://bradtethiopiaupdate.wordpress.com/.

STRUCTURE OF THIS BOOK

Aims and scope

The sites in this book only scratch the surface of the diversity that Ethiopia has to offer. In this book we have taken a pragmatic approach of largely concentrating on sites that are practical to visit in a relatively short visit to the country, and cover the majority of the region's most sought-after species. We have also added additional sites close to Addis Ababa that might be more feasible for anyone based in the capital, and some intruiging farther-flung sites for those with the time and stamina. Even so, we have been obliged to ignore much of the fascinating (but largely vast and inaccessible) mountainous north and forested south-west, and by necessity the prohibitively dangerous far eastern Ogaden region. BirdLife International's Important Bird Area directory (freely available on the internet at www.birdlife.org/datazone/ sites) provides an excellent overview of these tantalising areas.

Taxonomy and nomenclature

We follow the English names and taxonomy used in Redman *et al.*'s *Birds of the Horn of Africa*, with two exceptions: the English names Liben Lark and Ethiopian Bush-crow instead of Sidamo Lark and Stresemann's Bush-crow, which are preferred in the interests of their conservation. For mammals we follow the English names and taxonomy used in *The Kingdon Field Guide to African Mammals*. We occasionally highlight very distinctive bird subspecies by giving them distinct common names in inverted commas (e.g. 'Archer's' Francolin), and list their trinomial scientific names in the checklist at the end of the book (Appendix C). Trinomial scientific names are also given in Appendix B for distinctive mammal subspecies with well-established common names.

GPS coordinates

Although we have aimed to provide directions that are independent of having access to a GPS unit, we provide GPS coordinates for many locations where they might be most useful, and to help with pre-trip preparations on Google Earth. These coordinates were mainly recorded by the authors in the field, but some were extracted from satellite images provided by Google Earth. Note that these may be prone to an error margin of about 200 metres. Numbered coordinates in the text refer to the list in Appendix A (p.163). This list is available in electronic format suitable for uploading to a Garmin GPS unit by email from CS at spottiswoode@cantab.net.

Maps and place names

The maps in this book were produced from a combination of GPS coordinates and tracks made in the field by the authors, satellite imagery (Google Earth), topographical maps designed for aeronautical use (Defense Mapping Agency, St Louis, Missouri), and occasionally national park maps. They were made to be as accurate as possible, but the authors cannot take responsibility for any errors or subsequent changes. Tarred roads are indicated in orange, and unsurfaced roads in grey.

Note that spellings of Ethiopian place names are notoriously variable, and you may encounter variations of those we use in this book. In particular, the Oromo language (widely spoken in the southern half of Ethiopia and using a Latin alphabet) commonly repeats several letters within a word. Note too that towns rarely have signboards, and roadsigns in general are scarce.

TOP
FIFTY SITES

ADDIS ABABA REGION

1. Addis Ababa City
2. Entoto Natural Park
3. Gefersa Reservoir
4. Menagesha Forest
5. Meta Brewery
6. Muger Gorge
7. Gibe Gorge
8. Sululta Plains and surrounds

TOP 10 BIRDS

Blue-winged Goose
Rouget's Rail
Yellow-fronted Parrot
White-cheeked Turaco
Abyssinian Woodpecker
Abyssinian Longclaw
White-backed Black Tit
White-winged Cliff Chat
Abyssinian Slaty Flycatcher
White-throated Seedeater

Nearly all visitors enter Ethiopia via Addis Ababa, the third highest-altitude capital in the world. Addis is an enormous, sprawling and confusing city, but birders confined there on business need not despair: numerous endemics can easily be seen right within the city centre, and many excellent sites can be reached in day or half-day trips. Entoto Natural Park and especially Menagesha Forest both offer a good number of Ethiopia's forest endemics (notably the sometimes awkard-to-find **Yellow-fronted Parrot**) and the Muger Gorge is beautiful and provides several of the northern highland specials. Within a couple of hours from Addis, the Gibe Gorge offers birding with a distinctly more western Ethiopian feel, and offers amongst others access to one of the country's trickier endemics (**White-throated Seedeater**) as well as a star African bird (**Egyptian Plover**).

1. ADDIS ABABA CITY

Birding is surprisingly good within the vast and chaotic sprawl of Addis Ababa, and numerous endemics can be seen right in the city centre. **White-backed** and especially **Hooded Vultures** are, as in most Ethiopian towns, always in evidence overhead, and groups of **Wattled Ibis, Thick-billed Ravens** and **White-collared Pigeons** wing over the city centre. Many birders stay at the reasonably-priced Ghion Hotel (1 on map; GPS001), largely owing to its extensive gardens which are the best for birding of any of Addis's hotels. Several large Mountain Acacias *Acacia abyssinica* right in front of the main hotel entrance sometimes conceal a quietly foraging **Brown Parisoma**. Ghion Park, within the hotel grounds to the right of the main entrance (facing the hotel), is also worth a saunter and has some further Mountain Acacia trees. Endemic **Black-winged Lovebird, White-backed Black Tit** (not commonly) and **Abyssinian Slaty Flycatcher** all occur here, as well as many common highland species such as **Dusky Turtle Dove, Speckled Mousebird, Blue-**

Thick-billed Raven, one of Ethiopia's most outrageously distinctive endemics, is typically common around towns and cities. (Tasso Leventis)

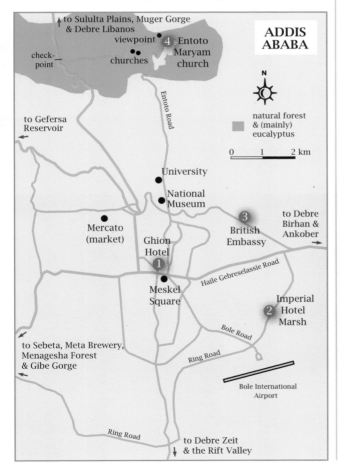

to Sululta Plains, Muger Gorge
& Debre Libanos
viewpoint **4** Entoto
Maryam
checkpoint · · churches · church

**ADDIS
ABABA**

N

to Gefersa
Reservoir

Entoto Road

natural forest
& (mainly)
eucalyptus

0   1   2 km

University

National
Museum

Mercato
(market)

3
British
Embassy

to Debre
Birhan &
Ankober

Ghion
Hotel
1

Haile Gebreselassie Road

Meskel
Square

Imperial
2 Hotel
Marsh

Bole Road

to Sebeta, Meta Brewery,
Menagesha Forest
& Gibe Gorge

Ring Road

Bole International
Airport

Ring Road

to Debre Zeit
& the Rift Valley

Brown Parisoma can be seen even in central Addis Ababa. (Dick Forsman)

Exciting endemics such as Rouget's Rail and Abyssinian Longclaw still hold out in central Addis Ababa, here at the Imperial Hotel marsh. (Claire Spottiswoode)

breasted Bee-eater, Red-rumped Swallow (which even breeds on the Bole International Airport buildings), **Mountain Thrush**, **Rüppell's Robin-chat**, **African Dusky Flycatcher**, **Montane White-eye**, **Tacazze Sunbird**, **Baglafecht Weaver**, and **Brown-rumped** and **Streaky Seedeaters**.

Small wetlands within the city can be surprisingly productive, although they are currently besieged by new construction projects. Perhaps the best of them is the marsh along a stream crossing the Ring Road near the Imperial Hotel (2 on map), in a kind of urban greenbelt south-east of the city centre, and a little north-east of its intersection with Bole Road (the airport road). Major construction is now underway here, so this site may soon become further degraded. In spite of disturbance and pollution, at the time of writing this was a good place for **Rouget's Rail**, **Abyssinian Longclaw** and other grass-

Rouget's Rail is an astonishingly confiding endemic rallid. (Tasso Leventis)

land birds. Approach the marsh from the north (i.e. from the Ring Road's intersection with Haile Gebreselassie Road – or you will be stuck on the wrong side of a dual carriageway), and pull off to the right on the small track at the greenbelt's southern extremity (GPS002). Immediately in front of this track is the marsh's only perennially flooded section, where even during the dry season **Rouget's Rail** may be found. Other interesting species in the moist grassland here include **Ethiopian Cisticola, Abyssinian Longclaw** and **Red-breasted Wheatear**, and **Erlanger's Lark** along the dry margins. **Thick-billed Raven** is commonly seen here.

Some of the best birding in Addis is in the well-wooded grounds of the British Embassy (3 on map) on the north-eastern side of the city centre, which are especially good for **Abyssinian Woodpecker** and **Abyssinian Catbird**; however, access is very difficult, but can be arranged through certain tour companies.

Silvery-cheeked Hornbill is loudly conspicuous in most of Ethiopia's forests. (Tasso Leventis)

2. ENTOTO NATURAL PARK

On the northern outskirts of Addis Ababa city, a small remnant patch of natural juniper forest (with scattered *Hagenia* and olive trees) exists in the otherwise largely eucalyptus-smothered Entoto Hills. The park can be entered from the main road leaving Addis to the north (towards e.g. the Sululta Plains, and ultimately Lake Tana). The park is signposted on the right (GPS003), just before the police checkpoint at the top of a hill. From this turn-off, follow a straight road uphill through a eucalyptus plantation for about 3 km to the remaining forest patches around the churches and viewpoint (4 on Addis Ababa map; GPS004) at the summit of the hill. Forest and woodland species that may be found here include **Black-winged Lovebird, White-cheeked Turaco, Banded Barbet, Abyssinian Woodpecker** (especially at the forest edge), **Abyssinian Oriole, Abyssinian Catbird, White-backed Black Tit, Abyssinian Ground Thrush** and, uncommonly, **Yellow-fronted Parrot. White-winged Cliff Chat** occurs at the forest edge and at roadsides (e.g. around the turn-off). Raptors here include **Lammergeier, Mountain Buzzard** and **Rufous-breasted** and **Great Sparrowhawks**. The park can alternatively be entered via the Entoto Maryam church, at the end of Entoto Road north of the city centre. The entrance lies just beyond the church.

Rüppell's Robin-chat, a shy but common species of thicker vegetation in much of Ethiopia. (Tasso Leventis)

3. GEFERSA RESERVOIR

Gefersa is a reservoir surrounded by eucalyptus plantation and grassland, 18 km west of Addis on the southern side of the road to Ambo and Nekemte. Access to the reservoir itself is not possible, but a good view can be obtained through the fence at its grassy western edge. Approaching from Addis on the Ambo road, drive past the reservoir entrance and, about 2 km further on, park next to the road at the far end of the reservoir (GPS005); avoid the temptation to stop sooner, where an inlet nears the road, as you will almost certainly be hurried on by an armed guard. Walk down a short slope for about 300 m. From here you can peer at the reservoir through the fence (ideally with a scope), and also birdwatch in short grassland around a stream. The dam itself is good for Palearctic waterfowl (Nov–Mar) such as **Garganey**, **Pintail**, **Tufted Duck** and **Northern Shoveler**, and year-round for resident species such as **Southern Pochard** and **African Black**, **Red-billed** and **Yellow-billed Ducks**. **Blue-winged Goose** used invariably to be seen here, but numbers appear to have declined steeply in recent years owing to hunting, and this is sadly no longer a reliable site. The grassland around the fence is good for **Wattled Ibis**, **Rouget's Rail** (less dependably than at the Imperial Hotel marsh, see p.24), **Grey-rumped Swallow**, **Red-breasted Wheatear**, **Abyssinian Longclaw** and **Black-headed Siskin** (also in the eucalyptus trees, where **Abyssinian Slaty Flycatcher** also occurs). During the dry season (Nov–Mar), small flocks of **Ortolan Bunting** occur in the short grass, and **African Snipe** visits the stream. Year-round, **African Hobby** can frequently be seen hunting over the grassland.

4. MENAGESHA FOREST

Menagesha Forest (also known as Menagesha-Suba Forest) allows access to a good diversity of forest species on an easy half-day trip from Addis Ababa. Nearly three thousand hectares of juniper forest lie amongst plantations on the eastern slopes of 3,385 m Mount Wechecha, an extinct volcano. The Emperor Zera Yacob (1434–1468), noticing the degradation of the forest around Mount Wechecha, initiated what was the first reforestation and conservation measure in Africa by having juniper trees planted here.

Key birds African Crowned Eagle, Yellow-fronted Parrot, White-cheeked Turaco, Abyssinian Ground Thrush, Abyssinian Catbird, Banded Barbet, Sharpe's Starling.

Key habitats Dry evergreen forest, dominated by juniper trees; altitude about 2,600 m.

Access The forest is about one hour's drive from Addis Ababa. Take the main road to Jimma, and just past the village of Sebeta (opposite the 27 km post), turn right. Keeping straight ahead here will take you to the Meta Brewery (see next site); to reach Menagesha, turn left 100 m past the turn-off (at the decaying signpost indicating 'Menagesha Suba National Park 16 km') and continue along this gravel road (which may be muddy and require 4WD after heavy rain) through 14.5 km of farmland and grassland, to Suba village. Turn

Tall juniper woods in Menagesha Forest are inhabited by Abyssinian Catbird, amongst several other endemics.
(Claire Spottiswoode)

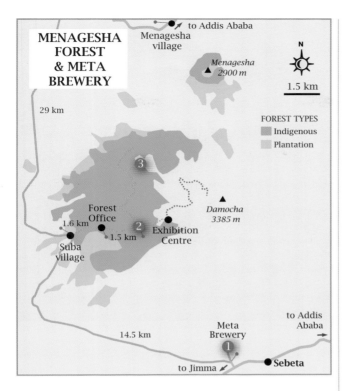

right here, along a track leading through 1.6 km of largely alien plantation before reaching the Forest Office (GPS006), where you need to pay a small entrance fee and can obtain a map of walking trails. It is also possible to approach the forest from the north, via Menagesha village (see map), but this road is slightly less reliable because it is prone to flooding after heavy rain.

Birding From the Forest Office, continue (by car, or easily enough on foot)

White-cheeked Turaco is much the more widespread of Ethiopia's two beautiful endemic turacos. (Nik Borrow)

Abyssinian Catbird, a characterful endemic babbler of Ethiopia's highland forests. (Nik Borrow)

uphill to a picnic site (2 on map) beneath a stand of tall, mature juniper trees. This is a good spot to park, bird and walk (try the track continuing uphill towards the waterfall, 3 on map). The juniper trees here are an excellent site for **Yellow-fronted Parrot** (especially in the late afternoon when they gather before roosting), **Abyssinian Catbird** and **White-backed Black Tit**. Also listen carefully for the repetitive song of **Abyssinian Ground Thrush**, usually given from high in the canopy in the morning and evening, and look out for a scarce **Abyssinian Woodpecker** around forest clearings such as at the picnic site (2 on map). As you drive or walk, look out for **Abyssinian Crimsonwing** feeding at the road edges. Other common forest and forest-edge species here include **White-cheeked Turaco, African Olive Pigeon, Narina Trogon, Banded Barbet, Abyssinian Oriole, Rüppell's Robin-chat, African Hill Babbler, Brown Woodland Warbler, Abyssinian Slaty Flycatcher** and **Montane White-eye**. Listen out for flocks of **Sharpe's Starlings** high in the canopy, and for the cries of **African Crowned Eagle** (which breeds here) and **Mountain Buzzard** overhead.

Other animals Guereza Colobus is common here, and antelope include Menelik's Bushbuck and Bush Duiker. Common Warthog and Yellow-spotted Hyrax may be seen in the forest, and Leopard is frequently heard at night by those camping at the picnic site.

5. META BREWERY

The Meta Brewery (GPS007), about 30 km south-west of Addis Ababa, has a 'Recreation Centre' (commonly called Meta Abo) containing a remnant patch of acacias. It is a particularly good site for the often tricky-to-find **Abyssinian Woodpecker** and **Spotted Creeper**. The site is open on Saturdays and Sundays

Abyssinian Woodpecker is a widespread but inconspicuous and sometimes hard-to-find endemic of open montane woods and forest edge. (Jacques Erard)

only, and an early start is recommended to avoid the crowds that accumulate from about 10 a.m. (on weekdays, when it is quieter, special written permission needs to be obtained from the Meta headquarters in Addis Ababa). For directions, please see previous site. Driving into the brewery, go past the factory (on your right) until the end of the road where there is a parking area and kiosk. Numerous paths wind through tall acacias on the surrounding hills. Look for **Abyssinian Woodpecker** and **Spotted Creeper** especially in the taller trees directly in front of the kiosk, on your left-hand side as you enter. Other interesting species in this area are **Black-winged Lovebird**, **Banded Barbet**, **White-winged Cliff Chat** and **White-backed Black Tit**. **Erckel's Francolin** is also found in the area, but largely in the surrounding outer grassy hills, away from the acacias and human activity.

6. MUGER GORGE

The Muger Gorge, with a slender but impressive waterfall near the village of Derba, is a good site close to Addis Ababa for species of rocky cliffs and gorges. To reach it, take the Sululta Plains/Lake Tana road north from Addis for 42 km, then at the southern outskirts of the village of Chancho (GPS008), turn west onto on a gravel road for 29 km to the village of Derba. Just past the village, take a small track to the right just before a cement factory (GPS009), and follow this for less than a kilometre to the edge of the gorge, from where the Muger Falls are visible. This provides a good vantage point to scan for such species as **Lammergeier**, **Verreaux's Eagle**, **Lanner** and **Peregrine Falcons**, **African Hobby** (occasionally) and **Nyanza Swift**. **Rüppell's Black Chat**, **White-winged Cliff Chat** and **White-billed Starling** are common along

Abyssinian Black Wheatear, a characteristic species of rocky hill slopes and escarpments. (Nik Borrow)

A female White-billed Starling, one of the several Ethiopian highland endemics occurring only north of Addis Ababa. (Jacques Erard)

the cliff edge. Scan the grassy slopes below the vantage point for **Erckel's Francolin**, which perches conspicuously on rocks when calling in the mornings and evenings; when it is not calling, scanning the grassy areas might reveal foraging birds. Troops of Geladas are resident here and are reasonably approachable.

7. GIBE GORGE

The beautiful Gibe Gorge can be visited in a day trip from Addis Ababa (provided an early start is made) along the main road to Jimma, and holds a number of species more characteristic of Ethiopia's western lowlands.
Key birds Egyptian Plover, Yellow-throated and Four-banded Sandgrouse, Clapperton's Francolin, Snowy-headed Robin-chat, Foxy Cisticola, Exclamatory

Paradise Whydah, Red-billed Pytilia, Bar-breasted Firefinch, White-throated Seedeater.

Key habitats Acacia woodland and scrub, rocky, wooded hillsides, riparian bush.

Access From Addis, take the Jimma road through Welisso (also known as Ghion) to Welkite, which is 150 km from Addis. This is a good quality tar road and the journey should take about two hours. From Welkite, continue along the main road towards Jimma; the road starts to wind down into the Gibe River gorge 25 km beyond Welkite, and birding proper starts here.

Birding From where the road starts to wind down the gorge, look carefully for small groups of **White-throated Seedeater** in the acacia trees and small bushes along the roadside (**Yellow-fronted Canary** is also common here) as well as another western species, **Stripe-breasted Seedeater**. Also keep an eye out from here on for **Little Rock Thrush** and **Exclamatory Paradise Whydah**. As the road drops, the habitat becomes more degraded and cultivated, and **Foxy Cisticola** and **Bush Petronia** (common) occur in the roadside scrub and grass, and **Vinaceous Dove** in taller trees. Rank areas of tall grass hold what are probably Ethiopia's easternmost **Moustached Grass Warblers**. Check open areas within the farmlands on either side of the road for groups of rocks that may turn out to be flocks of **Yellow-throated** or **Four-banded Sandgrouse** or, rarely, **Clapperton's Francolin**.

Thirty-six kilometres beyond Welkite, the road passes over the Gibe River bridge (GPS010). **Egyptian Plover** can be found here during Jun–Aug, when the Omo River floods their habitat further downstream, forcing the birds up the Gibe River. Park at the police post just beyond the bridge, and ask for permission to walk upstream along the river and scan exposed rocks for this stunning species. **Senegal Thick-knee** is likely to be seen in the process. **Bar-breasted Firefinch, Red-billed Pytilia** and **Abyssinian Waxbill** (the latter abundant) drink at pools along the river edge; look for these species especially in mixed grass and scrub. **Black-faced Firefinch** has also been seen here. **Snowy-headed Robin-chat**, again very much a western species here near the edge of its range, occurs in denser riparian thicket along this walk.

Other animals Hippopotamus is abundant in the Gibe River, and crocodiles also occur.

Egyptian Plover is a bird of sandbars in large rivers, along which it moves considerable distances. (Dick Forsman)

Abyssinian Longclaw
favours moist grassland
along highland streams.
(Tasso Leventis)

The endemic Blue-winged
Goose has recently become
threatened by hunting,
which has historically posed
little threat to Ethiopia's
birds. (Tasso Leventis)

8. SULULTA PLAINS AND SURROUNDS

North of Addis Ababa, undulating plateau grassland at about 2,600 m altitude stretches on either side of the main road north to Lake Tana, and will be crossed en route to several key birding sites (e.g. Debre Libanos and the Jemma Valley). The plains begin about 18 km north of Addis Ababa, and at all times of year roadside birding is very good all the way from here north to Sululta town (23 km from Addis) and Muka Turi village (78 km from Addis). These birding notes also apply to the similar terrain between Muka Turi and Lemi, and Lemi and Debre Birhan, on the way to the Jemma Valley from the west and east respectively (see p.37).

Common species of open grassland include **Wattled Ibis**, **White-collared Pigeon**, **Erlanger's Lark**, **Red-chested Swallow** (especially near culverts), **Banded Martin**, **Cape Rook**, **Red-breasted Wheatear**, **Moorland Chat**, **African Stonechat**, **Groundscraper Thrush** and **Black-headed Siskin**. During Nov–Mar, they are joined by Palearctic migrants such as **Isabelline**, **Pied** and **Northern Wheatears**, **Red-throated Pipit** and **Ortolan Bunting**. Moister grass along streams often holds **Blue-winged Goose**, **African Snipe**, **Abyssinian Longclaw** and, uncommonly, **Rouget's Rail** and **African Quailfinch**, and more uncommonly still, **Great Snipe**. **Spot-breasted Plover** also occurs in this habitat but is increasingly scarce, and most frequent in the area's major wet season (Jun–Aug). **Black-winged Plover** occurs more commonly. **Fan-tailed Widowbird** and **Yellow-crowned** and **Yellow Bishops** are also most in evidence during the wet season and after, when in breeding plumage. **Lammergeier** occasionally passes overhead, as well as **Steppe** (Oct–Mar) and **Tawny Eagles**, and **Augur Buzzard**. Stop especially at the point where the tar road crosses the Duber River (GPS011) just north of Sululta town. The cutting here holds **White-winged Cliff Chat**, and the marshy area on the southern (left-hand) side of the road **Abyssinian Longclaw**. Several more productive streams are crossed further north, approaching Muka Turi. One of the three only known breeding sites in Ethiopia (and also in the world) for the vanishingly scarce **White-winged Flufftail** is a small marsh not accessible from the

Erlanger's Lark forms part of a taxonomically confusing complex of species, but is now generally regarded as distinct and endemic to the Ethiopian highlands. (Tasso Leventis)

main road. It is critically sensitive to disturbance, and so for obvious reasons it should not be visited.

The Debre Birhan–Denneba area is that to which three **Northern Bald Ibises** (part of a party of four) have in recent years annually been satellite-tracked from their breeding grounds in Syria. Keep an eye out for them in this general region during August–February. Unfortunately, the exact site which the ibises frequent is inaccessible, and for conservation reasons not open to visitors: they have the best chance of persisting if a low profile is kept.

Groundscraper Thrush is often abundant in Ethiopia's highland grasslands. (Tasso Leventis)

Red-breasted Wheatear is a handsome and common bird of highland grassland; Ethiopia forms most of its range but it also occurs across the Red Sea in Yemen and surrounding areas. (Tasso Leventis)

THE NORTH-CENTRAL HIGHLANDS

9. Debre Libanos
10. Jemma Valley
11. Gemessa Gedel
12. Ankober Escarpment
13. Melka Ghebdu

TOP 10 BIRDS

Harwood's Francolin
Erckel's Francolin
Abyssinian Longclaw
Rüppell's Black Chat
Abyssinian Black Wheatear
White-billed Starling
Red-billed Pytilia
Black-headed Siskin
Ankober Serin
Yellow-throated Seedeater

The highlands north of Addis are riven with deep river gorges and dizzying escarpments, and birding in this spectacular setting is wonderfully easy and exciting. A number of Ethiopia's montane endemic species do not occur in the southern highlands such as the Bale Mountains, so a trip north of Addis is essential to see them. These are **Harwood's Francolin**, **Rüppell's Black Chat**, **White-billed Starling**, **Ankober Serin** and, in the Rift Valley lowlands at the escarpment's foot, **Yellow-throated Seedeater**. These aside, many other endemic and highland species can easily be seen. A very good two- to three-day loop might follow the sites below in the order in which they are described, starting with the Sululta Plains described in the previous chapter. Gemessa Gedel may not be essential, but is a useful back-up if Ankober Serin proves difficult at Ankober itself. If current road and security conditions permit (enquire first in Debre Birhan; 4WD is recommended), you can then link up with Awash (site 14) from Ankober in the east; if not, it is easy to retrace your steps from Ankober to Debre Birhan and then nip back to Addis Ababa along the tarred road.

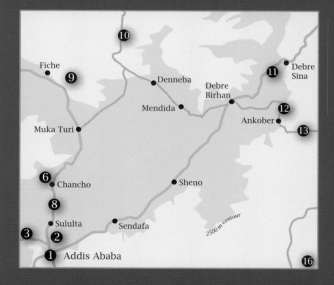

9. DEBRE LIBANOS

Debre Libanos is an Ethiopian Orthodox monastery on the precipitous lip of the Jemma valley, where some excellent forest and montane birding is very accessible (easily manageable, for example, in a day trip from Addis Ababa). The area provides easy and scenic access to several montane species not occurring in the southern highlands. The monastery itself, rebuilt in the 1950s by Haile Selassie after it was bloodily destroyed during the Italian occupation, is worth a visit too.

Key birds Nyanza Swift, Abyssinian Woodpecker, Banded Barbet, White-backed Black Tit, White-winged Cliff Chat, Rüppell's Black Chat, White-billed Starling.

Key habitats Montane grassland, rocky cliffs and gorges, olive-juniper forest.

Access Debre Libanos is less than two hours' drive from Addis Ababa, on the T3 tarred road to Debre Markos. Continue through the villages of Sululta and Muka Turi to 23 km beyond the latter, where the monastery is clearly signposted on the right (1 on map, p.38). The monastery itself (2 on map) lies 4.6 km farther along a gravel access road which is easily accessible by 2WD vehicle. The Ethio-German Park Hotel above the Portuguese Bridge offers nice accommodation.

A fine forest patch lies adjacent to the monastery at Debre Libanos.
(Claire Spottiswoode)

The Jemma Valley escarpment drops away near the Portuguese Bridge.
(Claire Spottiswoode)

Lammergeier can be astonishingly common in Ethiopia's northern highlands. (Dick Forsman)

African Wood Owl's distinctive duet is likely to be heard at night in any wooded part of the highlands. (Tasso Leventis)

Birding Excellent birding is possible right at the turn-off to the monastery from the tar road (1 on map). A short stroll north of here is the so-called Portuguese Bridge (actually built by Ras Darge little over a hundred years ago), which provides easy access to the spectacular brink of the Jemma valley. Park at the recently opened Ethio-German Park Hotel just north of the turn-off, and walk downhill to the bridge and beyond. From here there is an excellent view down through interminable layers of terraced cultivations to the distant silver shimmer of the Jemma River, nearly a kilometre below. The cliffs and boulder-strewn slopes immediately below the bridge are excellent for **Erckel's Francolin**, **Rüppell's Black Chat**, **White-winged Cliff Chat**, **Blue Rock Thrush** and groups of **White-billed Starlings**. Swarms of **Nyanza Swift** may whip past at eye level, giving good views of their transluscent secondaries and slim jizz, and rapidly outpacing the placidly gliding parties of **Rock Martin**. This is also a good vantage point for raptors, which are likely to include **Lammergeier** and **Steppe** (Oct–Mar), **Tawny** and **Verreaux's Eagles**.

The short (4.6 km) drive east from here to the monastery is famous for its Geladas. Several troops, each presided over by a leonine alpha male, are very likely to be seen placidly foraging at the roadside, although they may occasionally be hard to find. **Thekla Lark** and **Stout** and **Singing Cisticolas** will probably fail to distract attention from the baboons' resplendently pink

Banded Barbet is a widespread endemic, especially favouring fig trees. (Dick Forsman)

A troop of Gelada baboons, a species endemic to Ethiopia, is almost certain to be seen in the environs of Debre Libanos. (Callan Cohen & Michael Mills)

chests, blonde manes and daunting incisors. Approaching the monastery, check the enormous fig tree (GPS012) overhanging the road about 3 km from the turn-off for **Banded Barbet** and **White-billed Starling** (note that **Slender-billed Starling** also occurs here). The barbet and the starling are also fairly common around the monastery itself. Park here and pay an entrance fee before wandering off into the adjacent forest. Immediately to the right of the monastery gates, work your way south to a rocky streambed (where another impressive fig dependably yields **Banded Barbet**) and follow the roughly paved footpath up the slope into the forest beyond (beware that the area close to the monastery can be rather unhygienic: watch where you step). The forest is initially fairly open, and the fine old juniper trees are worth scanning for **Abyssinian Woodpecker**. Here and the church grounds themselves are especially good sites for **White-backed Black Tit**. Other species typical of mid-altitude Ethiopian forests and forest edge are **White-cheeked Turaco, Lemon Dove, Hemprich's Hornbill, Abyssinian Oriole, Rüppell's Robin-Chat, Abyssinian Slaty Flycatcher, Brown Woodland Warbler, Montane White-eye** and **Yellow-bellied Waxbill**. **Abyssinian Catbird** is present, but scarce here. **Lammegeier, African Goshawk, Rufous-breasted Sparrowhawk** and **Nyanza Swift** might appear in gaps in the canopy.

If you spend the night at the Ethio-German Park Hotel, listen out at dusk for **Cape Eagle Owls** hooting from the hotel surrounds. **African Wood** and **Abyssinian Owls** may also be heard here at night, and Spotted Hyaenas. **Other animals** A troop of Geladas is invariably present along the road between the Portuguese Bridge and the monastery – typically in the first kilometre or so from the turn-off – and usually allow good views.

10. JEMMA VALLEY

The Jemma River has created a vast and spectacularly impressive valley, over a kilometre deep in places, wending towards the upper reaches of the Blue Nile. At a certain point east of Debre Libanos it is crossed by a steep pass which has become the classic site for the endemic Harwood's Francolin. General birding is also extremely good here, and includes probably the best chance close to Addis Ababa of seeing **White-throated Seedeater** and **Red-billed Pytilia**.

Rüppell's Black Chat characteristically bobbing its tail; the white wing-flashes are visible only in flight. (Tasso Leventis)

Looking out over the Jemma Valley's terraced fields during the dry season. (Claire Spottiswoode)

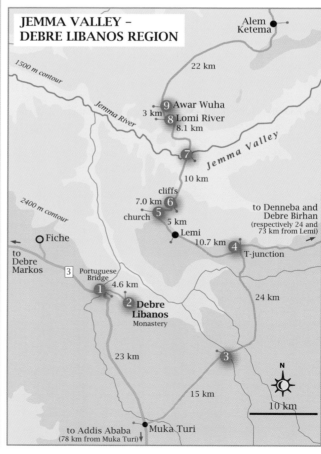

JEMMA VALLEY – DEBRE LIBANOS REGION

Alem Ketema

1500 m contour

22 km

Jemma River

9 Awar Wuha
3 km
8 Lomi River
8.1 km

7

Jemma Valley

10 km

cliffs
7.0 km 6
church 5
5 km
Lemi
10.7 km
4
T-junction

to Denneba and
Debre Birhan
(respectively 24 and
73 km from Lemi)

2400 m contour

○ Fiche

to
Debre
Markos

3 Portuguese
Bridge
4.6 km
1
2 **Debre
Libanos**
Monastery

24 km

23 km

3

15 km

N

10 km

to Addis Ababa
(78 km from Muka Turi)
Muka Turi

Rocky slopes such as these at the upper reaches of the Jemma escarpment are prime habitat for Harwood's Francolin.
(Claire Spottiswoode)

Key birds Fox Kestrel, Harwood's and Erckel's Francolins, White-winged Cliff Chat, Abyssinian Black Wheatear, Rüppell's Black Chat, Foxy Cisticola, White-billed Starling, Red-billed Pytilia, White-throated Seedeater.

Key habitats Rocky slopes, cultivations, acacia thornbush.

Access The Jemma Valley descent is reached via good-quality gravel roads from either Muka Turi (approaching from the south-west) or Debre Birhan and Denneba (approaching from the east). The pass itself has recently been reconstructed and is now a good-quality gravel road. Basic accommodation is available in Alem Ketema, a village 33 km beyond the Jemma river bridge, but it is very pleasant and convenient to camp in the valley itself. Alternatively, good accommodation is available at Debre Libanos (see p.35), but this is an hour and a half's drive away, so a very early pre-dawn start is needed to ensure a good chance of seeing Harwood's Francolin. Note that there is no accommodation in the village of Lemi, near the beginning of the pass.

Birding There is good birding along either approach road to the Jemma Valley, whether from Muka Turi or Debre Birhan, similar to that on the Sululta Plains (p.32). One especially good stretch on the eastern approach road from Muka Turi is the stream crossed at 3 on map (GPS013), and several further stream crossings north towards Lemi. If approaching from the east, look particularly along the several productive stream crossings between Debre Birhan and Mendida (e.g. at GPS014 or GPS015, respectively 6 km/17 km east

The endemic White-winged Cliff Chat sometimes occurs side-by-side with the geographically much more widespread Mocking Cliff Chat. (Tasso Leventis)

of Mendida, or 20 km/9 km west of Debre Birhan). Likely species include **Blue-winged Goose** and **Abyssinian Longclaw** in marshy meadows, and **White-winged Cliff Chat** in road cuttings, as well as the usual highland grassland assemblage including **Nyanza Swift, Banded Martin, Thekla** and **Erlanger's Larks, Red-breasted Wheatear** and **Black-headed Siskin**. The road eventually forms a T-junction with the Lemi-Debre Birhan road, and here it approaches cliff edges at the edge of the Jemma Valley (4 on map; GPS016), on either side of the village of Wekelo Antsokiya. A quick stop and scan here may well yield **Erckel's Francolin, Lammergeier, Verreaux's Eagle, Abyssinian Black Wheatear** and **Rüppell's Black Chat; Erlanger's Lark** is common in the adjacent fields. **Ankober Serin** has been seen here, although we are only aware of one record.

Just beyond Lemi village, the road drops over the valley lip. **Harwood's Francolin** occurs from the beginning of the pass onwards (also see below for the bridge area at the bottom of the valley), and is best searched for during the first hour or so of daylight, when crowing males perch conspicuously on large rocks, and small parties may be seen feeding out in the open on the terraced fields. You might consider engaging a local person to help; many people here know the bird (*soren* in Amharic) and its importance well, and are extremely good at spotting distant francolins. A good area to search is the vicinity of the small, blue-roofed church called Wula Gabriel (5 on map; GPS017), situated in a copse of olive trees on a promontory above the road about 5 km beyond Lemi (permission may be granted to camp here by the people round about, but be aware that the church is a short steep walk above the road; passing the church you will see the remnants of the old road down the valley, now largely reduced to a scree slope). Also scan the rocky slopes alongside and below the road particularly for the next 1–2 km, before a small village is reached. Beware that **Erckel's Francolin** is also numerous, but its rapid crowing is very different from the drawn-out grind of Harwood's; the two sometimes feed alongside one another, when Harwood's will be seen to be conspiciously smaller. Other common species of these rocky slopes are **Abyssinian Black Wheatear, Rüppell's Black Chat, White-winged** and **Mocking Cliff Chats** (sometimes a stone's throw from one another), **Long-billed Pipit, Singing Cistiocala, White-billed Starling** and **Cinnamon-breasted Bunting**. The rather scarce and local **White-throated Seedeater** occurs here too, feeding in small parties within the scrub and cultivations.

An especially fine view of a sheer-sided gorge is from about 12 km from Lemi (6 on map; GPS018), where a scan of the gleaming cliff-face might turn up **Fox** and **Common Kestrels**, both of which breed here, amongst **White-collared Pigeon, White-billed Starling** and formations of **Nyanza Swift**. **White-throated Seedeater** is also seen here. Throughout the pass, other widespread species of Ethiopian forest edge and moist bushland occur, including **Black-winged Lovebird, Hemprich's Hornbill, Blue-breasted Bee-eater** and **African Citril**. Despite the bird-scaring boys and women atop their curious pulpits, the adjacent crops, grassland and scrub teem with seed-eating birds such as **Red-collared Widowbird, Black-winged Red Bishop, African Silver-bill, Village Indigobird** and its host the **Red-billed Firefinch**, and this is also a peculiarly good area for the oddly distributed **Speckle-fronted Weaver** (unlikely to be seen anywhere else on a typical Ethiopian itinerary). Where the road passes through agricultural areas beyond the foothills, check exposed

Harwood's Francolin is a threatened endemic of the Blue Nile valley and its tributaries, such as the Jemma. (János Oláh)

trees for perched **Fox Kestrel**, especially in the middle of the day.

The rapid descent to the valley bottom at 1300 m (22 km from Lemi) soon brings an entirely new atmosphere. The bridge over the Jemma River (a sturdy Bailey bridge, 7 on map; GPS019) is the classic site for **Harwood's Francolin**, and although they can certainly be found here in the early morning, they are perhaps easier on the high slopes where the perspective given by the slope makes them easier to spot. A small track on the right-hand side just beyond the river is a good place to search; if the river is not too high, also try the rocky slopes of the low ridge at the confluence of the Jemma and a subsidiary. Along the river itself, **Goliath Heron, Woolly-necked Stork, Giant Kingfisher, Hamerkop** and **Senegal Thick-knee** occur.

The acacia thornbush here is generally good; also try the thicket-lined, potholed Lomi River, 8.1 km uphill beyond the bridge (8 on map; GPS020), which is particularly good for birds coming to drink in the morning and evening. This is a good place to search for **Foxy Cisticola** (search the thorny scrub on the ridges above the river), **Speckle-fronted Weaver, Crimson-rumped Waxbill, White-throated Seedeater** and **Red-billed Pytilia**, and with tremendous luck perhaps **Stone Partridge** (keep a careful eye at the road-sides) and **Bronze-winged Courser** (roosting under trees in the daytime). Other more characteristically western Ethiopian species found here are **Vinaceous Dove, Bush Petronia** and (rarely) **Black-faced Firefinch**. Palearctic migrants are often especially abundant in the Jemma valley, perhaps most of all on passage, and may include **White-throated Robin** (Aug–Oct and Mar–Apr) as well as the usual complement of wheatears, warblers and shrikes.

The Lomi River is an especially good site for endemic seedeaters such as White-throated Seedeater and Red-billed Pytilia. (Claire Spottiswoode)

A similarly productive wooded valley with fig and coffee trees, named Awar Wuha, lies on the right-hand side of the road 3 km farther on the ascent (9 on map; GPS021). This is especially good for **Red-billed Pytilia, White-throated Seedeater, Black-winged Lovebird** and **Bruce's Green Pigeon**. If you continue north out of the valley to Alem Ketema (via the village of Fitra, which is 18.5 km beyond the bridge), keep an eye out on this escarpment too for **Harwood's Francolin, Foxy Cisticola**, and **White-throated Seedeater**.

Other animals Geladas occasionally visit the upper reaches of the pass, although they and Olive Baboons are unpopular with farmers and tend to be chased away.

A party of Crimson-rumped Waxbills bathes in the Lomi Stream. (Tasso Leventis)

11. GEMESSA GEDEL

Gemassa Gedel (meaning broken cliff) is an excellent site for **Ankober Serin**, easily accessible alongside the main tar road from Addis Ababa to Tigray. From Debre Birhan, continue north for 44 km towards Kombolcha. At GPS022, on the right-hand side, there is an opening in the mountains less than 100 m from the road, yielding a view to a sheer cliff overlooking the Awedi River. **Ankober Serin** may be seen feeding in the fields between the tar road and the cliffs, or even on the left-hand side of the road away from the cliffs; if not, carefully scan the cliff-faces (on the mountain slopes on either side of the gap) for parties of serins, feeding and perching among the lichens. Beware that this area is often obscured by dense cloud, although usually with occasional clearings. Other typical highland species occur too, including **Lammergeier, Verreaux's Eagle, Rock Martin, Blue Rock Thrush** (Oct–Feb), **Moorland Chat, Cinnamon Bracken Warbler, White-billed Starling, Black-headed Siskin** and frequent troops of Geladas. **Abyssinian Black Wheatear** and **White-winged Cliff Chat** are especially common along the road between Debre Birhan and Gemassa Gedel, and general grassland birding is good between Debre Birhan and Addis Ababa (see sites 8 and 10 for details of the birds of this habitat).

12. ANKOBER

Mist-smothered Ankober shivers on the lip of a spectacular escarpment of the Awash Valley. It has long been a site of strategic importance and was the seat of government of Emperor Menelik II during the nineteenth century.

Explosively calling Cinnamon Bracken Warblers often manage to remain concealed even in the scantiest alpine bushes at high altitude. (Andy Swash)

ANKOBER & MELKA GHEBDU

Now a small ramshackle village, it was propelled back into fame by the discovery in 1976 by John Ash of a nondescript but intriguing new species of finch, **Ankober Serin**. Over the edge of the escarpment, in the baking acacia country below, is the best-known site for another endemic finch, the **Yellow-throated Seedeater** (see next site).

Key birds Rufous-breasted Sparrowhawk, Erckel's Francolin, Abyssinian Catbird, Ankober Serin.

Key habitats Alpine moorland, cliffs and cultivations; juniper-olive forest.

Access Ankober is reached via the substantial town of Debre Birhan, about 2 hours' drive (130 km) from Addis Ababa on a recently repaired tar road, in excellent condition at the time of writing. From here, Ankober village is

Ankober Serin is a bird of inhospitably cold and wind-blasted cliffs such as those in the foreground, here photographed at point 3 on the map.
(Claire Spottiswoode)

Ankober Serin, Ethiopia's most recently-discovered endemic bird.
(Richard Saunders)

Moorland Chat is an abundant and engaging bird over much of Ethiopia's highest altitudes. (Tasso Leventis)

another 40 km (one hour's drive) east on a reasonably good gravel road. A range of accommodation is available in Debre Birhan (the best in town is currently the Eva Hotel; more are under construction). In Ankober, excellent accommodation is available at the Ankober Palace Lodge (3 km beyond Ankober village; 5 on map), which is perched atop a steep hill (accessible only on foot; a moderate level of fitness is needed to reach it comfortably) on the exact site of Menelik II's imperial palace, and has correspondingly strategic views.

Birding The following account assumes that you approach Ankober from Debre Birhan in the west; distances are given from the start of the gravel road just north of Debre Birhan. The road from Debre Birhan crosses undulating open landscape, after 25 km gradually rising to a maximum of c.3,400 m, where it is worth watching out for **Rufous-breasted Sparrowhawk** as you pass through a large eucalyptus plantation (1 on map; GPS023). **Ankober Serin** habitat begins thereafter, from about 28 km to just outside of Ankober village. The road runs roughly parallel to the escarpment edge on your left, where there is a precipitous drop into the Rift Valley. The serin is a bird of harshly exposed cliff-faces, to which small groups cling, perching on ledges and tufts of tussock grass. Flocks also visit adjacent stony, ploughed fields to feed, so look out for them at the roadside (but note that **Brown-rumped** and **Streaky Seedeaters** and **Black-headed Siskin** are also common here). Walk up from the road to the escarpment edge, and carefully scan the rock-faces (preferably through a telescope), for example at 28.0 km and 30.0 km (respectively 2 and 3 on map; GPS024 and GPS025). The latter point, 3, is particularly good: work your way up to the escarpment edge along a rocky path through small fields, and scrutinise the steep cliffs on either side of the ravine at the summit. At 37.9 km (4 on map; just before the outskirts of Ankober village), there is especially easy access to good habitat, as the road runs very close to the cliff edge, but the previous sites are more reliable. This whole area is excellent for raptors, including commonly **Lammergeier** and **Verreaux's Eagle**, and **Rufous-breasted** and **Great Sparrowhawks** venturing over the moorland to hunt. **Thekla Lark**, **Moorland Chat** and **Cinnamon Bracken Warbler** are common. Check any flocks of starlings for **Somali Starling**, which has been recorded here, although as ever **Slender-billed** and **White-billed Starlings** are much more abundant.

The escarpment just below Ankober village (altitude 3,100 m) also provides fine birding. It descends in a series of switchbacks through open woods and terraced cultivations, and then a sequence of villages (see next site) to the Awash River on the distant horizon. This road has recently been rebuilt and at the time of writing was good-quality gravel. The wooded slopes of the promontory where the Ankober Palace Lodge is situated (3 km beyond the village, see above; GPS026) and the following 7 km or so of road beyond it have remnants of olive–juniper forests. Here **Erckel's Francolin** can be quite common and vocal in the early mornings, although hard to spot when crowing, and perhaps more likely to be flushed on foot (this species also occurs in the Ankober Palace Lodge grounds, and the staff may be able to point you towards one). **Cinnamon Bracken Warbler** and **Abyssinian Catbird** are conspicuously vocal along the road below the lodge, **Little Rock Thrush** sometimes occurs among the buildings, and **African Wood** and **Abyssinian Owls** may be heard at night. In the rock-strewn grasslands and cultivations, **Abyssinian Black Wheatear** and **Singing Cisticola** are common. Forest raptors such as **Mountain Buzzard** and **Rufous-breasted Sparrowhawk** may pass overhead. There are also recent records of **Somali Starling** from this stretch of road, so it is well worth checking the flocks of **Slender-billeds**.

Intensive terraced cultivations on the steep slopes below Ankober Palace Lodge.
(Claire Spottiswoode)

Little Rock Thrush has a limited distribution in East Africa, and especially favours wooded rocky areas.
(Tasso Leventis)

Other animals Troops of Geladas are regularly encountered along the cliff edge north of Ankober, where Starck's Hare and Ethopian Rock Hyrax are also likely to be disturbed. Ethiopian Wolf does occur in the highlands around Ankober, but is scarce here and unlikely to be seen.

13. MELKA GHEBDU

The Rift Valley below the Ankober escarpment is a world away from the mist-enveloped alpine moorlands still visible just forty minutes' drive to the north. Continuing down the escarpment road below Ankober (above; see also map on p.42), the road passes through the village of Aliyu Amba (13 km beyond Ankober Palace Lodge; GPS027), to a hot lowland (1,400 m) acacia-wooded valley. A minor stream crossing known as Melka Ghebdu (GPS028), 18.6 km from Ankober Palace Lodge, is improbably famous as the easiest site to find the endemic **Yellow-throated Seedeater**. Although recent surveys have revealed this species to be more widespread than previously known, Melka Ghebdu remains the most easily accessible site from Addis Ababa. The road crosses a small stream at 7 on the map on p.42, which leads into a slightly larger stream to your left. Walk along the rocky streambed or along the road beyond, looking out for singing males giving a rather unremarkable but typical serin-like song, or small foraging parties. Beware that **Reichenow's Seedeater** also occurs commonly here, but its distinctive wing-bars and facial markings are usually conspicuous. The stream often holds **Half-collared Kingfisher**, and the riparian thicket and drier acacia thornbush beyond is good for **Eastern Grey Plantain-eater** (alongside two relatives, **White-bellied** and **Bare-faced Go-away-birds**) and **Banded** and **Yellow-breasted Barbets** (listen for the latter's duet, which resembles a police siren). There is generally good acacia

Yellow-throated Seedeater occurs in the streamside vegetation at Melka Ghebdu.
(Claire Spottiswoode)

Yellow-throated Seed-eater remained unseen for over century after the first specimen was collected, before being rediscovered at Melka Ghebdu in 1989. (Andy Swash)

thornbush birding here; among some of the more notable species are **Clapperton's Francolin** (listen for its slow, grinding crowing), **Chesnut-crowned Sparrow-weaver** (a more typically western species in Ethiopia), **Black Scrub Robin** (Sep–Feb), **Rüppell's Weaver** and (with much luck) **Red-billed Pytilia**.

Yellow-breasted Barbet is often located by its oddly siren-like call. (Dick Forsman)

THE AWASH REGION

14. Road from Melka Ghebdu to Awash
15. Southern Awash National Park
16. Lake Beseka and Mount Fantale
17. Bilen Lodge
18. Ali Dege Plains
19. Harar Region and Babile Elephant Sanctuary

TOP 10 BIRDS

Somali Ostrich
Arabian Bustard
'Ethiopian' Cliff Swallow
Gillett's Lark
Red-winged Lark
Sombre Rock Chat
Ashy Cisticola
Somali Fiscal
Nile Valley Sunbird
Yellow-throated Seedeater

The arid Awash region of the north-eastern Rift Valley offers wonderfully diverse savanna and dry lowland birding, as well as good wildlife watching and starkly impressive volcanic landscapes. With respect to endemics it is essential only for the enigmatic – if unelectrifying – **Sombre Rock Chat**, but numerous other dryland species with wider distributions (particularly Sahelian species extending from West Africa) are more easily seen here than anywhere else in Ethiopia; these include **African Swallow-tailed Kite**, **Arabian Bustard** and **African Collared Dove**, as well as a Horn of Africa endemic, **Gillett's Lark**. A minimum of three days is needed to have a look around Awash National Park itself, and make a foray north-east to the arid and fascinating Bilen Lodge area. For most visitors, the Awash region will be a geographical dead end but for the link with Ankober (see site 14). However, the return journey to Addis Ababa is reasonably quick along the main tar road that links Ethiopia to the port of Djibouti. Beyond Awash and before Djibouti, this road skirts the remote Yangudi-Rassa National Park. It was established to protect a population of the critically endangered Somali Wild Ass, as well as numerous archaeological sites (Lucy was discovered nearby), but is less remarkable for birds. As elsewhere in Ethiopia, take great care in the Awash region to avoid pointing cameras at camels.

14. ROAD FROM MELKA GHEBDU TO AWASH

From Ankober and Melka Ghebdu (see sites 12 and 13) it is possible to continue directly through arid Afar country to the western flank of the Awash National Park. Although recently resurfaced, the road can still become impassable in the rainy season, so be sure to enquire about conditions in Debre Birhan or Ankober if travelling south (or Metahara if travelling north) before you set off. It is a little-used road, so take extra water in case of a breakdown, remain aware of potential security concerns and be sure that your driver knows the route as it can become confusing in places. Take care especially about 26 km beyond the village of Dulesa (GPS029; see below), at a tiny Afar settlement at GPS030, where it is easy to head off south-east towards the Awash River and eventually the town of Werer (near the main tar road to Djibouti), rather than south-west towards Metahara on the tar road to Addis. (See site 17 for two GPS landmarks near the latter, en route to Mt Fantale.)

The Awash region is one of the easiest places in the world to see the beautiful Arabian Bustard. (Jacques Erard)

Starting from Melka Ghubdu and driving south-east, the road continues to drop in altitude, and soon enters very arid open country. This is an excellent area for **Arabian Bustard**, and at least one sighting is extremely likely. Look especially from about 15 km beyond Dulesa (also called Dulecha) village (see map on p.51), and note that **Kori Bustard** can also occur in this region. The road crosses several wooded riverbeds leading towards the Awash River. **African Collared Dove**, a Sahelian species that is relatively localised in Ethiopia, can be quite common here. Look especially in the patch of beautiful tall acacias (GPS031) about 3 km north-east of the village of Boloyta (GPS032), but beware that **African Mourning Dove** is also common. **Somali Bulbul** is very common here too, and other possible species of dry watercourses and adjacent scrub in this area include **Buff-crested Bustard**, **Lichtenstein's** and **Chestnut-bellied Sandgrouse**, **Eastern Grey Plantain-eater**, **Red-fronted Warbler** and

Egyptian Vulture is happily still common over much of Ethiopia, and is especially frequent in the Awash area. (Tasso Leventis)

Nile Valley Sunbird. Egyptian Vulture can be especially numerous along this road. **Water Thick-knee** has been seen along a stream here, far north of its known range in Ethiopia. Lesser Kudu and large troops of Sacred Baboon may well also be seen, and there is always a small chance of sighting predators such as Lion and Leopard.

15. SOUTHERN AWASH NATIONAL PARK

Awash is Ethiopia's flagship national park, and one of the few where wild animals might still outnumber cattle and camels. Savanna birding here is very diverse, easy and entertaining, although it is quite rainfall-dependent and undoubtedly at its best after good rains. Aside from its diversity, Awash is also an excellent site for finding several species of acacia thornbush birds that are unlikely to be encountered elsewhere during a typical short visit to Ethiopia. At the time of writing and for some years prior, banditry was a considerable concern in the northern section of the park, north of the tar road (see next site). This account is therefore confined to the vastly safer and more commonly visited southern section of the park; note that you will be asked to take a game scout with you even in this part of the park.

Key birds Arabian Bustard, Hartlaub's Bustard, African Swallow-tailed Kite, Abyssinian Roller, Gillett's Lark, Red-winged Lark, 'Ethiopian' Cliff Swallow, Ashy Cisticola, Somali Fiscal.

Key habitats Acacia thornbush, grassy plains, riparian forest, cliffs and gorges.

Access Allow at least three hours (more often four or five, owing to Addis traffic) to reach Awash National Park from Addis Ababa, on a good tar road. There are a number of accommodation options in the Awash area. The towns of Metahara and especially Awash have many small hotels (the Genet Hotel in Awash is recommended), which are more or less equidistant from the park

The southern Awash National Park's open plains, here green after good rains and grazed by Beisa Oryx. (Claire Spottiswoode)

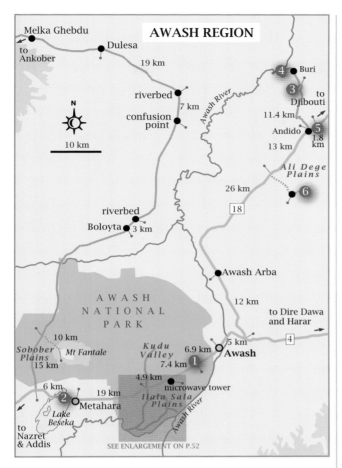

AWASH REGION

Melka Ghebdu

to Ankober

Dulesa

19 km

Buri

riverbed

7 km

Awash River

confusion point

to Djibouti

11.4 km

Andido

13 km

1.8 km

N

10 km

Ali Dege Plains

26 km

18

riverbed

Boloyta 3 km

Awash Arba

12 km

AWASH NATIONAL PARK

to Dire Dawa and Harar

Sobober Plains

10 km

Mt Fantale

15 km

Kudu Valley

6.9 km

5 km

Awash

7.4 km

4

6 km

19 km

4.9 km

microwave tower

Metahara

Ilala Sala Plains

Lake Beseka

Awash River

to Nazret & Addis

SEE ENLARGEMENT ON P.52

The rarely-seen display that betrays the Buff-crested Bustard's name. (Andy Swash)

gate and provide a very reasonable base. Within the park itself, there are three overnight options. Kereyou Lodge is composed of an unhappy regiment of ageing caravans, which are difficult to recommend, although the restaurant is superbly positioned on the cliff edge of the Awash gorge and is a fine spot for a lunch or breakfast stop. The newly built Awash Falls (Fuafuate) Lodge, which overlooks the falls, offers comfortable accommodation. In some ways best of all, a series of camping areas are strung along the northern shore of the Awash River near the park headquarters and falls, some (such as that named Zinjero) set in beautiful locations among groves of riparian fig trees and acacias. Camping here is wonderful, but be aware that there are no facilities here at all and that you will need to pick up an overnight scout from the nearby park headquarters, known as Gotu (see map on p.52). Excellent accommodation in the broader Awash area is also available at Bilen Lodge (p.58).

Birding Birding in Awash National Park is concentrated in three broad habitat types: the open acacia-studded grassland of the Ilala Sala plains, denser acacia thornbush, and the riparian forest along the Awash River. The Ilala Sala Plains are where game-watching is best. **Kori** and, less abundantly,

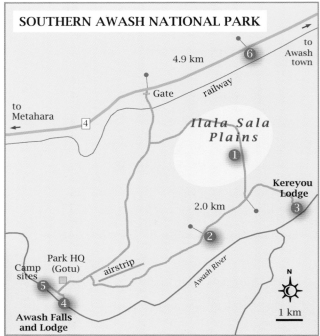

Hartlaub's Bustard is not uncommon on the Awash plains. (Andy Swash)

Hartlaub's Bustards and Secretarybird stride among the small herds of oryx and gazelle, against the distant backdrop of Mount Fantale. Arabian Bustard is occasionally seen here, but more reliably searched for elsewhere (see sites 14 and 17). (White-bellied and Black-bellied Bustards, by contrast, prefer the lightly wooded grassy plain edges, whereas Buff-crested Bustard occurs in thornbush.) African Swallow-tailed Kite hunts overhead on the plains during Nov–Apr (still scarce in Nov), Pallid and Montagu's Harriers can be common in winter, and Eastern Chanting Goshawk year-round. Other interesting

A male Kori Bustard beginning to inflate his throat as he gears up to display. (Andy Swash)

raptors here include **Pygmy Falcon** and **Northern White-faced Owl** (check the isolated stand of acacia trees around the small, sometimes dry water-hole at 1 on map; GPS033), and vultures including **Rüppell's**, **White-backed**, **Lappet-faced** and **Hooded**. Both **Singing Bush** and **Red-winged Larks** can be fairly easily seen, perched on a song post or scuttling at the roadside, but may also be very inconspicuous during dry periods. **Ashy Cisticola** also sings from small bushes. **Somali Fiscal** is quite common here, sharing vantage points with **Abyssinian Roller** and **Southern Grey Shrike**.

The southern and western areas of the park are somewhat more densely wooded, with less grass cover and taller acacias. This is prime habitat for **Gillett's Lark**, which favours the slightly more broken country closer to the Awash River (search, for example, in the vicinity of 2 on map; GPS034); it feeds inconspicuously on the ground, and sings or calls thinly from the tops of large thornbushes. This is also a good area to search for **Ashy Cisticola**. Stony, more sparsely vegetated areas are frequented by **Black-headed Plover, Chesnut-bellied** and occasionally **Lichtenstein's Sandgrouse, Chestnut-backed** and **Chestnut-headed Sparrow-larks, Rosy-patched Bush-shrike** and migrant wheatears.

Red-and-yellow Barbet is invariably seen in the vicinity of termite mounds, in which it burrows. (Tasso Leventis)

More widespread typical species of such dry acacia thornbush country are **Buff-crested Bustard, Blue-naped Mousebird, Abyssinian Ground Horn-bill, Black-billed Woodhoopoe, Abyssinian Scimitarbill, Yellow-breasted, Red-fronted** and **Red-and-yellow Barbets, Somali Bulbul, Grey Wren-warbler, Masked Shrike** (Sept–Apr), **White-crested Helmetshrike, Slate-coloured Boubou, White-headed Buffalo-weaver, Rüppell's Weaver, Eastern Paradise** and sometimes **Steel-blue Whydahs**, and occasionally **Nile Valley Sunbird**. The drier, denser thornbush in the vicinity of the entrance gate is also good for such species. Throughout the park, flocks of bee-eaters pass liquidly overhead, including **White-throated** (Apr–Sep), **Madagascar** and **Northern Carmine Bee-eaters** (which also favour Kereyou camels as foraging vantages).

The ageing Kereyou Lodge (3 on map; GPS035) is spectacularly situated in dry, rocky acacia country at the edge of the Awash Gorge. It is famously the location of several sightings (spanning Sep–Feb, and all made since 1988) of

Rosy-patched Bush-shrike's sliding, high-pitched calls are a classic sound of Ethiopia's drier, open bushlands. (Paul Donald)

what is tentatively known as **'Ethiopian' Cliff Swallow** – possibly, or possibly not, conspecific with the Red Sea Swallow known only from a single corpse found under a Sudanese lighthouse in 1984. (They have also been sighted at nearby Lake Beseka and Mount Fantale, see next site.) While scanning optimistically from the lodge's verandah, **Fan-tailed Raven** and **Bristle-crowned Starling** may pass by; it is also a predictably good vantage point for raptors, and **Ovambo Sparrowhawk** and **Sooty Falcon** have been sighted here. A telescope might reveal **Goliath Heron** (and crocodiles) along the Awash River far below. **Gillett's Lark** occurs in the dry bush in the vicinity of the lodge.

Dense riparian bush and beautiful old fig trees around the Awash Falls (4 on map; GPS036) and, especially, in the vicinity of the campsites (5 on map) provide excellent birding. Typical species include **Black-billed Barbet, Eastern Grey Plantain-eater** (as well as **White-bellied Go-away-bird**), **Bruce's Green Pigeon, White-rumped Babbler, Rüppell's Starling,** and seasonal migrants such as **European Golden Oriole** and loudly bubbling **Thrush Nightingale.** This area is also good for raptors of denser woodland such as **Bat Hawk, Little Sparrowhawk** and **Shikra**. You might be lucky enough to flush a **Dwarf Bittern** from overhanging trees at the river fringes. The campsite is also coincidentally an area especially favoured by Lion, whose spoor may often be seen here. Look after your food supplies, or Olive Baboons and Grivet Monkeys will rapidly remove them. Beyond the campsite fringes and in the scrub across the river are species typical of drier acacia thornbush mentioned above.

If you wish to do a night drive, confirm this first with the park authorities, who will ask you to take a game scout, and may specify which areas are currently safe to visit. Success is very variable, but on a good night, **Slender-tailed Nightjar** can be common, as throughout much of Ethiopia, and **Dusky** (in rocky areas along the Awash River), **Plain** and **Nubian Nightjars** are all scarce possibilities. **Star-spotted Nightjar** can be fairly common on the Ilala Sala plains, especially their western end, and in the vicinity of the airstrip. **Double-banded Courser** is also possible, especially between the gate and the

Beisa Oryx, a fine antelope of north-eastern Africa. (Claire Spottiswoode)

park headquarters, and **Heuglin's Courser** throughout the park. Owls could include **Northern White-faced** and **Greyish** and **Verreaux's Eagle-owls**; the campsites and riverine trees around the falls are excellent places to look for **African Scops Owl**.

En route from the park gate to Awash town or Bilen Lodge (see site 17), through increasingly more arid country, also scan the vicinity of the microwave tower at the park's north-eastern corner (6 on map; GPS037) for **Arabian Bustard**, but beware that **Kori Bustard** also occurs in this transitional habitat. Nearby, another good area to search for **Arabian Bustard** is the first 5–6 km of the entrance road to Geda Camp, the turn-off to which is clearly signposted 7.4 km from the microwave tower towards Awash (1 on small-scale map of Awash region, p.51).

Other animals The Ilala Sala plains are famous for their herds of Beisa Oryx and Soemmering's Gazelle, albeit mixed among flocks of Kereyou camels. Common species of denser bush include Lesser and (less commonly) Greater Kudu, Common Warthog and Salt's Dik-dik. Lion is likely to be heard at night, especially along the Awash River, and Bat-eared Fox, Aardwolf, Spotted Hyaena, Wild Cat and Leopard are all possibilities on night drives.

16. LAKE BESEKA AND MOUNT FANTALE

Mount Fantale is a mini-Ngorongoro above the road to southern Awash National Park. It is a volcano and last erupted in the nineteenth century; the lava flow on its southern slopes has formed the ever-expanding Lake Beseka. This stark black landscape is crossed by the road to Awash, and is famously one of the few places where the scarce and poorly-known **Sombre Rock Chat** may reliably be seen. At the time of writing, an escort of two armed scouts was required to visit the summit of Mount Fantale and other parts of the Awash National Park north of the tar road, such as the Kudu Valley.

A *Sterculia* tree grows in the rugged lava landscape below Mount Fantale; this is Sombre Rock Chat's favoured habitat. (Claire Spottiswoode)

The well-named Sombre Rock Chat; the photograph shows its distinctive pale-edged undertail-coverts that distinguish it with certainty from Blackstart and Brown-tailed Rock Chat (both below). (Dick Forsman)

Brown-tailed Rock Chat is easily confused with Sombre Rock Chat, but has plain undertail-coverts, alas hidden here. (Tasso Leventis)

Blackstart is also common on lava flows in the Awash area, and can look unexpectedly similar to Sombre Rock Chat in the typically harsh light conditions. (Jacques Erard)

Key birds Western Reef Heron, Gillett's and Desert Larks, Sombre Rock Chat, Blackstart, Nile Valley Sunbird, Yellow-throated Seedeater, Striolated Bunting.
Key habitats lava flow, lake, acacia thornbush on rocky slopes.
Access Lake Beseka is bisected by the main tar road to Djibouti, and birding is easy at the roadside. Mount Fantale, by contrast, is a substantial undertaking, and park rules dictate that one must take along two armed scouts (for a small fee). The last 10 km of road, a slow, grinding ascent to the lip of the volcano's crater, is torturous and rocky, and the whole journey from southern Awash National Park is likely to take two to three hours one way, including birding stops, so the trip is deservedly unpopular with drivers. You might compromise and walk the last stretch. To reach this road, take the dirt road north from the tar road 6 km west of Metahara, sign-posted 'Sobober Camp' (GPS038). Ten kilometres further, there is an inconspicuous turn-off to the right (GPS039), among tall acacias (ignore an earlier turn-off), which leads up the mountain. The Kudu Valley, east of Fantale, has generally good acacia thornbush birding not unlike that in the southern part of the park (especially check open scrubby areas for **Gillett's Lark**), but again an armed escort is needed.

Birding Lake Beseka holds a good variety of widespread waterbirds in addition to, fairly regularly, **Western Reef Heron** and **Ferruginous Duck** (Oct–Apr). The lake is most interesting, however, because of the lava flow that has created it. This is a fascinating landscape of jumbled black chunks of lava interspersed with gnarled *Sterculia* trees and a few other tenacious shrubs. **Sombre Rock Chat** can be found anywhere in the lava flow, either north or south of the main road; search especially in the vicinity of the small tracks leading north and south from the tar road 2 km west of Metahara (GPS040), near a green signboard from Metahara Sugar Factory wishing one a good journey. Beware, though, that **Blackstart** is common here and can appear more similar than one might expect. About 500 m up the track on the northern side of the road, a shallow, sparsely vegetated sandy valley lies to the west of the track; these sandy flats can yield **Temminck's Courser**, **Desert Lark** (here near its southern limit in Ethiopia) and, occasionally, winter influxes of **Bimaculated Lark** and **Pale Rockfinch**. Any flowering trees along the deep, narrow gorge beyond

Western Reef Heron is typically a coastal bird, but occasionally drifts inland and is regularly seen at Lake Beseka. (Jacques Erard)

might produce **Nile Valley Sunbird**; also watch out here for flushed **Greyish Eagle-owl**, and troops of Sacred Baboon. Both **Striolated** and **Cinnamon-breasted Buntings** occur, as do flocks of **Bristle-crowned Starlings**.

If venturing up Mount Fantale, keep an eye out on the Sobober Plains (see map on p.51) for **Arabian Bustard**, which occurs here alongside **Kori Bustard**. Also keep an eye on the thornbush on the way up for **Yellow-breasted Barbet**, **Gillett's Lark**, **Long-billed Pipit**, **Boran Cisticola**, **Somali Fiscal** and the very range-restricted **Yellow-throated Seedeater**. The view from the summit across the steaming 3.5 km-wide crater of Mount Fantale is spectacular. Less so is **Sombre Rock Chat**, which also may be seen at the crater rim, and occasionally in rocky areas on the drive up. **Rüppell's Vulture**, **Lammergeier**, **Lanner Falcon** and **Bristle-crowned Starling** fly along the cliff-faces, and also keep an eye out for an infrequent **Fox Kestrel**.

Another lava flow (improbably known as 'Garibaldi'; GPS041) is crossed by the main road 27 km south-west of Metahara, where **Blackstart, Bristle-crowned Starling, Striolated** and **Cinnamon-breasted Buntings** and Sacred Baboon may be found. There is a report of **Sombre Rock Chat** here, although other recent searches have failed.

Other animals The northern part of Awash National Park is the best area to search for Sacred Baboon. Big troops come to drink at the (only) dam in the Kudu Valley in late afternoons, and troops are sometime also seen on the Lake Beseka lava flow (especially in the very early morning), and along the track up Mount Fantale. Parties of Ethiopian Rock Hyrax also occur on the lava flow and mountain, and Lesser Kudu is widespread in thornbush; Greater Kudu is nowadays scarce.

17. BILEN LODGE

Bilen Lodge allows easy access to the wonderfully rocky, arid, thorny Afar country to the north-east of Awash National Park, where birding is excellent. The lodge was constructed in consultation with the Afar community and is located alongside the Bilen Hot Springs, where Wilfred Thesiger camped in the 1930s. Between here and the distant Asebot Volcano, to the south-east, are the rather degraded and unprepossessing Ali Dege Plains (see below), which are, however, good for one of the Awash region's star birds, **Arabian Bustard**.

Key birds Somali Ostrich, Arabian Bustard, African Swallow-tailed Kite, Grasshopper Buzzard, Spotted Thick-knee, Lichtenstein's and Four-banded Sandgrouse, African Collared Dove, Yellow-breasted Barbet, Black Scrub Robin, Nile Valley and Shining Sunbirds.

Key habitats Arid, rocky thornbush, and dry open plains.

Accommodation at Bilen Lodge is in Afar-style rooms, surrounded by dry bushland that is especially productive during migration.
(Claire Spottiswoode)

Access To reach Bilen Lodge, take the tar road from Awash to Djibouti and 40 km beyond Awash Arba. Here, at the small village of Andido (GPS042), turn left onto a rough track signposted to the camp. From here it is an 11.4 km drive north to the hot springs and lodge, along the western side of a low rocky ridge. Bilen Lodge (GPS043) is located on a low rise near the hot springs and

Arabian Bustard habitat along the access road to Bilen Lodge. (Claire Spottiswoode)

overlooking a large area of reedbeds to the west. The lodge has 15 pleasant en-suite chalets in Afar architecture, and a good restaurant. They can arrange various activities including swimming in the hot springs, camel trekking, and visiting an Afar village. Bookings are through Village Ethiopia in Addis Ababa. The Ali Dege plains (next site) lie to the right of the main road as you approach the Bilen Lodge turn-off.

Birding Approaching Bilen Lodge, one passes through prime country for **Arabian Bustard**. Keep an eye out for them at the roadside as you travel north from the Harar/Djibouti road fork, especially in the bushy arid country beyond Awash Arba village (GPS044; see also Ali Dege Plains, next site). The gravel road leading from the tar road to Bilen Lodge is especially good, and they are sometimes even seen on the lodge outskirts. Other species worth looking out for along the gravel access road towards the lodge include **White-bellied Bustard**, **Lichtenstein's Sandgrouse**, **Spotted Thick-knee** and migrant **Grasshopper Buzzard**.

The beautiful Lichtenstein's Sandgrouse is readily seen in the arid, rocky bushland around Bilen. (János Oláh)

Shining Sunbird can be abundant around Bilen, as in many areas of dry bushlands on rocky ground.
(Andy Swash)

Very good birding may be had simply by strolling around the arid thornbush within and around the Bilen Lodge grounds, particularly during migration seasons. acacia thickets that are in flower are particularly good for sunbirds such as **Nile Valley** (sometimes abundant) and **Shining Sunbirds**, and migrant warblers, including **Upcher's** and **Ménétriés's Warbler**. **Black Scrub Robin** is also regularly seen here; search especially in denser patches of thicket. **Yellow-breasted Barbet** and **Ethiopian Swallow** breed in the camp buildings, the former digging their burrows directly into the mud walls. Apparent patches of rocky ground that begin to shuffle away deliberately are likely to be **Lichtenstein's** or (more rarely) **Four-banded Sandgrouse**. General acacia birding is very good, with characteristic species including **White-throated** and **Northern Carmine Bee-eaters**, **Von der Decken's**, **Eastern Yellow-billed** and **African Grey Hornbills**, **Blue-naped Mousebird**, **Abyssinian Roller**, **Red-fronted Barbet**, **Somali Bulbul**, **Yellow-bellied Eremomela**, **Grey-headed Batis**, **African Grey Flycatcher**, **Chestnut Weaver** and **Golden-breasted Starling**. The restaurant is a good vantage point from which to scan with a scope the marshes and reedbeds that lie to the north-west, and this could turn up a variety of waterbirds including **Western Marsh Harrier** and **Collared Pratincole** feeding over the reeds.

African Collared Dove occurs near the hot springs, especially in riparian vegetation along the small stream crossing the Bilen Lodge access road opposite the hot springs. If you fail here, then also try the dry riparian woodland along the nearby Awash River (4 on map), where it is relatively common. An armed escort (arranged by the lodge) is necessary to visit the river, which is a 5 km drive northwards via the village of Buri (3 km from the lodge) and which otherwise provides similar birding to that around the lodge.

It is not safe to do extensive night drives in the area, but you might be granted permission to travel (accompanied by a guide) a short distance back down the entrance road. **Slender-tailed Nightjar** can be seen here, or hawking insects around the lodge lights at dusk, or flushed from day roosts, and there are records of **Star-spotted Nightjar.** Verreaux's and **Greyish Eagle-owls** and **Northern White-faced Owl** are present, and **African Scops Owl** seems to be resident within the grounds. Recently, there have been a number of daytime sightings of scarce wintering (Nov–Mar) **Egyptian Nightjars** in the vicinity of the lodge.

Other animals There are some star mammals in the vicinity of Bilen Lodge, especially Gerenuk – which you are likely to encounter delicately browsing along the final stretch to the camp – and the marvellous Naked Mole-rats famed for their insect-like, highly social colonies reproductively dominated by a single specially elongated 'queen'. You will see their conical mounds even within the camp grounds, and with patience – especially after rain, when digging mole-rats let off whale-blows of sand – it is possible to see them occasionally poke their extraordinary naked and blind heads above the surface. Lion and Spotted Hyaena are resident around the camp and likely to be heard at night, and other mammals include Common Warthog (abundant), Lesser Kudu, Unstriped Ground Squirrel and (although rarely seen) Caracal.

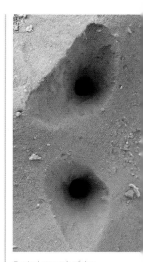

Conical mounds of the extraordinary Naked Mole-rat, studied in evolutionary biology labs throughout the world and occurring wild at Bilen Lodge.
(Claire Spottiswoode)

18. ALI DEGE PLAINS

The Ali Dege Plains are overgrazed and badly encroached by mesquite (*Prosopis juliflora* – a plague in the Afar region, known locally as the 'Devil Tree'). The plains are nonetheless a good area to search for **Arabian Bustard**. While scanning the plains, you may also see **Kori Bustard**, **Somali Ostrich** (rarely), **Egyptian Vulture**, **Secretarybird**, **African Swallow-tailed Kite** (usually in big groups when present), **Saker Falcon** (a scarce winter migrant, with occasional influxes), **Double-banded Courser** and flocks of **Chesnut-backed** and **Chestnut-headed Sparrow-larks**. Occasionally, there may be influxes of large numbers of irruptive species such as **Yellow-throated Sandgrouse**, **Bimaculated Lark** and **Pale Rockfinch**. There are also historical records of **Heuglin's Bustard** from the eastern part of the plain, nearest Asebot Mountain. One of the dwindling few Ethiopian populations of Grevy's Zebra occurs on the Ali Dege plains, as do Soemmering's Gazelle and Beisa Oryx.

Lappet-faced Vulture is declining throughout Africa, but is happily still fairly common throughout much of Ethiopia. (Tasso Leventis)

The plains can be scanned from several points. The easiest is from the main road 2 km beyond (i.e. towards Djibouti) the turn-off to Bilen Lodge, at the 275 km mileage post from Addis (5 on map; GPS045). Alternatively, you can attempt the tracks running east of the main road 13 km before the turn-off to Bilen Lodge (6 on map; GPS046). There is a rather confusing network of tracks which can be followed in the general direction of the plain, but it is probably only advisable to attempt these with any confidence if accompanied by a local guide. This area is inhabited by a mixture of tribes (Afar and Somali) and is not necessarily safe.

19. HARAR REGION & BABILE ELEPHANT SANCTUARY

Harar is about as far along the road to Somalia as most tourists ever venture. The portion of the Ogaden beyond has been too risky to visit for quite some time, which is especially unfortunate considering that it nears the Somalian type locality of **Archer's Lark**, closely related to the Liben Lark and not seen with certainty since its discovery in 1922. Harar, fortunately, is safe to visit, although usually in pursuit of history and hyaenas rather than birds. It is a famously atmospheric city, with a strongly Islamic feel, and a history of generations of 'hyaena-men' who to this day feed hyaenas by hand outside the city walls at dusk. These are the main reasons to visit, and the birding is typical of dry, rocky country at mid-altitude. Roadside stops between Dire Dawa and Harar might produce **Somali Fiscal**, **Bristle-crowned Starling**, **Blackstart**, **Little Rock Thrush** and **Red-fronted Warbler**, and the area seems particularly good for Palearctic migrants including **Upcher's Warbler** and **Common Rock Thrush**. Sacred Baboon becomes commoner as one moves east of Awash,

African Orange-bellied Parrots often nest in holes in termite mounds. (Tasso Leventis)

and might be seen at the roadside anywhere up to Harar. Note that well-known Lake Alemaya, on the northern side of the road 21 km west of Harar, is now sadly mostly dry and no longer much good for birding, but keep an eye out for it from around GPS047.

The Babile Elephant Sanctuary and the nearby Valley of Marvels – so called for its multitude of very impressive balancing rock formations – can be visited as a day trip from Harar. The turn-off to the Babile Elephant Sanctuary is 18 km east of Harar on the main road to Jijiga, at Bisidimo (from where there is a single century-old record of **Salvadori's Seedeater**, well north of its current range), but inconveniently you will first need obtain permission and collect a game scout from the sanctuary office in Babile village, another 12 km farther east (see the Bradt Guide for full details of access, and how best to locate the elephants). Species of this stark, rocky sanctuary include **Pygmy Falcon, Black-headed Plover, Dwarf Raven, Little Rock Thrush, Rosy-patched Bush-shrike** and the generally uncommon (in Ethiopia) **Green-winged Pytilia**. The Valley of Marvels is yet further south-east along the road to Jijiga, and crossed by it 5–10 km south-east of Babile village. Dry country birding is good here too, and species have included **Verreaux's Eagle, Bare-faced Go-away-bird, Shining** and **Hunter's Sunbirds**, and **White-bellied Canary**.

Care is needed to distinguish Hunter's Sunbird from the more widespread Scarlet-chested, with which it widely overlaps. Hunter's typically prefers drier country, but its range in Ethiopia isn't fully understood. (Tasso Leventis)

THE CENTRAL RIFT VALLEY

20. Debre Zeit Lakes
21. Lake Koka to Meki
22. Lake Ziway
23. Lake Langano: Western shore
24. Lake Langano: South-eastern shore
25. Abiata-Shalla National Park
26. Wondo Genet
27. Lake Awassa

TOP 10 BIRDS

Bat Hawk
Black Crowned Crane
Yellow-fronted Parrot
Black-winged Lovebird
Banded Barbet
Thick-billed Raven
Abyssinian Oriole
Spotted Creeper
African Hill Babbler
Abyssinian Ground Thrush

The Rift Valley is also southern Ethiopia's main transport axis, and all visiting birders will travel down it en route to the endemic-rich southern lowlands. Much of the Rift Valley is heavily transformed by industry, grazing, flower plantations and other agriculture, but birding is still extremely productive and diverse. It is exceptionally good along its string of lakes surrounded by arid savannas, and patches of remaining forest along escarpments bordering the valley. The lakes and savannas are excellent for general Afrotropical bird diversity, and in Nov–Mar for Palearctic migrants (especially ducks, waders, gulls and passerines). Some of Ethiopia's more reliable sites for the endemic **Yellow-fronted Parrot** are found in the fringing forests.

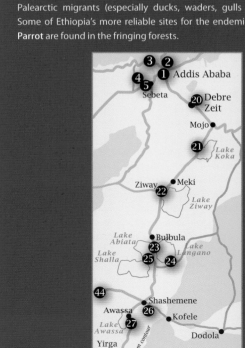

20. DEBRE ZEIT LAKES

Debre Zeit (also known as Bishoftu, its Oromiffa name) is a large sprawling town and airforce base 50 km south-east of Addis Ababa, through which one passes en route either down the Rift Valley or east towards Awash. It is situated in a volcanic area and surrounded by lakes, which can make a very productive birding stop if time allows. Most of the lakes fill volcanic craters, and have steep, rocky and often wooded sides.

Much the best lake for birds, though, is not a crater lake at all: Lake Cheleleka is a shallow, ephemeral pan with a broad and very variable shoreline, just north-west of the town centre. Resident species include **Knob-billed** and **Red-billed Ducks, Southern Pochard, African Pygmy-goose** and **White-backed Duck** (the last two especially among emergent vegetation at its fringes, particularly along its eastern shoreline), and Palearctic migrants (Nov–Mar) can include **Pintail, Garganey, Northern Shoveler, Ferruginous Duck, Tufted Duck, Ruff, Black-tailed Godwit, Gull-billed Tern** and flocks of **Common Cranes** that may number in the hundreds or even thousands. To reach it, turn north off the main road at GPS048; follow this road over a railway, and after about 350 m you will see the beginning of the lake on your left. The road skirts its eastern margin and subsequent floodplain, and various small tracks lead closer to the water's edge, e.g. around 1 on map, 2 km from the turn-off. Alternatively, turn north of the main road 1.2 km to the west of here, at the signpost for 'Genesis Farms' (GPS049). Continue for about 1 km until you see the lake on your right (around 2), then scan from the road or walk down one of the footpaths amongst vegetable fields to the water's edge.

Malachite Kingfisher is commonly seen quietly perching on reedy fringes of all the Rift Valley lakes. (Dick Forsman)

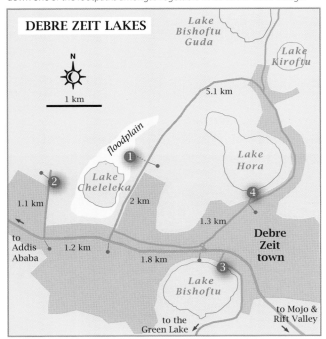

DEBRE ZEIT LAKES

N

1 km

Lake Bishoftu Guda

Lake Kiroftu

5.1 km

floodplain

Lake Cheleleka

Lake Hora

1.1 km

2 km

1.3 km

to Addis Ababa

1.2 km

1.8 km

Debre Zeit town

Lake Bishoftu

to the Green Lake

to Mojo & Rift Valley

Lake Cheleleka is a very productive waterbird site close to Addis Ababa, despite being nearly surrounded by the ever-expanding town of Debre Zeit. (Claire Spottiswoode)

Lake Bishoftu, just south of the town centre, is alkaline and very deep, and has a small wintering population of **Ferruginous Duck**, reliably present during Mar–Nov, as well as other Palearctic ducks, and resident species such as **Cape Teal** and **Southern Pochard**. It is most easily viewed from the Dreamland Resort (2 on map), a hotel at its eastern rim; to reach it, turn south at the sign on the main road and drive up to the hotel on the crater rim. The densely bushed hillside below the restaurant terrace is good for **Black-winged Lovebird**, **Banded Barbet**, both **White-winged** and **Mocking Cliff Chats**, and **Rüppell's Weaver**.

A short distance due north of Debre Zeit town are some further crater lakes, Hora (very saline), Kiroftu and Bishoftu Guda, which are also worth a look if you have time. Lake Hora lies just to the east of Lake Cheleleka, and its shoreline is reached via the Lake Hora Recreation Area (4 on map). **Pink-backed Pelicans** and **Great Cormorants** nest on trees and cliffs along its margins, and a pleasant variety of other waterbirds occur. The Green Lake (GPS050) is 5 km south of town and positioned in an exceptionally deep and steep-sided crater, and is so-named because of the algae that thrive in its alkaline water, making it anaerobic and inhospitable to fish. Greatly variable (but occasionally vast) numbers of algae-feeding **Lesser Flamingos** occur here, and it is also good for a variety of resident and Palearctic duck species sometimes again including **Ferruginous Duck**. To reach the Green Lake, turn off as for Lake Bishoftu (above), follow this road part the Dreamland Resort, skirting the eastern side of Lake Bishoftu, and continue for about 5 km. Access has on occasions been forbidden on account of the nearby airforce base.

Rüppell's Weaver is nearly endemic to the Horn of Africa, and common near water in many parts of Ethiopia's Rift Valley. (Andy Swash)

21. LAKE KOKA TO MEKI

Lake Koka (also known as Lake Gelila), with its impressive volcanic backdrop, is skirted by the main tar road down the Rift Valley, just south of Mojo. Despite appearances it is not volcanic in origin like the other Rift Valley lakes, but rather a vast reservoir formed by the damming of the headwaters of Awash River, here a long journey from its ultimate end in the Danakil Depression in Ethiopia's far north-east. The lake nudges the road in several places between the towns of Mojo and Meki (30–35 km north of Meki); stop and scan particularly at the point where the Awash River flows into the lake (GPS051), 23.2 km from the turn-off south at Mojo, and also at the extensive wetland area crossing the road 3.4 km farther on (GPS052). Bird numbers vary greatly between seasons and years, but when the water is visible it is well worth pausing here to scan from the roadside. A pair of **Black Crowned Cranes** may often be found standing in the dense aquatic vegetation where the road crosses the Awash River. Other waterbirds can include **Saddle-billed** and **Yellow-billed Storks**, **Goliath Heron**, **Greater Flamingo**, **Hottentot Teal**, **Red-billed Duck**, **Southern Pochard**, and in season Palearctic migrants such as **Garganey**, **Green** and **Wood Sandpipers**, **Whiskered** and **White-winged Terns** and **Black-tailed Godwit**.

Superb Starling is an abundant bird of Ethiopia's drier lowlands; here, an adult collects maggots, puffin-style, for its hungry brood. (Paul Donald)

The vast area of farmed plains that lies between the towns of Alem Tena (38 km from Mojo) and Meki is also important for Palearctic species, including sometimes large numbers of **White Stork**, **Common Crane** and **Common** and **Lesser Kestrels**. This area is good for Afrotropical species too, including **African Swallow-tailed Kite** (largely Nov–Apr), **Abdim's Stork**, **Four-banded Sandgrouse** and **Chestnut-backed Sparrow-lark**. The best area is roughly 11 km south of Alem Tena (c.9 km north of Meki, GPS053). Along the roadside all the way down the Rift Valley, look out for parties of **Chestnut-bellied Sandgrouse**, **Abyssinian Ground Hornbill** and **Chestnut Sparrow**, the latter very inconspicuous when not in breeding plumage (females resemble other sparrow species).

Abyssinian Ground Hornbill is still wonderfully common in lowland Ethiopia, despite its need for large trees in which to nest. (Tasso Leventis)

22. LAKE ZIWAY

The town of Ziway lies on the western shore of the lake (pronounced Zwhy). The lakeshore can be reached along a dual-carriageway track that turns east off the main tar road through town next to the Bekele Molla Hotel and Shell fuel station. Follow this track 800 m to a short causeway leading into the lake, which provides a good vantage point from which to scan the lake and fringing vegetation of reeds and thickets. You can also take the last turning to the left before the water's edge, which leads about 1 km to a recreation area which also provides a good vantage – particularly for Hippopotamus (and Yellow-spotted Hyrax, which occur in the fig trees and buildings). Waterbirds are abundant and relatively tame and approachable at both places, making this a particularly good place for photography. You might also be able to hire a small boat from a local fisherman. Common species include **Eastern White Pelican**, **Gull-billed Tern** (Sept–May and often overwintering), large numbers of **Marabou Stork**, **Hamerkop**, **Black Heron**, **Spur-winged Plover**, **White-faced** and **Fulvous Whistling Ducks**, **Hottentot Teal**, **African Darter**, **Long-tailed Cormorant** and **Black Crake**. **White-backed Duck** and **African Pygmy-goose** are likely to be found by carefully scanning the emergent vegetation with a telescope; with more luck still, one might detect a **Lesser Jacana** (but beware of young **African Jacanas**) – this is one of the few known sites for this species in Ethiopia. **Saddle-billed Stork** occasionally visits, and **African Rail** might be heard from the reeds. During Nov–Apr, resident **Grey-headed Gulls** are joined by Palearctic migrants such as **Lesser Black-backed** and **Black-headed** and, more rarely, **Pallas's** and **Heuglin's Gulls** can occur here; **Slender-billed Gull** has even been recorded. **Lesser Swamp Warbler**, **Vitelline Masked Weaver** and in winter Palearctic migrants such as **Sedge Warbler** lurk in the fringing vegetation.

Yellow-billed Stork occurs around the shallow margins of many Ethiopian lakes. (Tasso Leventis)

23. LAKE LANGANO: WESTERN SHORE

The Rift Valley lakes of Langano, Abiata and Shalla are all situated close together in dry, open acacia savanna. Birding along the western shore of Lake Langano is very productive, and makes a wonderful introduction to the East African savannas for any birder new to the region. There are also good sites for several widespread species that can be surprisingly tricky to find elsewhere. Lake Langano is also one of the sites where the still-mysterious 'Ethiopian' **Cliff Swallow** has been sighted a number of times (see also site 15).

Key birds Clapperton's Francolin, Heuglin's Courser, Northern White-faced Owl, Grey-headed Woodpecker, Red-throated Wryneck, Banded and Red-fronted Barbets, Little Rock Thrush.

Key habitats Acacia savanna, low wooded cliffs, open lake shoreline.

Access Birding along Langano's western shore is easiest around the two hotels on the lake's western shore. These are respectively the Bekele Molla Hotel (turn-off 137 km south of Mojo, at GPS054 and opposite the Abiata-Shalla National Park signboard; a good campsite is also available here), and the Wabe Shabelle Hotel (turn-off 123 km S of Mojo, at GPS055). Both are reached along gravel tracks running 3 km east of the main Addis–Moyale tar road to the lake shore.

Birding The Bekele Molla Hotel is situated at the base of some low cliffs. Birding in the hotel grounds is very productive (check larger trees for **Hemprich's Hornbill**, **Banded**, **Red-fronted** and **Black-billed Barbets**, **Red-throated Wryneck**, **Black-winged Lovebird** and **Abdim's Stork**), as is the adjacent acacia woodland. A stroll through the woodland (e.g. along the track running parallel to the entrance road, at the base of the low cliffs, or along the lake shore north of the hotel) is likely to produce many species typical of taller acacia, including **Blue-naped Mousebird**, **Black-billed Woodhoopoe**, **Striped**

Blue-breasted Bee-eater tends on average to occur at higher altitudes than Little Bee-eater, but there is much overlap. The Ethiopian subspecies *lafresnayii* is very distinctive and may in fact be more closely related to the Cinnamon-chested Bee-eater of East Africa. (Tasso Leventis)

Tall acacia woodland near the Bekele Molla Hotel at Lake Langano; birding in this habitat can be spectacularly productive. (Claire Spottiswoode)

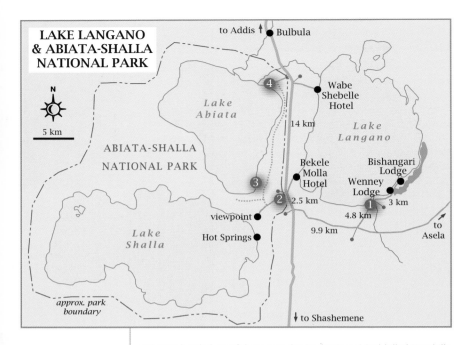

**LAKE LANGANO
& ABIATA-SHALLA
NATIONAL PARK**

to Addis ↑ ● Bulbula

N

5 km

*Lake
Abiata*

ABIATA-SHALLA

NATIONAL PARK

④

● Wabe
Shebelle
Hotel

14 km

*Lake
Langano*

Bekele
Molla
Hotel

Bishangari
Lodge

Wenney
Lodge

③

② 2.5 km

viewpoint ●

● Hot Springs

*Lake
Shalla*

①   3 km

4.8 km

9.9 km

to
Asela

*approx. park
boundary*

↓ to Shashemene

and **Grey-headed Kingfishers**, **Von der Decken's** and **Red-billed Hornbills**, **Bearded**, **Nubian** and **Grey-headed Woodpeckers**, **Red-fronted Barbet**, **Buff-bellied Warbler**, **Mouse-coloured Penduline-tit**, **Grey-headed** and sometimes **Black-headed Batises**, **White-crested Helmetshrike**, **Rüppell's Starling**, **Rüppell's**, **Little** and **Chestnut Weavers**, and perhaps **Crimson-rumped Waxbill**. **Boran Cisticola** occurs, but is outnumbered by the common **Rattling Cisticola**, from which it is best distinguished by call as well as by its duller crown. Rank undergrowth may attract foraging parties of seedeaters and during Nov–Mar denser tangles might have migrant warblers such as **Common** and **Thrush Nightingales**. **Common Kestrel**, **Fan-tailed Raven**, **Mocking Cliff Chat** and **Abyssinian Black Wheatear** occur on the cliffs, among hawking **Blue-breasted Bee-eater** and galloping Ethiopian Rock Hyrax. At

Care is needed to separate Black-headed Batis from the much commoner Grey-headed Batis. Confusingly, Black-headed's head is typically slate-grey, rather than ash-grey in the Grey-headed. (Dick Forsman)

dusk and dawn, listen for **Verreaux's Eagle-owl** calling from the taller trees at the base of the cliff; they are quite active in the evenings and are often seen before dark. **Freckled Nightjar** calls from the cliffs and may perch on the hotel roofs at night. **Saker Falcon** (a winter visitor to Ethiopia) has been seen in this vicinity.

The Wabe Shabelle Hotel is set in rather arid, sparse savanna, but has well-watered grounds and the lusher vegetation within the hotel compound can be very productive; it is well known for **Little Rock Thrush**, which is often present among the buildings. **Rüppell's Weavers** sometimes nest here in large numbers. The staff often keep track of active owl roosts, and may be able to point you towards **Verreaux's** and **Greyish Eagle-owls**, **Barn Owl** and **Northern White-faced Owl**. Small parties of **Slender-tailed Nightjar** can usually be found roosting in the hotel compound; look especially in the vicinity of the rubbish dump to the left of the car park, about 30 m from reception. The open ground beyond here is also worth scanning for **Temminck's** and **Heuglin's Coursers**, **Four-banded Sandgrouse** and **Clapperton's Francolin**. The lake shoreline is mainly gravel beach and not very birdy, but **Senegal Thick-knee** may be seen and, in winter, **Gull-billed Tern** and (although less frequently than at Abiata-Shalla, see site 25) **Pallas's**, **Heuglin's**, **Black-headed** and **Lesser Black-backed Gulls**.

Left: Boran Cisticola (left, Tasso Leventis) and Rattling Cisticola (right, Jacques Erard) often occur alongside one another in Ethiopia. Boran can be distinguished its duller and greyer crown, as well as by its gentler call.

Greyish Eagle-owl is often seen by day in the grounds of the Wabe Shabelle Hotel at Lake Langano. (Dick Forsman)

Clapperton's Francolin's range extends westwards as far as Nigeria, but it is far from abundant within Ethiopia, and is thought to have declined in numbers. Lake Langano is still a good site for it. (Nik Borrow)

Rüppell's Starling prefers taller woodland and can be locally abundant in the Rift Valley. (Tasso Leventis)

Grey-backed Fiscal is a very social bird, occurring in noisy and probably cooperatively breeding parties in open, grassy woodland. (Tasso Leventis)

24. LAKE LANGANO: SOUTH-EASTERN SHORE

Access to the moister south-eastern shore of Lake Langano is via two privately run eco-lodges, Bishangari and Wenney (Guereza Colobus in Oromiffa). Bishangari Lodge is located in a beautiful setting among tall fig trees, with natural forest both within the lodge compound and on the low hills beyond it, and birding is excellent throughout.

Key birds Scaly Francolin, Yellowbill, White-cheeked Turaco, Narina Trogon, Yellow-fronted Parrot, Scaly-throated Honeyguide, Abyssinian and Grey-headed Woodpeckers, African Hill Babbler, Abyssinian Ground Thrush, Green-backed Twinspot.

Key habitats Acacia woodland, fig forest, medium-altitude montane forest.

Access The turn-off (GPS056) to Bishangari and Wenney Lodges is 139.5 km south of Mojo. This gravel road eventually leads to the town of Asela, but turn off it after 9.9 km (GPS057), following the signs, and the dabs of orange paint on roadside trees. The distance to Bishangari Lodge is 20 km in total from the tar road, and the latter stretches may require 4WD at times. Note that at one point a bridge over a stream (1 on map on p.70, GPS058) consists of an open-ended former shipping container, which restricts the maximum height of vehicles (luggage might need to be temporarily removed from roof-racks). Wenney Lodge is 2 km beyond this bridge, and Bishangari 1 km further. Bishangari Lodge can also be reached by boat from the Bekele Molla Hotel on the lake's western shore (see previous site). Accommodation at Bishangari is not cheap but highly recommended: the bungalows are extremely comfortable, the food good, and horse trekking, mountain biking, boat trips and birding guides are available; ask especially for Teesho or Hakim at Bishangari, or Hirpo Dube at Wenney Lodge. Although this account concentrates on Bishangari Lodge, birding at the somewhat cheaper Wenney Lodge is similar and also very good. Wenney, however, has less easy access to the forest.

Birding Very good birding is possible even along the entrance road to the lodges: the mixture of large acacia and fig trees along the final c. 6 km of track in particular (e.g. in the vicinity of the 'container' bridge, 1 on map), can be very productive. Species may include **Bare-faced Go-away Bird, Black-**

Both resident African and Palearctic migrant subspecies of Peregrine Falcon occur in Ethiopia. This African individual is devouring an African Thrush behind Bishangari Lodge. (Tasso Leventis)

winged Lovebird, Banded, Double-toothed, Black-billed and **Red-fronted Barbets**, **Red-throated Wryneck**, **Grey-headed Woodpecker**, **Little** and **Rüppell's Weaver**, **Reichenow's Seedeater** and even **Narina Trogon**. Keep an eye out for a day roosting **Heuglin's Courser** in open areas, such as around the Bishangari compound entrance.

Bishangari Lodge is set at the edge of a small patch of forest, where it grades into sparse acacia savanna at the lake edge shore. Behind this small forest patch is a large grassy area of former lake bed where **Woolly-necked Stork**, **Wattled Ibis** and **Grey-backed Fiscal** occur, and beyond this a large area of natural forest extending north along the lake shore. Footpaths lead from the lodge to a gate at the back of the compound, and you should engage a guide to take you to a network of footpaths within the larger forest patch beyond. Excellent forest birding is possible here, and many of the key species occur even in the small forest patch within the lodge grounds: these include **Scaly Francolin** and **Abyssinian Ground Thrush**, both of which lurk in the understorey right around the lodge buildings. Other forest species include

Shy but quietly trilling parties of Green-backed Twinspot can be found, with a little patience, in the wonderful natural forest behind Bishangari and Wenney Lodges. (Tasso Leventis)

The indigenous forest around Bishangari and Wenney Lodges has a heavily grazed understorey, but is still superb for birds. (Lajos Németh)

Yellow-fronted Parrot, White-cheeked Turaco, Narina Trogon, Lemon Dove, Scaly-throated Honeyguide (listen for its loud, mechanical trill), Abyssinian Woodpecker, African Hill Babbler, Abyssinian Oriole and Grey and Red-shouldered Cuckooshrikes. Yellowbill is present but not common; listen for its curious shrieking call. Parties of Green-backed Twinspot trill softly in understorey tangles and may be flushed from the path edges, sometimes intermingled with African Firefinch. The hard-to-see Scaly Francolin crows loudly in the early mornings. It is perhaps most easily seen in the larger forest patch, where the heavily grazed understorey is fairly open, but sometimes also ventures out onto the lodge paths. Mottled and Nyanza Swifts and Black Saw-wing pass over the canopy.

Also ask at the lodge for directions to the short (< 2 km) walking trail from the lodge along the lake's edge. This leads to an area of an area of vegetated lakeshore with tall reeds, where Hippopotamus and a wide variety of water-birds can be seen. These may include Purple Heron, Saddle-billed Stork, Greater Flamingo, Purple Swamphen and Lesser Swamp Warbler, and in winter a collection of Palearctic waders, gulls and terns. This is a particularly pleasant walk in the early mornings and evenings.

25. ABIATA-SHALLA NATIONAL PARK

This national park can provide good birding, especially for Palearctic migrants, but is somewhat degraded and of uncertain future. The two lakes differ strongly in character: Lake Shalla fills a volcanic caldera and is deep and sterile, whereas Lake Abiata is very shallow and brackish. Once Ethiopia's answer to Kenya's Lake Nakuru, Lake Abiata is sadly rapidly shrinking owing to industrial water extraction, and is ringed by a broad dry plain of former lakebed.

Key birds Greater and Lesser Flamingos, many Palearctic waders and gulls, Kittlitz's Plover, Black Crowned Crane, Abyssinian Black Wheatear.

Key habitats Acacia savanna, saline lakeshore.

Access The main park entrance is directly opposite the Lake Langano Bekele Molla Hotel turn-off (see site 23; GPS054). The park headquarters are at the gate, and you will be asked to take a game scout in your car, which is anyway recommended to ensure a hassle-free drive to the lake. Lake Abiata is more easily reached from a second park entrance near Bulbula (details below).

Birding Directly surrounding the main (southern) park entrance is an area of

Lesser Flamingos trawl along the rapidly receding shoreline of Lake Abiata. (Nik Borrow)

relatively intact savanna, owing to having been formerly fenced for Somali Ostrich farming (an introduced population now breeds in the park). This extends about 2 km from the gate (2 on map on p.70), and provides good acacia birding. Species include **Black-bellied Bustard, Greyish** and **Verreaux's Eagle-owls, Abyssinian Ground Hornbill, Black-billed Woodhoopoe, Black Scimitarbill** (generally an uncommon bird), **Bearded, Nubian** and **Cardinal Woodpeckers, Red-throated** and (during Nov–Mar) **Eurasian Wrynecks, Foxy Lark, Buff-bellied Warbler, White-winged Black Tit** and Grant's Gazelle. From the gate the road continues to a viewpoint (GPS059) overlooking Lake Shalla (and some nearby hot springs), and a turn-off leads north to Lake Abiata. Lake Shalla's tremendous depth means that it is not particularly good for birds, except for **Sacred Ibis** and **Eastern White Pelicans** that breed on the islands. The road from here north to Lake Abiata is very degraded (shown as a dotted line on the map) owing to heavy industrial traffic, and may be exceptionally dusty during the dry season and impassable in the wet. It passes along some low sandy cliffs where **Abyssinian Black Wheatear** occurs, and through degraded woodland and scrub that is good for **Stone-curlew** (occasionally large numbers in winter, Oct–Apr), and **Temminck's** and **Double-banded Coursers** and Grant's Gazelle year-round. Vehicles need to stop a few hundred metres from the lake shore (around 3 on map) to avoid getting stuck in the deceptively firm dry lake margins; see below for likely species.

The lakeshore of Abiata itself is more easily reached via the northern park gate, signposted just before Bulbula. This road is in better condition and passes through farmland before reaching the lake after about 3 km. A game scout collected at the gate will assist you to avoid getting your vehicle stuck in mud, either by accident or by misleading directions from people hoping to dig you out. The end of this road (around 4 on map) was at the time of writing quite a long way (2–3 km) from the water's edge, and birding is hugely variable, depending on water levels. However, the walk can be worth it for **Black Crowned Crane** (year round), **Wattled Crane** (rarely, but especially during Nov–Dec), **Common Crane** (Nov–Mar) and thousands (sometimes hundreds of thousands) of both **Greater** and **Lesser Flamingos** and migrant Palearctic waterfowl such as **Northern Shoveler**. The shoreline can be extremely good

Algae-feeding Lesser Flamingos (foreground) tend to outnumber invertebrate-feeding Greater Flamingos (with straight neck) at Lake Abiata. (Tasso Leventis)

Pygmy Falcon is an apparently cooperatively polyandrous species in which the male (pictured) is less brightly plumaged than the chestnut-backed female. (Tasso Leventis)

for waders: **Kittlitz's Plover** is always common, and during Nov–Mar joined by Palearctic migrants including **Ruff**, **Little Stint**, **Curlew Sandpiper**, **Ringed** and **Little Ringed Plovers** and, more rarely, small numbers of **Red-necked Phalarope** and **Kentish**, **Caspian**, **Lesser Sand**, **Grey** and even (with increasingly regularity) **Pacific Golden Plovers**. This is also a good spot to scan for Palearctic migrant gulls including **Pallas's**, **Heuglin's**, **Black-headed** and **Lesser Black-backed Gulls**. Other migrants such as **Barn Swallow** and **Yellow Wagtail** may also congregate here in huge numbers on passage. **Barbary Falcon**, scarce in Ethiopia, has been seen here.

26. WONDO GENET

Wondo Genet is a hot spring resort in some wooded hills fringing the eastern side of the Rift Valley near Shashemene, and is heavily frequented by weekend traffic from Addis Ababa. Its main attraction is easy access to mid-altitude montane forest, offering a host of endemic species, within straightforward road access and adjacent to a good hotel, and with excellent local guides available. The forest is, however, under severe pressure from charcoal burning and clearing for agriculture.

Key birds African Crowned Eagle, Yellow-fronted Parrot, Black-winged Lovebird, Half-collared Kingfisher, Narina Trogon, Banded and Double-toothed Barbets, Abyssinian Woodpecker, Spotted Creeper, African Hill Babbler, Abyssinian Ground Thrush, Abyssinian Oriole, Sharpe's Starling, Green-backed Twinspot.

Narina Trogon, named by François Levaillant after his Khoikhoi mistress and, presumably, correspondingly splendid.
(Tasso Leventis)

Tall, open woodland at the edge of what remains of Wondo Genet's natural forest. Spotted Creeper much favours this habitat.
(Claire Spottiswoode)

Key habitats Mid-altitude montane forest (sadly large parts have been cleared in recent years), secondary forest; altitude about 1,800 m.

Access From the Rastafarian stronghold of Shashemene, take the well-signposted gravel road east for 14 km to the village of Wosha, and turn left at the sign onto a final 3 km stretch to the hotel and hot springs. The hotel is run by the Wabe Shabelle chain and boasts a preposterously spaceship-shaped restaurant. It can be very busy at weekends, when advance booking is advised. On leaving the Wabe Shebelle Hotel with binoculars, one is sure

Abyssinian Ground Thrush is inconspicuous but sometimes surprisingly confiding at Wondo Genet and elsewhere. (Dick Forsman)

to be accosted by one or more local guides reciting lists of desirable species. Many of them are knowledgeable and sharp-eyed and well worth engaging (also to keep crowds of children at bay); ask particularly for Nuru, or alternatively for Mekonen Tassew or Mekonen Mulu.

Birding Two forested valleys extend up from the hotel/hot spring area, and although their natural forest is sadly heavily degraded, many excellent forest birds can still be found. The left-hand (northern) valley, named Geriramo, is reached via a track heading uphill immediately in front of the hotel compound entrance; follow it past some houses and up the eastern flank of the valley. It initially passes through open, regenerating areas that until a few years ago were pine plantations, then enters some rather degraded forest comprising tall, widely spaced trees, with much rampant secondary growth beneath. This is good habitat for some species of woodland and forest edge, such as **Black-winged Lovebird**, **Grey-headed Woodpecker**, **Banded Barbet**, **Lesser Honeyguide** and rarely **Wahlberg's Honeybird**, **Red-shouldered Cuckooshrike**, **Spotted Creeper** and especially **Abyssinian Woodpecker**. Look out for **Yellow-fronted Parrot** especially from here onwards. Pairs (typically) are often seen flying over, screeching noisily, in the early morning and late evening, and often rest on exposed branches. Other species associated with fruiting trees are **Banded** and **Double-toothed Barbets**, **Slender-billed Starling** and **Sharpe's Starling**, which is typically seen perched on exposed branches of tall trees, often giving its thin, remarkably metallic warbling song. Other reasonably common and vocal forest birds here include **African Emerald Cuckoo**, **White-cheeked Turaco**, **Silvery-cheeked Hornbill**, **Narina Trogon**, **Grey Cuckooshrike**, **Abyssinian Oriole**, **African Hill Babbler**, **Abyssinian Slaty Flycatcher** and **Montane White-eye**. **Nyanza Swift** and **Black Saw-wing** are likely to pass overhead. Search the understorey for **Abyssinian Ground Thrush**, which is not uncommon here, and the path edges for **Green-backed Twinspot** although commoner seedeaters of the secondary growth are **Yellow-bellied Waxbill**, **African Firefinch** and **African Citril**. **Scaly Francolin** is very vocal in the mornings, and you might be lucky enough to locate one within sight of the path.

To reach the right-hand (southern) valley, take the track that turns uphill at the bottom of the hotel drive (above the swimming pool entrance), and follow it up a series of switchbacks to a small stream (GPS060), where a mineral water

African Hill Babbler lurks in dense tangles, often along streams, but gives away its presence with a fluty song. (Tasso Leventis)

Guereza Colobus is amazingly abundant in most of Ethiopia's forests. (Tasso Leventis)

factory was under construction at the time of writing. Above the factory site are some earth cliffs where **Half-collared Kingfisher** breeds, and **Little Rock Thrush** may be seen. From here a footpath leads across an open area with several beautiful large trees (including figs), which are especially good for **Banded** and **Double-toothed Barbets, White-winged Cliff Chat** and **Spotted Creeper**. It then crosses a stream where **African Hill Babbler** can be particularly common in the rank vegetation, and then steeply ascends the side of a valley. The natural forest here is also extremely good for similar species to those mentioned above for the Geriramo valley, and your guide may offer to show you an **African Crowned Eagle** nest.

In the early morning when frolicking crowds are absent, the area around the hot springs swimming pool is worth checking for **Half-collared Kingfisher**; also search along its outlet stream, by taking the footpath 100 m below the swimming pool entrance, down to a weir; also look out for **Giant Kingfisher** and **Mountain Wagtail** here. **Abyssinian Catbird** has been seen here, although it is strangely rare at Wondo Genet.

The grounds of the Wabe Shabelle Hotel can themselves be very productive. **Yellow-fronted Parrot, Black-winged Lovebird, Banded** and **Double-toothed Barbets** and **Sharpe's Starling** all pass through, especially when trees are fruiting, and flowering trees attract many sunbirds, especially **Beautiful, Tacazze** and **Scarlet-chested Sunbirds. Abyssinian Woodpecker** is occasionally seen here, and groups of **Green-backed Twinspot** may feed quietly on the lawns and paths, but are not always present. Dawn chorus is likely to include, less euphoniously, **Thick-billed Raven** and **Silvery-cheeked Hornbill**. At dusk, keep an eye out for **Bat Hawk** anywhere in this area. Other scarcer forest raptors include **Ayres's Eagle** and **Great** and **Little Sparrowhawks**; the latter is often seen and heard in the canopy of the trees in the hotel grounds. **Western Banded Snake-eagle** has been seen in the area, but is by no means common. **African Wood Owls** call in the grounds at night. **Montane Nightjar** calls from the open areas of regenerating forest above the hotel, and there have been single records of **Plain Nightjar** and **Buff-spotted Flufftail** nearby, so keep an ear out for these scarce nocturnal species.
Other animals Guereza Colobus is common.

27. LAKE AWASSA

The large town of Awassa makes a very pleasant stopover en route south to bush-crow country, and is excellent in its own right for a good variety of woodland and waterbirds. Birding is concentrated around a scatter of small sites, including the two large hotels on the lakeshore. The two hotels provide straightforward access to the shoreline and adjoining woodland, as well as protecting some large riparian trees.
Key birds Black Crowned Crane, Lesser Jacana, Bat Hawk, Blue-headed Coucal, Red-throated Wryneck, Spotted Creeper, Abyssinian Waxbill.
Key habitats Swampy and open lakeshore; reedbeds; riparian trees; mixed woodland.
Access and birding Numbers refer to the small-scale map of Awassa town on p.80, and sites are simply arranged north to south as though approaching from Addis, rather than in order of importance.

A careful scan of lily-covered lake edges is likely to reveal a quiet pair of African Pygmy Goose. (Dick Forsman)

1. Road to Wondo Tika On the very northern outskirts of the Awassa urban area, before reaching the Tikur Wuha river (below), turn onto a track leading westwards from Kedist Mariam (St Mary's) Church (GPS061). Follow this dirt road for about 2 km until it reaches Lake Awassa, and then north along its shores for another couple of kilometres. This is the best area around Awassa for **Black Crowned Crane**, and is also particularly good for **Lesser Jacana**, amongst other more widespread waterbirds.

2. Bridge over Tikur Wuha River A short distance (1.2 km) south of Kedist Mariam Church (see above), the main road passes over a bridge (GPS062) with a police checkpoint, just before reaching Awassa town proper. Stop at the checkpoint, and ask permission from the police to scan for birds from bridge. The grassy marshy area at the river's edge (especially on the western side) is well worth scanning for a nice variety of widespread waterbird species such as **Goliath Heron, Fulvous Whistling Duck, African Pygmy-goose, African Jacana**, and occasionally small groups of **Black Crowned Crane**.

3. United Africa Hotel (formerly the Wabe Shabelle Hotel Number One) The more northerly of the two Lake Awassa hotels probably offers the better lakeshore habitat. To reach the shoreline, go out of the gate at the back of the hotel compound, and walk north (right) along the footpath that follows a slightly raised dyke wall (a on map). This area can be full of activity from women washing and passing groups of children, but is usually still very good for waterbirds. The emergent vegetation along this marshy shoreline is one of the few reliable sites in Ethiopia for **Lesser Jacana**, and is also good for **African Pygmy-goose, Hottentot Teal, White-backed Duck** and **Malachite, Pied** and

Black-winged Lovebird is a common species of well-wooded country throughout much of Ethiopia; this is a female. (Tasso Leventis)

Spotted Creeper has a fascinating geographical distribution, widely divided between Africa and India; Awassa and Wondo Genet are both excellent places to search for it. (Andy Swash)

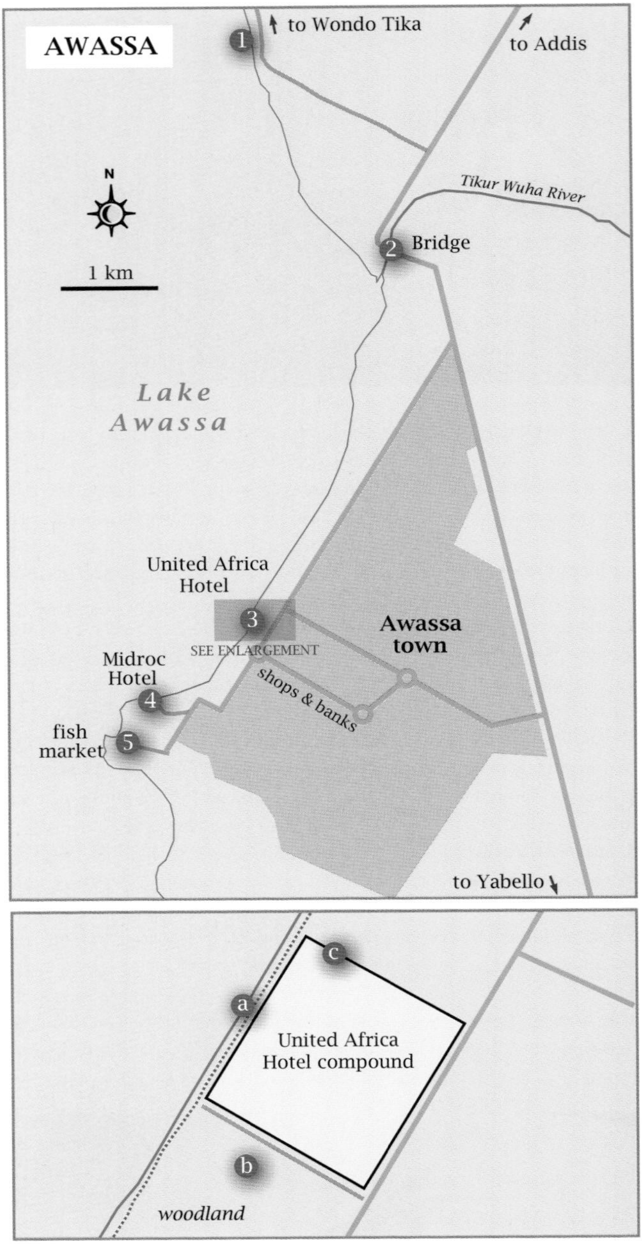

AWASSA

to Wondo Tika

to Addis

1

Tikur Wuha River

2 Bridge

Lake Awassa

United Africa Hotel

3

SEE ENLARGEMENT

Awassa town

Midroc Hotel

4

shops & banks

fish market

5

to Yabello

c

a

United Africa Hotel compound

b

woodland

Giant Kingfishers. Blue-headed Coucal is often seen flopping heavily from the reeds and sedges, where **Grosbeak Weaver, Yellow-mantled Widowbird** and **Abyssinian Waxbill** forage; look for parties of the latter in any moist, swampy areas. To reach an area of productive acacia woodland, turn south (left) at the gate; the woodland (b) begins just beyond the southern boundary fence of the hotel compound. This is a particularly good site for **Spotted Creeper**, as well as **Red-throated** and (seasonally) **Eurasian Wrynecks, Little Weaver**, and various widespread species of moist woodland such as **African Pygmy** and **Woodland Kingfishers**. Palearctic migrants might include **Upcher's, Barred, Olive-tree** (scarce in Ethiopia) and **Marsh Warblers, Thrush Nightingale** and **Isabelline Shrike**. The tall trees in the hotel area are favoured by scarce raptors such as **Western Banded Snake-eagle** and **Bat Hawk**; keep a watchful eye for the latter especially at dusk, when its curious, ominous shape can be seen coursing up the lake shore. By day, big trees are often festooned with **Black-winged Lovebird, Silvery-cheeked Hornbill** and **Slender-billed Starling**; look especially in figs for **Double-toothed** and **Banded Barbets**. **Thick-billed Ravens** are usually much in evidence around the compound. **Verreaux's Eagle-owl** often roost in the tall alien *Casuarina* trees in the north-western corner of the compound (c). **Northern White-faced Owls** are occasionally present in the thorn-trees along the western edge of the compound, and can be searched for with a spotlight at night.

4. Midroc Hotel (formerly the Wabe Shebelle Hotel Number Two) This hotel is nicely positioned right at the water's edge, but the shoreline is slightly less productive than at the United Africa. Woodland birding is very similar. Both hotels are currently plotting major building plans, so conditions may change in future.

5. Awassa fish market The fish market can be a colourful scene, as squabbling hordes of waterbirds pillage scraps from landing fishermen and busily filleting market-keepers. It has become a local tourist attraction, and a small entrance fee is payable. There is much activity especially in the mornings, as fresh fish are brought in and the posses of **Eastern White Pelicans, Grey-headed Gulls** and **Great Cormorants** are at their most hysterical. Macabre groups of **Marabou Storks** also gather here. Away from the chaos of the market proper, **Giant, Pied** and **Malachite Kingfishers** are ever-present, **Goliath** and **Black Herons** quietly stalk the lakeshore, and sombre pairs or parties of **Senegal Thick-knee** loiter in quieter spots. There is a fine tract of woodland (GPS063) just to the north of the fish market, and a stroll here has a good chance of turning up **Spotted Creeper, Red-throated** and (in winter) **Eurasian Wrynecks, Grey-headed** and **Nubian Woodpeckers, Woodland** and **Grey-headed Kingfishers**, and **Banded** and **Double-toothed Barbets**.

Marabou Storks are ubiquitous in the Rift Valley; a watchful Malachite Kingfisher is in the foreground. (Lajos Németh)

The Awassa fish market, where scores of pillaging waterbirds profit from local fishermen. (Nik Borrow)

THE BALE MOUNTAINS AND BEYOND

28. Bale Mountains National Park: Dinsho Region
29. Bale Mountains National Park: Sanetti Plateau
30. Bale Mountains National Park: Harenna Forest
31. Sof Omar
32. Imi and the Ogaden

TOP 10 BIRDS

Ruddy Shelduck

Spot-breasted Plover

Wattled Crane

Cape Eagle-owl

Abyssinian Owl

Abyssinian Woodpecker

Abyssinian Catbird

White-backed Black Tit

Abyssinian Longclaw

Salvadori's Seedeater

The Bale Mountains in Ethiopia's southern highlands are a vast and beautiful mountain range easily accessible by vehicle. There is also a well-established network of trekking routes for those with the time and energy. Birding here is easy, full of montane endemics, and complemented by star mammals and spectacular backdrops. The Bale massif's southern slopes are covered by the extensive, wet Harenna Forest (site 30), and in-between the high Afro-alpine moorland of the Sanetti Plateau with its wolves and eagles (site 29). In a 4WD vehicle, it is possible to drive directly south from the Bale Mountains to the dry lowlands of extreme southern Ethiopia (see next section). This journey from the town of Goba across the plateau and down through the Harenna Forest to Dolo Mena and Negele is surely one of the most spectacular drives in Africa. In less than a day one passes through every stratum of montane and alpine vegetation before dropping through an awesome 35 km of forest and eventually emerging, after a descent of nearly 3,000 m in altitude, into the camel-dotted thorny lowlands. Away from this route, this section also includes two lowland sites east of Bale, Sof Omar and the Imi region of the Ogaden. The former is a good lowland site especially famed for **Salvadori's Seedeater**, the latter a difficult and risky destination only advisable with much local support.

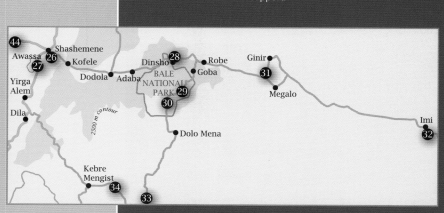

28. BALE MOUNTAINS NP: DINSHO REGION

The Bale National Park headquarters are at Dinsho on the massif's northern slopes, which are dominated by *Hagenia*–juniper woodland providing excellent birding. Dinsho is also where any trekking can be arranged, and park fees paid in advance for a visit to the Sanetti Plateau and Harenna Forest (see sites 29–30).

Key birds Spot-breasted Plover, Wattled Crane, Rouget's Rail, Abyssinian Owl, Cape Eagle-owl, Abyssinian Woodpecker, Red-billed Chough, Abyssinian Ground Thrush, Abyssinian Catbird, White-backed Black Tit, Brown ('Bale') Parisoma.

Key habitats *Hagenia*–juniper woodland and wet forest, Afro-alpine heathland, tussocky montane streams.

Access Dinsho is 400 km from Addis. Allow at least four hours for the journey from Shashemene, or more including birding stops. The road can become very slow-going after heavy rains, but was being rebuilt at the time of writing and may soon be much improved. Accommodation (pleasant dormitory rooms and a campsite) is available at Dinsho Lodge at the Bale National Park headquarters just outside Dinsho; alternatively, Dinsho is 42 km (allow at least an hour, more if wet) from the Wabe Shabelle Hotel in Goba (see site 29). Dinsho should be accessible at all times of year in 2WD vehicles, although the road to the Web Valley (see below) is typically inaccessible during the rainy season, even by 4WD. Dinsho is also the starting point for many trekking routes, and where park fees should be paid prior to visiting the Sanetti Plateau (see next site).

Birding The long journey from Shashemene can be livened up by several sites en route. On leaving Shashemene the road rapidly climbs out of the Rift Valley, and by the town of Kofele settles onto highland grassland at an altitude of about 2,400 m. Roadside birding is very good all the way to Dinsho. In particular, on either side of the town of Dodola (respectively 71.7 and 83.3 km from the start of the gravel road outside Shashemene; GPS064

The Ethiopian subspecies *albofasciatus* of African Stonechat is startlingly black and white in plumage; immatures such as this bird, however, have a little familiar rufous on the breast. (Jacques Erard)

Several endemics inhabit the juniper woods of the Bale Mountains, here near Goba in September with a *Kniphofia* substratum in flower. (Claire Spottiswoode)

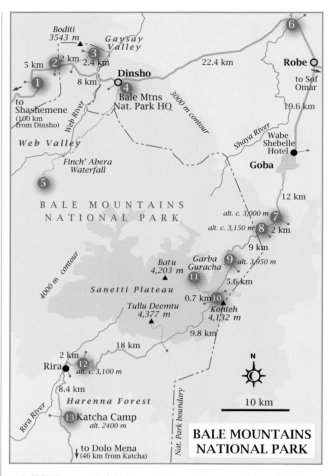

Ethiopian Cisticola was recently split from the much more widespread Winding Cisticola, and occurs mainly in moister highland scrub (Jacques Erard)

and GPS065 respectively), the road intersects groves of beautiful Mountain Acacias *Acacia abyssinica* at about 2,400 m, where **Brown Parisoma** can usually be found working its way through the tree canopies (especially interesting for imminent comparison with the Bale *griseiventris* subspecies on the slopes of the Sanetti Plateau, see p.90). Check the numerous other stream crossings en route for **Blue-winged Goose, Wattled Ibis** and **White-collared Pigeon** and sometimes **Abyssinian Longclaw**. Common species of the highland grassland and agricultural fields throughout this area include **Black-winged Plover, Cape Rook, Erlanger's Lark, Red-breasted Wheatear, Groundscraper Thrush, Yellow Bishop, Red-collared** and **Fan-tailed Widow-bird, Black-headed Siskin, Red-billed Oxpecker** atop cows and donkeys and, during Oct–Mar, many Palearctic migrants including **Red-throated Pipit** and **Northern, Pied** and **Isabelline Wheatears; Cyprus Wheatear** has also been seen here. During the dry season (late Dec onwards), many fields are burnt and attract large numbers of raptors including **Western Marsh, Pallid** and **Montagu's Harriers, Grasshopper** and **Long-legged Buzzards** and **Common** and **Lesser Kestrels.**

With the help of local guides, Montane Nightjar can be seen at day roosts around Dinsho. (Nik Borrow)

Continuing beyond Adaba towards Dinsho, the *Podocarpus* and juniper-wooded valley of the Ashiro stream (112.7 km from Shashemene, just as the road rapidly begins to gain altitude; GPS066) is also worth a stroll for a chance of **Abyssinian Woodpecker** and with much luck a roosting **Abyssinian Owl**, as well as the rather easier **Abyssinian Catbird** and **White-backed Black Tit**. These species can also be searched for on the impressively wooded hillsides alongside the steep section of road immediately beyond here, at about 119–127 km (rising in altitude from about 2,800 m to 3,300 m), which is an area known locally as Sebsibe Washa. This is also an excellent stretch for raptors, including **Martial Eagle** and **Lammergeier**. Emerging from this woodland, the pass skirts a sculptured sandstone outcrop on your left and enters alpine moorland as it peaks around 3,600 m, before dropping in altitude on the final approach to Dinsho. This pass provides a first taste of Bale's alpine specials such as **Red-billed Chough**, **Rouget's Rail** and **Malachite Sunbird**.

The Bale Mountains foothills on the approach to Dinsho, with juniper trees scattered among pastures and cultivations. (Claire Spottiswoode)

As the road drops down into the Gaysay Valley (to about 3,100 m), scan for **Cape Eagle-owl** at the point where the road passes close to cliff edges on the eastern (right-hand side approaching Dinsho) side of the road, 14 km before Dinsho (156 km from Shashemene), at GPS067 (1 on map). An owl is often present in a hollow in the section of cliff directly below the road. If not, the children of the group of huts at the base of cliffs will often show its whereabouts for a small tip, but please ask them not to throw stones to flush it; please also take care not to disturb the owls by approaching too closely. **Somali**

In Ethiopia as in much of Africa, Red-billed Oxpeckers are threatened by livestock dips, but are still relatively common in the Bale foothills. (Tasso Leventis)

Moorland Francolin occurs patchily across eastern Africa's montane areas, and the Bale Mountains National Park is one of the few places where it is readily seen. (Dick Forsman)

Starling has also been reported here, but requires confirmation; **Slender-billed Starling** is common.

The vicinity of the pond on the left-hand side of the valley at 2 on map (151 km from Shashemene; GPS068) is excellent for **African Snipe**, **Spot-breasted Plover** (particularly during the northern winter when birds may descend in good numbers from higher altitudes), **Blue-winged Goose** and **Rouget's Rail**; also search similarly moist habitat in the vicinity of the Web River crossing 7 km further (at GPS069). Short grasslands here and elsewhere in the valley hold abundant **Moorland Chat**, the occasional **Red-breasted Wheatear**, common **Abyssinian Longclaw** and **Thekla Lark** (**Erlanger's Lark** also occurs but is less common at such high altitudes) and, occasionally protruding nervously from their burrows, the curiously blunt heads of Giant Root-rats.

This final 11 km of the Gaysay Valley before Dinsho is also an excellent area for mammal-watching. Here is the first chance of spotting an Ethiopian Wolf, since one pack lives in this valley. Many other large mammals are easily seen near the road, oblivious to passing trucks, including an excellent chance of Mountain Nyala (endemic to the Bale massif), and the more widespread Bohor Reedbuck and Common Warthog. With a great deal of luck, a crepuscular Caracal or Serval Cat might be spotted. **Chestnut-naped Francolin** and, a little less commonly, **Moorland Francolin**, are easily seen at the roadside. Around most drainage lines, **Rouget's Rail**, **African Snipe** and **Blue-winged Goose** will easily be seen, as well as the occasional **Spot-breasted Plover**. **White-collared Pigeon** and **Wattled Ibis** are common, and flocks of **Black-headed Siskin** settle among the grass and heath. The taller heathlands are especially good for **Ethiopian Cisticola**, the strikingly black-and-white Ethiopian highland race of **African Stonechat**, **Yellow Bishop** and **Cinnamon Bracken Warbler**. Throughout the Dinsho area, **Augur Buzzard** is abundant, and **Lammergeier** regularly seen. Other raptors may include **Lanner Falcon**, **African Goshawk**, **Brown Snake-eagle**, **Tawny**, **Steppe**, **Martial** and (very scarcely) **Eastern Imperial Eagles**.

Hagenia–juniper woodland extends down the sides of the Gaysay Valley, away from the road. One scenic and accessible spot to walk can be reached by taking the rough track (4WD only) that extends north from the Bale National Park signboard (GPS070), next to the small building 8 km west of Dinsho. Follow this track across a small stream and until it starts to contour along the wooded slopes. A particularly good valley is 2.4 km along this track (3 on map). **Abyssinian Catbird** and **White-backed Black Tit** are common here, and with some dedicated searching one has a good chance of locating **Abyssinian Woodpecker**. Note that **Grey-headed Woodpecker** also occurs here, so tapping does not necessarily indicate Abyssinian. **Cinnamon Bracken Warbler** and **Yellow-bellied Waxbill** hop about the understorey.

Rather denser woodland, dominated by juniper and *Hagenia* trees, occurs around Dinsho Lodge (4 on map; the turn-off is at GPS071, at the eastern outskirts of Dinsho village). Although **Abyssinian Woodpecker** prefers more open woodland, it has also been seen around forest edge and clearings in this area. **Abyssinian Catbird** is very common around the lodge; volleys of calling (interspersed by long silences) are heard throughout the day. **Abyssinian Ground Thrush** might be seen bounding along the mossy forest floor, or calling (confidingly, but from a difficult-to-detect position high in a juniper tree) in a series of short, simple motifs, occasionally varying. Groups of **White-backed Black Tit** move through the *Hagenia* and juniper trees, prising off bark. **Brown Woodland Warbler** and **Yellow-crowned Canary** are very common, and **Black-winged Lovebird** is likely to screech overhead; although **Yellow-fronted Parrot** has been recorded here, it is seen only rarely. **Cinnamon Bracken Warbler** call explosively from rank tangles, and Menelik's Bushbuck and Mountain Nyala pick their way through clearings. At night, **African Wood Owl**, **Montane Nightjar** and occasionally **Abyssinian Owl** may be heard. The lodge staff, particularly Abdela Husa, keep tabs on day roosting sites for all these species, so be sure to enquire.

Abyssinian Owl is a difficult bird anywhere, but again with local help might be found roosting around Dinsho. (Andy Swash)

An excellent day trip from here is to the Web Valley (5 on map; about a 30 km round trip), when possible, which is unlikely during the rainy season (May–Oct). Birding is similar to that on the Sanetti Plateau (see next site): two pairs of **Wattled Cranes** breed here, and it is also a fine area to search for **Golden Eagle**, **Spot-breasted Plover** and Ethiopian Wolf.

Flowering Giant Fennel (*Ferrula*) and Red-hot-pokers (*Kniphofia*) cover the Gaysay Valley near Dinsho during the rainy season, here in June. The juniper-*Hagenia* slopes beyond are excellent habitat for Abyssinian Owl, Abyssinian Woodpecker and Mountain Nyala. (Claire Spottiswoode)

A superb male Mountain Nyala, now nearly endemic to the northern flanks of the Bale Mountains. Despite its tiny global population, it is easily seen around Dinsho. (Dick Forsman)

Other animals The Gaysay Valley is especially good for mammals, which include Common Warthog (abundant), frequent herds of Mountain Nyala especially along its forested margins, Bohor Reedbuck, and always a chance of spotting a Serval Cat or Ethiopian Wolf. Dinsho is an excellent place to watch Menelik's Bushbuck, a long-haired subspecies endemic to Ethiopia.

29. BALE MOUNTAINS NP: SANETTI PLATEAU

The Sanetti Plateau is an extraordinary landscape that is easily accessible by road from the town of Goba, beneath its northern slopes. The alpine moorlands of the plateau itself support the only known sub-Saharan breeding populations of three Palearctic species, **Ruddy Shelduck**, **Golden Eagle** and **Red-billed Chough**, and are famous for their population of the world's most endangered canid, the Ethiopian Wolf. Clear days are common but there can be a lot of mist on the plateau during Nov–Dec, a time popular with birders; during the rainy season (Jun–Aug), the wildflowers can be superb but again you risk being mist-enshrouded. The wet escarpment beneath the southern side of the plateau is covered by the vast Harenna Forest (see next site).

Key birds Ruddy Shelduck, Golden Eagle, Moorland Francolin, Spot-breasted Plover, Wattled Crane, Abyssinian Woodpecker, Red-billed Chough, Abyssinian Catbird, White-backed Black Tit, Brown Parisoma.

Key habitats *Hagenia*–juniper woodland and wet forest, Afro-alpine moorland, alpine tarns, tussocky montane streams.

Access Approaching from the north, the Sanetti Plateau is accessible by high-clearance 2WD vehicle, via the town of Goba. Goba lies 42 km east of Dinsho (see previous site), at the base of the Bale escarpment (altitude 2,650 m). Note that the Dinsho–Goba road is typically in slightly poorer condition than the Shashemene–Dinsho stretch (which was being tarred at the time of writing). The best place to stay in Goba is the Wabe Shabelle Hotel, on the right-hand side of the road just as one enters town from Dinsho. Be sure to have paid your park fees in Dinsho beforehand, as you might be asked to show a receipt at the park entrance just below the plateau.

Approaching from the south, the Sanetti Plateau is accessible only by 4WD vehicle (which is essential to ascend its southern escarpment), via a road

These *Hypericum* (St John's-wort) woods above Goba are the favoured habitat of the *griseiventris* subspecies of Brown Parisoma, endemic to the Bale Mountains. (Claire Spottiswoode)

Giant Lobelias *Lobelia rynchopetalum* growing at 4,000m on the Sanetti Plateau. (Richard Saunders)

through the Harenna Forest. The nearest moderately comfortable accommodation at this end is in Negele (see site 35). At the time of writing the road from Negele to Dolo Mena (see also the Genale River, site 33) had just been rebuilt and was largely good-quality gravel; however, the road from Dolo Mena to Sanetti can be in poor condition after heavy rain and may occasionally become impassable (enquire locally). In a 4WD it is possible to drive from Goba to Negele in a day trip, but this necessarily rather rushes the stunning trip over Sanetti and through Harenna. Ideally, do the journey over two days and camp in the Harenna Forest (see next site).

Birding Approaching Goba from Dinsho, consider a brief stop at the Shaya River crossing (6 on map on p.84), where a scan might turn up **African Black Duck** and the riparian trees hold **Abyssinian Ground Thrush**. On the western outskirts of Goba itself, a nocturnal stroll around the wooded grounds of the

Spot-breasted Plover frequents alpine tarns at the highest altitudes on the Sanetti Plateau, as well as around Dinsho. (Tasso Leventis)

The Bale endemic *griseiventris* subspecies of Brown Parisoma, sometimes considered a full species; the yellow base to its bill is simply pollen from gleaned *Hypericum* flowers. (Tasso Leventis)

A few pairs of Wattled Cranes are usually present along marshy streams on the Sanetti Plateau and the Web Valley. (Nik Borrow)

Wabe Shabelle Hotel might turn up a calling **Abyssinian Owl**, and marshy areas in the grounds or below the hotel entrance are likely to hold **Rouget's Rail** and **African Black Duck**.

The following account assumes that you cross the Sanetti in a north–south direction; to obtain distances from Dolo Mena rather than Goba, if you cross from south to north, subtract them from 112. The road to the Sanetti Plateau begins to climb steeply as soon as it leaves Goba town, passing through strikingly different bands of vegetation types. Initially it passes through blocks of eucalyptus and juniper plantation then, immediately above this, through beautiful open *Hagenia*–juniper woodland (10–12 km from Goba's Wabe Shebelle Hotel; 7 on map and circa GPS072), which is one of the better places to search for **Abyssinian Woodpecker**. Other typical Ethiopian endemics of this habitat are also likely to be seen here, such as **White-backed Black Tit**, **Abyssinian Catbird**, **Abyssinian Slaty Flycatcher** and **White-cheeked Turaco**, and **Verreaux's Eagle** and **Mountain Buzzard** might be seen overhead. Look out for an improbable sighting of **Taita Falcon**, which has been recorded here.

The road then climbs out into a mosaic of terraced pastures, homesteads, stands of herbs, and scattered woody, yellow-flowered St John's-wort *Hypericum revolutum* trees (8 on map and from GPS073; about 13 km from Goba, at an altitude of about 3,300 m). This is perhaps the easiest place anywhere to see the *griseiventris* race of **Brown Parisoma**, which is endemic to the Bale Mountains, and decide for yourself whether it is likely to be a full species as sometimes suggested. It may take a bit of time to detect, working its way quietly through dense tangles of *Hypericum*, and occasionally giving its harsh, somewhat sunbird-like alarm call. **Cinnamon Bracken Warbler** and **Rouget's Rail** dart about the edges of the dense heath understorey, and **Ethiopian Cisticola** and **African Stonechat** perch excitedly above it. In the mornings and evenings, coveys of **Moorland** and **Chestnut-naped Francolins** can be very frequent here.

The road continues to rise through dense scrub where francolins remain frequent, and passes a Bale National Park boom and signboard. A few kilometres beyond here the heath changes to lower, sparser *Helichrysum* (everlasting flower) moorland dotted with rocks, tarns and Giant Lobelias *Lobelia rynchopetalum*, as the road flattens out onto the 4,100 m Sanetti Plateau. The impressive stands of Giant Lobelias (such as that just before the plateau edge) attract nectarivores such as **Tacazze** and **Malachite Sunbirds** and **Slender-billed Starling**. There is some confusion as to whether **Somali Starling** may occasionally occur here too. Certainly, it is well worth carefully checking any long-tailed starlings for the diamond-shape tails and (in females) unmarked ash-grey head of Somalis. Otherwise there are rather few passerines on plateau, although **Thekla Lark** and **Black-headed Siskin** are abundant. Where the road flattens out opposite a microwave tower is the first group of many alpine tarns (9 on map), most of them flooded only during about Aug–Jan but some, including one here, year-round. Scan here for pairs or loosely scattered groups of **Spot-breasted Plover,** picking their way along tarn edges or pacing the adjacent moorland. Here too are likely to be the first of many **Blue-winged Goose, Yellow-billed Duck** and perhaps **Ruddy Shelduck**, joined in Oct–Mar by good numbers of Palearctic-breeding migrants including **Green Sandpiper, Eurasian Wigeon, Pintail** and **Northern Shoveler**. Keep an eye out here for **Wattled Crane**, although they are perhaps most often seen in the open moist valley at 10 on map (GPS074), where further **Spot-breasted Plovers** are also likely.

Sub-Saharan Africa's only **Red-billed Chough** populations exist here on Bale and in the Simien Mountains, one of the many Palearctic relics (including birds, plants and insects) seemingly clinging on in Ethiopia's alpine moorlands. Choughs can be seen anywhere on the plateau, probing open short grass areas or flying over. Another intriguing such relic is the small population of **Golden Eagle**, which was discovered here in the 1980s and is now quite regularly seen. **Eastern Imperial Eagle** is a scarce Palearctic migrant, but the Sanetti Plateau is one of the few places in Ethiopia where they are relatively regularly seen. The commonest raptor on the plateau is, as ever, **Augur Buzzard**.

Just south of 10, a rough track (GPS075) on the western side of the road eventually leads to a spectacular cliff-face and lake called Garba Guracha (11 on map). Travelling a short distance down this track is worthwhile in order to

The Ethiopian Wolf is the world's most endangered canid and, although fewer than 250 persist in the Bale Mountains, a sighting is almost guaranteed; here a wolf hunts a Giant Root-rat, its favoured prey.
(Greg Davies)

Klipspringer is often seen on the southern edge of the Sanetti Plateau. (Tasso Leventis)

reach a particularly fine couple of tarns, near some park buildings about 1 km from the turn-off (but beware that these may dry out by late winter). When they contain water, an amble on foot to and around these tarns is well worthwhile for **Spot-breasted Plover**, **Wattled Crane** and waterfowl. The low cliffs above the eastern tarn have breeding **Lanner Falcon**, abundant Ethiopian Rock Hyrax, and a small chance of picking out a roosting **Cape Eagle-owl**. Garba Guracha itself is about an hour's walk (the track is too rough to drive) beyond the park huts.

The beautiful and imperilled Ethiopian Wolf is almost certain to be seen on a trip across Sanetti. Individuals, pairs or small groups might be spotted anywhere along the road and especially in the northern half of the plateau, often in the general vicinity of meadows and valleys where their rodent prey are most common (see Other animals). In general, the northern part of the plateau is perhaps the most scenically diverse and full of life, so if short of time concentrate your efforts here. You might find that you speed up through the southern part, beyond the turn-off to Tullu Deemtu (at 4,377 m the highest point in southern Ethiopia; it is possible to drive to the top but the road is very poor), which at the time of writing was increasingly encroached by livestock grazing. About 44 km from Goba, the road re-enters heath zone and begins sharply to drop over escarpment and down into the vast Harenna Forest (see next site).

Other animals A number of endemic mammals are easily seen on the Sanetti Plateau. The most conspicuous of them are the alert, whistling Ethiopian Meadow Rats, which are abundant and belong to a genus endemic to Ethiopia (*Stenocephalemys*). Starck's Hare is also endemic to Ethiopia's alpine moorland and can at times be common and conspicuous. Apart from Ethiopian Wolves, which are almost certain to be seen in a few hours' birding on the plateau, careful scanning usually also reveals their favourite prey, the bizarre, blunt-headed Giant Root-rats peering understandably nervously from their burrow entrances. These belong to an intriguing rodent genus (*Tachyoryctes*) endemic to east Africa's highlands. Rocky outcrops are often sprinkled with Ethiopian Rock Hyrax. Serval Cat is quite frequently seen on the plateau, especially at dawn and dusk. The heathlands of the southern escarpment, above the Harenna Forest, are especially good for Klipspringer, and Leopard has been sighted here too.

Giant Root-rat, a member of a bizarre genus of rodents confined to eastern African highlands, and the most important prey of the Ethiopian Wolf. (Dick Forsman)

30. BALE MOUNTAINS NP: HARENNA FOREST

The Harenna Forest is the largest single forest block in Ethiopia, and probably the most biodiverse locality in the Ethiopian highlands. It is still very poorly explored biologically and yet is already under threat, especially in its moister upper reaches, from logging and cultivation. The 35 km drive through all the vegetation zones of the forest's 1,500 m altitudinal span is still an incredible experience, and all the more so when sandwiched between the Afro-alpine moorlands of the Sanetti Plateau above, and desiccated *Acacia–Commiphora* thornbush lowlands beneath.

Key birds Abyssinian Woodpecker, African Hill Babbler, Abyssinian Ground Thrush, Abyssinian Catbird, White-backed Black Tit, Brown Parisoma, Sharpe's Starling, Abyssinian Crimsonwing.

Key habitats A drive through Harenna passes through all the forest altitudinal zones, from tree heath and lichen-draped St John's Wort at its upper margins around 3,200 m altitude, through cloud-forest dominated by *Hagenia* and *Podocarpus* trees at around 2,400 m, and eventually emerging into drier forest with a more open canopy around 1,800 m.

Access The Harenna Forest is bisected by the Goba–Dolo Mena road; see also under previous site. A 4WD vehicle is recommended at all times of year, and especially during the rains. The nearest hotel accommodation is in Goba to the north and Negele to the south, but ideally camp at a beautiful forest clearing at 2,400 m altitude known as Katcha Camp (13 on map on p.84; GPS076); camping fees are payable at the national park headquarters at Dinsho (see site 28).

Birding As for the Sanetti Plateau, the following account assumes travelling in a north–south direction; to obtain distances from Dolo Mena rather than Goba if you cross from south to north, subtract them from 112. As road drops over the brink of Sanetti and descends through a series of switchbacks,

The Harenna Forest covers a dizzying range of altitudes on the Bale Mountains' southern slopes. Here, a stream runs near Katcha Camp at 2,400m.
(Richard Saunders)

Sharpe's Starling gives its improbable warbling song from high in the tree canopy. (Andy Swash)

look out for **Plain Martin** breeding in the road cuttings, and **Chestnut-naped Francolin** and **Ethiopian Cisticola** in the dense scrub. The road then passes through a belt of dense Tree Heath *Erica trimera* before entering the upper margin of Harenna. Here the forest is dominated by gnarled, contorted and mist- and lichen-draped St John's-wort trees *Hypericum revolutum*, much opened up for pasture. At about 3,100 m asl (12 on map on p.84 and vicinity of GPS077; 53 km from Goba), the St John's-wort intergrades into taller *Hagenia* forest and becomes another excellent area to search for **Abyssinian** and **Grey-headed Woodpeckers**, **White-backed Black Tit**, and the *griseiventris* race of **Brown Parisoma** (see Goba, above). The road then passes through the small, invariably wet village of Rira (where basic food is available), and enters tall montane forest, now sadly much disturbed by grazing and tree extraction.

At 64.1 km from Goba, a white Amharic signboard (GPS078) on the eastern side of road marks a small track leading 1 km across a large forest clearing, lined by *Hagenia* trees and timidly picking Menelik's Bushbuck, to the beautiful streamside spot called Katcha 'Darwin' Camp (13 on map on p.84). Whether or not you are camping, this is a very good spot to walk a little and search for birds. It is one of the few dependable sites for **Abyssinian Woodpecker**: scan the *Hagenia* branches carefully for quietly foraging birds. **Abyssinian Catbird** and **Abyssinian Ground Thrush** are also quite common in the vicinity of the camp, and are likely to be detected by their songs, often given throughout the day. The ground thrush typically gives a simpler and more repetitive song than does the more widespread and conspicuous **Mountain Thrush**, but they seem sometimes to mimic one another, so most thrush songs are worth investigating! Evenings and mornings offer the best chance of overflying **Yellow-fronted Parrot**, as well as the commoner **Black-winged Lovebird**. Undergrowth at the campsite edges and along the entrance track, as well as anywhere along the road through the forest (look out for birds flushing at the roadside), commonly yields inconspicuous seed-eaters such as **Abyssinian Crimsonwing**, **Green-backed Twinspot**, the more evident **Yellow-bellied Waxbill**, **Black-and-white Mannikin** and **African Citril**, and explosively singing and alarming **Cinnamon Bracken Warbler**. In winter, the clearing around Katcha is a good site for **Tree Pipit**. If camping at Katcha

The *unduliventer* subspecies of African Goshawk, endemic to the Ethiopian highlands and distinguished by its conspicuous white tail-spots. (Dick Forsman)

White-backed Black Tit is an Ethiopian endemic that especially favours open juniper or *Hagenia* woods at higher altitudes, such as at Harenna's upper margins. (Andy Swash)

you are likely to hear **Montane Nightjar** and **African Wood Owl**, although searching for them at night might be tempered by also hearing Leopard and Spotted Hyaena.

Other characteristic forest species here and elsewhere in Harenna include **White-cheeked Turaco, Narina Trogon, African Emerald Cuckoo, Silvery-cheeked Hornbill, African Hill Babbler** (best located by its fluty call), **Abyssinian Oriole, Grey Cuckooshrike, Brown Woodland Warbler, Abyssinian Slaty Flycatcher, Brown-throated Wattle-eye, Olive Sunbird, Montane White-eye** and **Slender-billed Starling**. Listen for the oddly metallic yet canary-like warbling of flocks of **Sharpe's Starling**, singing from high in the tree-tops. Frequently seen forest raptors include **African Goshawk** (likely to be heard and seen displaying over Katcha at dawn, showing the white tail-bars peculiar to the endemic Ethiopian subspecies *unduliventer*), **Great Sparrowhawk** and **African Crowned Eagle**. **Scaly Francolin** occurs, but is inconspicuous when not crowing. As one descends, the forest grows drier, the understorey is increasingly dominated by coffee plantations, and eventually the road

Tall forest in the lower reaches of Harenna, dissected by the Goba to Dolo Mena road. (Claire Spottiswoode)

Parties of Yellow-bellied Waxbills are a common sight at forest edges in Ethiopia. (Tasso Leventis)

emerges into proper cultivations and makes a startlingly rapid transition into dry, lowland thicket and thornbush near the town of Dolo Mena.

If continuing from Dolo Mena to Negele, look out for 'scree slopes' of the bizarre, rock-like spherical storage organs of *Pyrenacantha malvifolia* plants, particularly in the low-lying valley about 20 km from Dolo Mena. Birding is very diverse along this road, and can include (to name just a few) **Abyssinian Ground** and **Von der Decken's Hornbills**, **Red-and-yellow Barbet** (where columnar termite mounds occur for nesting), **Boran Cisticola**, and **Golden-breasted** and **White-crowned Starlings**. Keep a close eye out for **Salvadori's Seedeater**, which has occasionally been sighted along this road.

Pyrenacantha malvifolia is cultivated around the world by succulent enthusiasts, but comes from eastern Africa and grows abundantly around Dolo Mena. (Lajos Németh)

Troops of Olive Baboons frequent the lower reaches of Harenna, as do, much more scarcely, Giant Hog and several species of large carnivore. (Claire Spottiswoode)

Other animals Lion, Wild Dog, Serval Cat, African Civet, Bush Pig and Giant Hog all occur in the Harenna Forest and have all been seen at the roadside on scarce occasions; Leopard and Spotted Hyaena are usually heard at night while camping at Katcha. Bale Monkey is a dark, thick-furred subspecies of Grivet Monkey that is often considered a full species, and a threatened one at that. It is confined to the bamboo forest zone (2,400–3,000 m) of the Bale massif, and at Harenna is shy and uncommon. By contrast, Guereza Colobus is typically common and conspicuous here. The Harenna Shrew is, so far as is known, endemic to a tiny area in the upper reaches (*Hagenia* zone) of the forest, and is Critically Endangered.

31. SOF OMAR

At Sof Omar is one of the deepest caves in the world, 15 km long, formed where the Web River cuts through limestone on its way to the Genale River, in the lowlands east of the Bale Mountains. It is renowned to many as a Muslim shrine, and to fewer as a good site for **Salvadori's Seedeater**. It is a long rattling drive east of Goba, and best done as a day trip from there, although one may camp near the caves. If going for the day, make a very early start, as it can get hot and quiet here from mid-morning onwards. While this is undoubtedly a good site for the seedeater, it is perhaps less essential now that more accessible sites for it have come to light (see Negele and Filtu, sites 35 and 36 respectively). The caves are just beyond the village of Sof Omar, which is reached via the town of Robe, 10 km north of Goba on the road from Dinsho. Turn left at the traffic circle in central Robe, continue 60 km to the village of Goro, and a further 40 km to the village of Sof Omar. Just beyond the village and before reaching the caves, the road descends sharply through a limestone valley with fossil-rich cliffs, where **Brown-tailed Rock Chat** and **Bristle-crowned Starling** are likely to be seen. Just as the road bends sharply to the left (1 on map; GPS079), look out for a small footpath on the right-hand side, which is worth a stroll for all the specials listed below. Perhaps 200 m further, a motorable track leads off left down through dense acacia thicket in the valley bottom to the Sof Omar caves, and parallel to it a smaller footpath (2). All of this is prime country for **Salvadori's Seedeater** (as well as **Reichenow's Seedeater**). Males sing from conspicuous exposed

The Web River enters the sandstone labyrinth of the Sof Omar caves, named after a Muslim leader who took refuge in them eight centuries ago.
(Claire Spottiswoode)

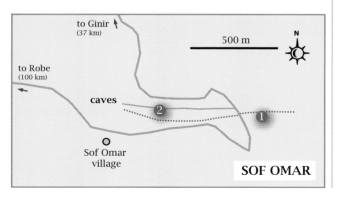

Dodson's Bulbul is one of the several well-marked forms of Common Bulbul often considered as separate species; it occurs in the dry lowlands of eastern and southern Ethiopia.
(Tasso Leventis)

perches (with their typical canary-like songs), and small groups often forage low in the vegetation. These thickets also offer **Northern Brownbul**, **Pygmy Batis**, **Lead-coloured Flycatcher** (localised in Ethiopia), as well as the usual panoply of acacia species including **Von der Decken's Hornbill**, **Dodson's Bulbul**, **Northern Grey Tit**, **Little Rock Thrush**, **Grey-headed Batis**, **Shelley's** and **Golden-breasted Starlings** (particularly at the top of the gorge), **Shining Sunbird**, **Purple Grenadier**, **Somali Bunting** and migrant warblers. **Fischer's Starling** has been recorded here, but is decidedly scarce. Sacred Baboon has been seen along the road from Goba.

32. IMI AND THE OGADEN

The arid lowlands of eastern Ethiopia make up a vast and fascinating but unfortunately largely inaccessible region, owing to security conditions. From Sof Omar (see site 31), it is possible to venture east to the arid thornbush lowlands between Ginir and Imi, where the habitat resembles that of the Bogol Manyo area (see site 37) and birds may include **White-winged Dove**, **Somali Bee-eater**, **Golden Pipit**, **Somali** and **Philippa's Crombecs**, **Yellow-vented Eremomela**, **Magpie Starling** and **Parrot-billed Sparrow**. However, this is a long way and the region is relatively unstable, so the security situation needs to be carefully investigated before venturing so far east. Before travelling as far as Imi (GPS080) it is also essential first to obtain official paperwork authorising passage, from the local authorities in Robe. From Imi, a road runs south to Dolo Odo (GPS081; see site 37) via Hargele, but this region is dangerous at present, and is likely to remain so. **Little Brown** and **Heuglin's Bustards** have been seen in several places all along this road, and especially in the vicinity of Hargele. East of Imi and towards Gode and Kelafo, approaching Ethiopia's eastern border with Somalia, **Little Brown Bustard** is known to occur reasonably commonly. However, the security situation is precarious, and the region should be avoided unless reliable new information suggests otherwise. Other interesting species reportedly frequent in this eastern region include **Somali Wheatear** and **Somali Sparrow**, and uncommonly **Donaldson Smith's Sparrow-weaver**.

One of a few known photographs of Little Brown Bustard, here photographed in Somalia but also occurring in broad yet largely inaccessible areas of eastern Ethiopia. (John Miskell)

THE SOUTHERN LOWLANDS

33. Upper Genale River
34. Wadera–Kebre Mengist
35. Negele and the Liben Plain
36. Filtu Region
37. Bogol Manyo Region
38. Dawa–Wachile Region
39. Arero Forest
40. Yabello Region
41. Mega and Soda
42. Agere Maryam

TOP 10 BIRDS

Prince Ruspoli's Turaco
African White-winged Dove
White-tailed Swallow
Liben Lark
Short-tailed Lark
Somali Wheatear
Philippa's Crombec
Ethiopian Bush-crow
Juba Weaver
Salvadori's Seedeater

South of the Bale Mountains, Ethiopia drops away steadily in altitude. Defining features are the Genale and Dawa River drainages, descending from the highlands to baking dry border country at a few hundred metres above sea level. Much of this region is covered by arid, camel- and cattle-infested *Acacia–Commiphora* thornbush and savanna, with some patches of juniper forest in the higher foothills. It is another nucleus of remarkable bird endemism, recognised as a global Endemic Bird Area containing six restricted-range species: **Nechisar Nightjar** (see next section), **Prince Ruspoli's Turaco**, **Liben Lark**, **White-tailed Swallow**, **Ethiopian Bush-crow** and **Salvadori's Seedeater**; all but the first of these are readily seen. Moreover, many more species are very difficult to see anywhere else in the world, owing to fraught security in Somalia and northern Kenya; these include **African White-winged Dove**, **Philippa's Crombec** and **Juba Weaver**. The sites in this section are ordered as if travelling south over the Bale Mountains, beginning in the Negele region and following a roughly clockwise route first south-east towards the Somali border around Bogol Manyo, and then west to Arero and Yabello. At least a week would be well spent in this region, remembering that a full day's travel should be allowed between Negele and Bogol Manyo.

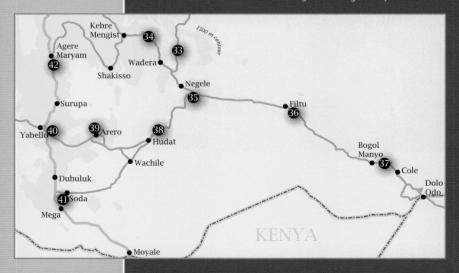

33. UPPER GENALE RIVER

Swift flocks of long-tailed Golden-breasted Starlings are a common sight in southern Ethiopia's dense bushlands. (Paul Donald)

The northern reaches of the Genale River can be reached from the road from Dolo Mena (below the southern Bale escarpment) to Negele. This road crosses the Genale River proper at a substantial Bailey bridge (watch out for sometimes missing timber, which local children will replace for a small fee) just north of Genale village and, 2.8 km farther on, a smaller, usually largely dry tributary at a sandy drift just south of it (27 km from Negele, or 123 km from Dolo Mena; 1 on map on p.103; GPS082). In the vicinity of the latter are many impressive fig trees where, particularly in the dry season, **Prince Ruspoli's Turaco** is sometimes seen. Best of all, ask here for turaco guide Adem Dube (you are likely to be surrounded by people on arrival), who might be summoned by a bellow upstream, and who keeps track of the birds' whereabouts. He may also guide you up a beautiful rocky, wooded valley to the

The sandy, fig-lined tributary of the Genale River made famous by its population of Prince Ruspoli's Turacos. (Claire Spottiswoode)

east, where the birds seem to be present year-round. Other species attracted to fruiting figs are **Bruce's Green Pigeon**, **Black-billed Barbet** and many starlings, including **Bristle-crowned** and **Golden-breasted Starlings. Brown-tailed Rock Chat** occurs on the rocky slopes and may venture down into the valley. Also keep an eye out for the turaco in any roadside trees in this area, towards both Dolo Mena and Negele, especially perched on exposed branches early in the morning. It has a surprisingly broad habitat tolerance for such a localised species, and occasionally ventures into even fairly dry acacia thornbush.

34. WADERA–KEBRE MENGIST FORESTS

The direct road from the Rift Valley tar road to Negele (as opposed to via Arero, see site 39) passes through a patchily forested highland area where **Prince Ruspoli's Turaco** occurs. The bird is probably less dependably found here than at Arero Forest, Negele and Genale (see sites 39, 35 and 33), owing to the larger area to search, but this area can be a useful backup if you miss it elsewhere. This escarpment region is fairly heavily populated and much is degraded or under cultivation, but some good tracts of forest (altitude 1,600–2,000 m) remain, especially in sheltered valleys. Beware that **White-cheeked Turaco** is very common here, and has a similar call to Ruspoli's; worryingly, hybrids have been sighted in this area. General forest birding is also good, and other interesting species include **African Crowned Eagle, Narina Trogon, Yellow-fronted Parrot, Grey Cuckooshrike, African Hill Babbler, Brown Woodland Warbler, Abyssinian Oriole, Abyssinian Slaty Flycatcher** and **Sharpe's Starling**; marshy clearings hold **Rouget's Rail, Red-collared Widowbird** and **African Citril**. There are a number of forested valleys along the 52 km stretch between Wadera and Kebre Mengist (e.g. 3, 22 and 30 km from Wadera; respectively GPS083, 084 and 085), but keep an eye out for Ruspoli's at the roadside anywhere between Kebre Mengist and Wadera, even in unlikely-looking degraded farmbush. The same applies along the minor road from Shakisso to Agere Maryam; this is the most direct practicable route between Negele and Yabello if, as occasionally happens, the security situation precludes travelling via Arero (see site 39).

The typically liquid calls of the endemic Abyssinian Oriole provide a backdrop to most of Ethiopia's higher-altitude forests. (Nik Borrow)

35. NEGELE AND THE LIBEN PLAIN

The Liben Plain ('Diida Liiben' in Borana), a unique and isolated patch of grassland east of the town of Negele, is famous as the only place in the world where the **Liben** (formerly known as **Sidamo**) **Lark** occurs. Described in 1968 by Christian Erard, this highly distinctive and unusual lark is already a bird on the brink of extinction. Recent surveys estimate that fewer than 250 individuals survive, while their scrap of remaining habitat (< 3,000 hectares) is rapidly diminishing owing to bush encroachment, excessive cattle grazing and crop planting. At the time of writing one of these few remaining birds could readily be located in the right place and without excessive disturbance. General grassland birding is also good.

Key birds Hartlaub's and Kori Bustards, Somali Courser, Prince Ruspoli's Turaco, Liben Lark, Somali Short-toed Lark, White-crowned Starling, Salvadori's Seedeater.

Key habitats Open short grassland, with sparsely scattered thornbushes (altitude c.1,600m). The surrounding area is mixed and whistling-thorn woodland.

Access Note that Negele is also known as Negele Borana, to distinguish it from Arsi Negele in the Rift Valley. Directly opposite the turn-off to Arero is a military camp which has previously caused difficulties to birders searching for Liben Larks. It seems now to be largely derelict and less likely to pose hassles, but remains in use to a certain extent and it is absolutely necessary to avoid its immediate vicinity. The best hotel in Negele is the Green Hotel (take the first right on entering town from the north, and be sure to ask for the rooms on the right of the compound, which have en suite bathrooms); reasonable accommodation and good food are also available at the Nile Hotel.

Birding Liben Lark prefers grassland with very few or no shrubs, particularly at

A Liben Lark in mid song-flight, showing its extravagantly elongated hind-claw. The bird's name has been recently changed from the geographically erroneous Sidamo Lark at the specific request of the Liben Plain's Borana inhabitants. (Andy Swash)

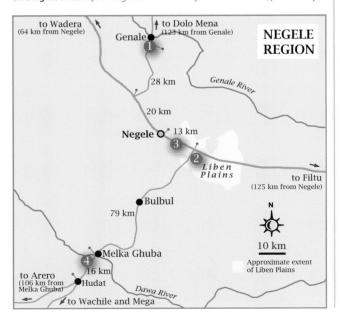

to Wadera (64 km from Negele)
Genale
to Dolo Mena (123 km from Genale)
NEGELE REGION
28 km
Genale River
20 km
Negele 13 km
Liben Plains
to Filtu (125 km from Negele)
Bulbul
79 km
N
10 km
Approximate extent of Liben Plains
Melka Ghuba
16 km
to Arero (106 km from Melka Ghuba)
Hudat
Dawa River
to Wachile and Mega

Borana settlements on the Liben Plain. This 30 km² patch of imperilled grassland is the world range of the Liben Lark. (Paul Donald)

the western side of the plains. In dry periods when the plain is heavily grazed, it may concentrate in any remaining patches of taller grass. Good areas to search are 1–2 km from the Arero turn-off, along both the Arero and Filtu roads (ie, around 2 on map). Try especially along the first 700 m or so down the small track leaving the Arero road 0.8 km from the junction, at GPS086. Early mornings are best (especially 06h30-09h30), when males are likely to give their somewhat skylark-like hovering song-flights, about 10 m above the ground, resembling a fly on the horizon before parachuting down after about 20 seconds; at closer range, their greatly elongated hind-claws can be seen dangling conspicuously during these flights. Males appear to sing year-round, although perhaps less frequently during winter. Their short and largely stationary song flight contrasts with the long, high, circular and somewhat chirruping song-flights of **Somali Short-toed Lark**, which is common here. When flushed, Somali Short-toed Larks can be easily distinguished by their rather nasal flight call (Liben Lark gives, rarely, a rather melodious *tseep-eeep-eeep-eeep*, reminiscent of a Pectoral-patch Cisticola), and when on the ground, relatively heavy pinkish bill, conspicuous whitish eye-ring, heavily streaked rather than scalloped mantle, and generally pot-bellied and horizontal posture. The alternative way to find a Liben Lark (such as at other times

Liben Lark has a distinctively upright posture, with a pale neck and beautifully scalloped back. (Tasso Leventis)

Somali Short-toed Lark can be pestilentially common on the Liben Plain, giving short nasal calls when flushed. (Paul Donald)

of day than morning) is to walk until you spot or flush one; they tend not to fly, but run quickly and rodent-like through the grass, occasionally standing upright to scan the surroundings, showing their pale, triangular-looking head, markedly scalloped back and pale central crown-stripe. A scope is useful for obtaining good views of their plumage characters.

Passerines in the open grasslands are rather few, and the other characteristic terrestrial species aside from these larks are **Pectoral-patch Cisticola** and **Plain-backed Pipit**. Flocks of **White-crowned** and **Wattled Starlings** follow the cattle, **Dwarf Raven** may pass overhead or squabble around cattle dung, and **Taita Fiscal** perch on small shrubs. Both **Crowned** and **Black-winged Plovers** are common; **Somali Courser** also seems attracted to bare roadsides, although **Temminck's Courser** is usually more commonly seen. **Kori Bustard** can be remarkably abundant. In the rainy season, widely spread males can be seen giving their balloon-like display, showing neck feathers that in this region are typically stained reddish by the soil. **Hartlaub's Bustard** is also regularly seen here, but is much less conspicuous and numerous; look especially in longer grass, such as in the vicinity of the seemingly derelict military camp (which should not be approached too closely). There are old records of the scarce **Heuglin's Bustard** here, especially in the sparsely wooded areas at the plain edges, but we are not aware of any recent sightings. **White-bellied Bustard** certainly does occur in this latter habitat. Small groups of **White-tailed Swallow**, typically a bird of the Yabello–Mega area (see sites 40 and

Grey-capped Social Weavers build their small colonies of loose straw nests on the wooded margins of the Liben Plain. (Tasso Leventis)

A Dwarf Raven makes off with a trophy cowpat on the Liben Plain. This near-endemic to the Horn of Africa occurs in open areas throughout much of southern and eastern Ethiopia, especially in the dry lowlands (Tasso Leventis)

Shelley's Starling can be locally common around Negele and Yabello, sometimes occurring in large flocks. (Paul Donald)

41), have been seen following herds of cattle on the plains at several times of year, and recently have been especially frequently seen in the vicinity of Diida Liiben Ranch about 2 km west of the Arero turn-off, in the woodland between here and Negele town. Note, however, that **Ethiopian**, **Wire-tailed** and (throughout the year) **Barn Swallows** are common. Frequently seen raptors on the plains include **Tawny Eagle**, **Black-chested Snake-eagle**, **Lanner**, and **Lesser** and, at times, **Grey Kestrels**. **Quail-plover** was seen five times in one day in June 2007 in the more arid eastern sector of the plains. Where the plains become lightly wooded at their eastern and southern edges, **Flappet Lark**, **Somali Fiscal**, **Grey-capped Social Weaver** and **Shelley's Rufous Sparrow** occur; **Golden Pipit** has also been recorded in this area and presumably this habitat, but we are not aware of any recent records. There is also a recent report of **Cyprus Wheatear** from the plain.

Prince Ruspoli's Turaco occurs, remarkably, in relatively sparse thicket along a drainage line halfway between Negele town and the Liben Plains (3 on map; GPS087), 6.3 from the Arero turn-off, or 6.5 km from the T-junction and

The breathtakingly beautiful Prince Ruspoli's Turaco can be unexpectedly easy to see at a site close to Negele. (Jacques Erard)

police checkpoint in Negele town where one branches off onto the Filtu road. This is a very reliable site. Scan for turacos perched in the open on exposed branches in the early morning and evening, often calling, or stroll through the habitat to search for them. They often perch quietly in the canopy, and when flushed fly only a short distance to the next clump of thicket where they can be relatively easily relocated (but are usually very hard to find in the main hours of daylight). Also try the bushy area 700m west (towards Negele) of here. Until recently this species was much more widespread in the Negele area, but deforestation has in recent years taken a heavy toll on its habitat of dry juniper woods, and almost none now remains. Other species of these thicketed drainage lines include **Grey-headed Bush-shrike**, **Slate-coloured Boubou** and **Black-headed Batis**.

Between the Liben Plain and Filtu (see site 36), and indeed even within Negele town, look out for **Salvadori's Seedeater**; the most likely confusion is with the common **Reichenow's Seedeater**. **Ashy Cisticola** (uncommon) and **Shelley's Starling** also occur at the plains edges, and the latter can be quite abundant between here and Melka Ghuba (see site 38).

Other animals Although oryx and gazelle grazed the plains until as recently as the 1970s, the only ungulates at present are cattle in vast numbers. Wild Cat may occasionally be flushed while one is searching for larks at dawn.

Reichenow's Seedeater is the most likely species to be confused with Salvadori's Seedeater (which often doesn't show the striking plumage shown on p.161); note its wing-bars and facial markings. (Andy Swash)

36. FILTU REGION

Filtu is a small town about mid-way between Negele and Bogol Manyo; the time of writing, the road between Filtu and the Somali border was, surprisingly, in better condition than that between Negele and Filtu. This road was built by Mussolini in the 1930s, but trucks and tanks have reduced it to a painfully slow and bumpy cobbled surface.

Look out for **Salvadori's Seedeater** in the acacia thornbush country anywhere between Negele and Filtu; groups may be flushed from the roadside, showing the lack of wing-bars that distinguishes them from **Reichenow's Seedeater**. They also occur in thornbush/cultivation mix, such as 88 km from Negele. **Grasshopper Buzzard** has been seen at the roadside in this area a number of times. Filtu village itself, likely to provide a lunch stop or opportunity for official permissions en route to Bogol Manyo, is much livened up by **White-crowned Starling**, **Dwarf Raven** and sometimes **Speke's Weaver**, all of which occur in the village centre; the arid open surrounds are also good country for **Egyptian Vulture** and **Ethiopian Swallow**.

Accommodation does exist in Filtu, although it is decidedly basic; a potential silver lining to finding oneself here for the night is an early start in the splendid *Commiphora* woodland that occurs along the road towards Bogol Manyo, about 30–60 km east of Filtu. A stop around (for example) 32–35 km beyond Filtu (i.e. around GPS088) might turn up such excellent *Commiphora*-dwelling species as **Bare-eyed Thrush**, **Scaly Chatterer**, **Pygmy Batis**, **Pringle's Puffback**, **Banded Parisoma**, **Red-naped Bush-shrike**, **Shining Sunbird** and **Northern Grosbeak-canary**, as well as more widespread species of the arid southern lowlands such as **Tiny Cisticola**, **Grey Wren-warbler**, **Red-fronted Warbler**, **Pale Prinia**, **Rufous Chatterer**, **Three-streaked Tchagra**, **Northern**

The nominate subspecies of Gillett's Lark occurs in the Filtu region; closer to Bogol Manyo, it is replaced by the poorly differentiated *degodiensis* form that until recently was considered a full species.
(Claire Spottiswoode)

White-crowned Starling is very common in southern Ethiopia, but otherwise occurs only in Somalia and the remote fringes of northern Kenya.
(Tasso Leventis)

Grey Tit, **Mouse-coloured Penduline-tit** and **African Grey Flycatcher**. Localised species which can be seen here include **Gillett's Lark** and **Salvadori's Seedeater**, which can be locally common. **Golden Pipit** has also been seen here.

37. BOGOL MANYO REGION

Bogol Manyo is an uninviting scattering of buildings in rocky lowland country (altitude about 300 m) approaching Ethiopia's junction with Kenya and Somalia; it would be unremarkable were it not the type locality of '**Degodi Lark**'. Described in 1971, it was not seen again for 20 years. A recent study has indicated that it should be regarded as conspecific with **Gillett's Lark**, but this should not dissuade one from making the (not inconsiderable) effort of visiting this arid, far-flung region which is packed with exciting, predominantly Somali species.

Key birds Heuglin's Bustard, Somali Courser, Lichtenstein's and Black-faced

Rocky hills with sparse acacia and *Commiphora* bushes in the Cole area; this is prime country for Somali Wheatear.
(Claire Spottiswoode)

Sparsely-vegetated range-lands on the road to Melka Suftu, with Somali dwellings at right. This is excellent habitat for Somali Courser and Heuglin's Bustard. (Claire Spottiswoode)

Sandgrouse, African White-winged Dove, Somali Bee-eater, Gillett's Lark, Somali Wheatear, Philippa's Crombec, Yellow-vented Eremomela, Somali Fiscal, Juba Weaver, Magpie and White-crowed Starlings, Black-bellied and Shining Sunbirds.

Key habitats Sparse, arid *Acacia–Commiphora* savanna; watercourses lined with dense acacia thicket; rocky hillsides. Altitude 180–400m.

Access Bogol Manyo is a very considerable journey from anywhere else. Allow a full day's drive from Negele, giving time for a few birding stops. It is advisable to enquire about security situation before visiting, and permission to sleep at Bogol Manyo should ideally first be obtained in Filtu. Depending on local conditions, it may or may not be required to be accompanied by a soldier. Birders have traditionally camped in Bogol Manyo village, but be warned that you might be charged an extortionate sum to do so. You might prefer to try your luck in Cole village, farther down the road towards Somalia, which is slightly larger and offers food, drink and possibly a cheap hotel. Conditions around Dolo Odo, near the Somali border, are also variable. Take particular care not to linger in the vicinity of the army camp at Bur Amino (GPS089), between Cole and Dolo Odo. If you visit Dolo Odo itself or sites near to it (see below), declare your presence to the police there and request permission to move around the area.

Birding Much of the road approaching Bogol Manyo from the north-west along the Addis Ababa road from Filtu is lined with familiar dense *Acacia–Commiphora* bush. However, a marked change in habitat is apparent a few kilometres beyond Bogol Manyo. Trees become sparser and large areas of bare reddish earth and short grass begin to appear. This is a good point at which to keep an eye out for **Heuglin's Bustard** (improbable but possible), as well as other typical species of arid plains such as **Somali Courser**; this is also good country for **Chestnut-headed Sparrow-Lark** and **Crowned Plover**. The acacia trees and hut roofs in Bogol Manyo village (GPS090) itself commonly

Magpie Starling is a nomadic and unpredictable bird, but the Bogol Manyo area is one of the more reliable places in Ethiopia to see it. Occasionally it may gather in enormous flocks. (Nik Borrow)

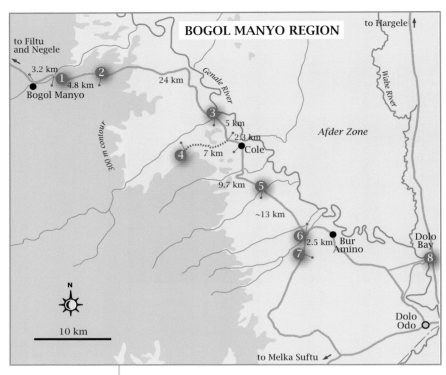

hold **African White-winged Dove** among more widespread species such as **Laughing** and **Mourning Doves**. The bare rocky area immediately around the town is worth scanning for **Short-tailed Lark**.

The road from here to Cole (GPS091; the next village, 20 km beyond Bogol Manyo and close to the Genale River), and somewhat beyond it, is all excellent birding country. Walks up acacia-lined watercourses are usually very productive. In particular, check the tall thicket lining the river crossings at 1 and 3 on map (respectively 3.2 and 32 km beyond Bogol Manyo; GPS092 and GPS093 respectively) for **African White-winged Dove**; the former can also be a good site for **Juba Weaver**, although these move around and may not always be

The Bogol Manyo region is one of the few places in the world where Somali Wheatear may be searched for in relative safety. (Debbie Pain)

The fabulous Golden Pipit occurs thinly in the dry thornbush of the Bogol Manyo–Filtu region. (Claire Spottiswoode)

present. Any pools of standing water at these crossings will attract many **Chestnut-bellied** and **Black-faced Sandgrouse** coming to drink, and perhaps the occasional **Lichtenstein's**. The latter tends to prefer a somewhat stonier substrate and is often seen sitting quietly under a tree in the rocky vicinity of watercourses. **Water Thick-knee**, a localised bird in Ethiopia, occurs here.

If you wish to judge its taxonomic status for yourself, the *degodiensis* subspecies of **Gillett's Lark** is fairly common between Bogol Manyo and Cole, favouring open *Acacia–Commiphora* thornbush on broken ground. The vicinity of the type locality (2 on map; GPS094) is 11 km beyond Bogol Manyo, where the lark occurs at high density. It has also been seen in the woodland immediately around Bogol Manyo village, and up to 17 km north-westwards from here on the road to Filtu. The lark occurs at least as far beyond Bogol Manyo as the area around Cole village, 40 km down the road towards the Somali border. A good patch of habitat is accessible up to 7 km along the old mining track (turn-off at GPS095) that heads south-west of the tar road, to 4 on map. This is an excellent track for birding: it is very good for **Philippa's Crombec**, and **Somali Wheatear** has recently been seen here a number of times, including in the company of fledged young. **Fischer's Starling** has been seen around the turn-off.

Other small watercourses are also well worth exploring for many of this area's sought-after birds. In the vicinity of Cole, also try for example the one intersecting the main road at 5 on map (GPS096). This is also a good site for **Philippa's Crombec** as well as **Yellow-vented Eremomela**, although both can

The *degodiensis* form of Gillett's Lark, until recently considered a distinct species. However, it has been found to be poorly differentiated with respect to morphology, voice and genetics
(Claire Spottiswoode)

The extraordinarily elegant Gerenuk is often seen browsing upright on its hindlegs, and is not uncommon from Yabello and Mega to Bogol Manyo. (Tasso Leventis)

easily be confused with **Yellow-bellied Eremomela**, which is common here; also beware of possible confusion, unlikely as it may seem, with **Northern Crombec**. Other characteristic species of this habitat are **Shining** and **Eastern Violet-backed Sunbirds**, **Rufous Chatterer**, **Parrot-billed Sparrow** and, less commonly, **Somali Bee-eater** and **Golden Pipit**. **Magpie Starling** can be common (as well as the commoner **White-crowned Starling**), and pairs and groups frequent this habitat as well as open bushland, especially around fruiting bushes.

Note that it is unfortunately not permitted to birdwatch or walk in the vicinity of the bridge over the Genale River that is visible just east of Cole. If the current security situation permits a night-drive – which is unlikely at the time of writing – possibilities include **Donaldson Smith's** (common), **Slender-tailed** and **Dusky Nightjars**.

If time and security circumstances allow, venturing beyond Cole towards Dolo Odo (on the Somali border) offers a better chance of encountering **Heuglin's Bustard**. In particular, the first 5 km of so of the minor road (turn-off at 6; GPS097) leading south-west from the main Negele–Dolo Odo road to Melka Suftu (farther south on the Kenyan border) is especially good for this species; stop at any minor vantage point and scan open areas. **Somali Courser** can also be amazingly common along this road, and patches of scrub hold **Philippa's Crombec** and **Yellow-vented Eremomela**. Open areas such as around 7 on map (GPS098) are excellent for **Somali Courser**, **Chesnut-bellied**, **Lichtenstein's** and **Black-faced Sandgrouse**, and **Short-tailed Lark** among the abundant **Chestnut-headed Sparrow-larks**.

If you want to approach the border any closer than a short distance down the Melka Suftu road, it is strongly advisable first to check in with the local authorities at Dolo Odo (GPS081) to obtain appropriate paperwork, and ideally a knowledgeable guide. Clearance from Dolo Odo is necessary to visit the riparian vegetation along the Genale River, best accessible at Dolo Bay (also known as Woldiya) (8 on map; GPS099). This is only a short distance north of Dolo Odo, but note that the main access road (the northerly of the two shown) can sometimes be flooded. Dolo Bay is a very reliable site for **Juba**

Weaver and **African White-winged Dove**, both of which can be common here, and **Magpie Starling** and occasionally **Fischer's Starling** occurs in the open areas along the access track.

East of the Genale River lies the tantalising expanse of the Ogaden and its **Little Brown Bustards**. It is physically possible to traverse this region along the road north from Dolo Odo to Imi, although the security situation there is dangerous and it cannot be recommended (see also site 32).

Other animals Günther's Dik-dik is abundant, and Unstriped Ground Squirrel common. Gerenuk occurs in the denser bush and is quite commonly seen at the roadside. Cheetah is occasionally seen along the Melka Suftu road, and Lions do occur in the region too. You may see the mounds of Naked Mole-Rats; see site 17 for more on these.

38. DAWA–WACHILE REGION

The road from Negele to Wachile, via the villages of Bulbul, Melka Ghuba and Hudat, passes through some excellent arid *Acacia–Commiphora* country as well as the Dawa drainage system. Birding here is easy, diverse and very enjoyable, and provides several species otherwise accessible only in the more remote Bogol Manyo region.

Key birds Vulturine Guineafowl, African White-winged Dove, Dwarf Raven, Bare-eyed Thrush, Pygmy Batis, Black-bellied Sunbird, Juba Weaver.

Key habitats Dense *Acacia–Commiphora* thicket, sparse *Commiphora* woodland, riparian thicket, sparse acacia scrub; altitude below 1,000 m.

Access The road from Negele to Wachile was at the time of writing reasonably good-quality gravel (4WD not required). From Wachile, it used to be possible

A male Juba Weaver, endemic to the Genale and Wabe Shabelle drainages of Ethiopia and Somalia (see p.159 for a female). (Jacques Erard)

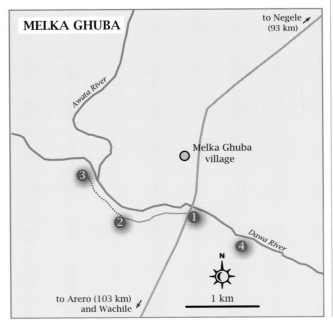

MELKA GHUBA

to Negele (93 km)

Awata River

Melka Ghuba village

3

2

1

4

Dawa River

N

to Arero (103 km) and Wachile

1 km

African White-winged Dove, a specialist of riparian acacia woodland along the Genale and Wabe Shabelle drainages. (Nik Borrow)

A characteristically well-concealed Scaly Chatterer. (Tasso Leventis)

to drive directly to Yabello via Arero. However, at the time of writing and for a year or two previously, this road was heavily damaged and no longer passable, requiring the journey to Yabello to be completed via the good quality gravel road south-west to Soda (see site 41), and from there up the tar road north to Yabello. This is not a great inconvenience as the road quality and birding are both very good on this alternative route.

The nearest accommodation is in Negele (see site 35) and Yabello (site 40), and the journey between the two is feasible in a day, including birding stops. If you wish to camp, inform the nearest village head or police outpost of your intentions; they will also be able to advise you of any local security concerns. Note that flare-ups occur quite frequently between the Borana, Gugii and Somali ethnic groups which meet in this region (Hudat, for example, is populated entirely by Somalis). It is best to enquire about the broader security situation before visiting. If this area is impassable, Yabello and Negele can still be linked via Kebre Mengist and Shakisso (allow a full day of travel; see also site 34). **Birding** Birding in *Acacia–Commiphora* thicket anywhere between Negele, Wachile and Soda is excellent. Throughout this region, a stop in any lively-looking *Acacia–Commiphora* thicket could turn up specials of drier *Commiphora*-dominated thornbush such as **Bare-eyed Thrush**, **Somali Crombec**, **Yellow-vented Eremomela**, **Red-fronted Warbler**, **Banded Parisoma**, **Pale Prinia**, **Red-naped Bush-shrike**, **Pygmy Batis**, **Pringle's Puffback**, **Black-capped Social Weaver**, **Northern Grosbeak-canary** and **Hunter's Sunbird**, with **Spotted Palm-thrush** along thicker drainage lines. Flocks of **Vulturine Guineafowl** are likely at the roadside, and **Eastern Chanting Goshawk**, **Golden-breasted Starling** and **Chestnut Weaver** can be common. **Philippa's Crombec** has been reported from this area and it would be useful to establish how widespread it might be, considering how little is known about this (largely Somali) species and its conservation status.

Wooded drainage lines are especially productive: try the river crossing (GPS 100) 72 km from Negele, where **African White-winged Dove** occurs. Best of all, devote a couple of hours to the area around the well-known bridge

over the Dawa River just south of the little village of Melka Ghuba, 93 km from Negele (4 on small-scale map on p.103). To reach a good place to walk, turn west 100 m south of the bridge (1 on large-scale map on p.113; GPS101), and follow a small track to its end. The dense *Commiphora* bush along this initial stretch is particularly good for **Red-naped Bush-shrike, Scaly Chatterer, Pygmy Batis** and **Pringle's Puffback**. The track peters out (washed away by floodwaters) after a kilometre; park here (2 on map) and follow the human and goat footpaths onwards upstream along the banks of the Dawa for another kilometre or so (3 on map). The riparian acacia and other thornbush thicket can be very productive. Notably, **African White-winged Dove** is fairly common (listen for its distinctively dove-like but unique, rapidly cooing call) in the taller riparian trees. **Juba Weaver** regularly occurs and breeds here in small colonies in riverside trees and thicket (in, e.g., November), but is sometimes absent, and inconspicuous when not in breeding plumage: look out for its markedly bicoloured bill. **Yellow-backed Weaver** was recorded once here in September 1997, although not more recently to our knowledge. Check any flowering trees carefully for **Black-bellied Sunbird**, which regularly (but not reliably) occurs, alongside more widespread relatives such as **Collared, Eastern Violet-backed** and **Shining Sunbirds**. There is also a track down the south bank of the river east of the road (4), which can be especially good for **Yellow-vented Eremomela, Somali Crombec** and, along the banks of the Dawa, **Water Thick-knee** (localised in Ethiopia).

The area around Wachile (GPS102) and Hudat (GPS103) villages is rather sparsely vegetated, and very good for **Dwarf Raven** and sometimes **Magpie Starling**. There are a few tall trees in Hudat village, where **White-winged Dove** can also occur. **Steel-blue Whydah** is regularly seen around Wachile, especially along the first few kilometres of the road from Wachile to Soda (see site 41), which at the time of writing was the best route to take to Yabello. *Commiphora* thicket along the Wachile–Soda road can be very productive, providing similar species to those listed in the first paragraph above. It is particularly good for **Scaly Chatterer**, which especially favours places where a

Commiphora trees on the banks of the Dawa River at Melka Ghuba. (Claire Spottiswoode)

dense, tangled understorey has developed under the *Commiphora* trees.
Other animals Günther's Dik-dik is common throughout this region. Nile Crocodile occurs in the Dawa River at Melka Ghuba, so swimming is not recommended.

39. ARERO FOREST

Arero forest is the assumed type locality for **Prince Ruspoli's Turaco**, the first specimen of which was discovered in the eponymous prince's collecting bag after an elephant killed him on the banks of the Omo River in 1893. It is probably the most reliable site to find this species, being a well-defined area that can be searched quite thoroughly (see also the broader Negele region, sites 33 to 35). However, Arero lies on the edge of an area prone to disputes

Tall juniper trees in Arero forest. (Claire Spottiswoode)

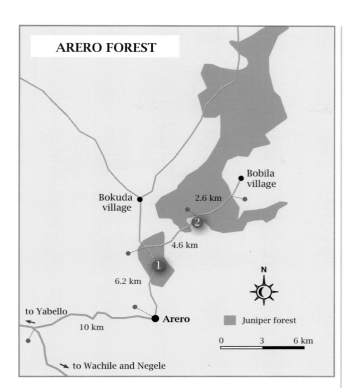

ARERO FOREST

Bobila
village

Bokuda
village   2.6 km

4.6 km

6.2 km

N

to Yabello

10 km   **Arero**   Juniper forest

0   3   6 km

to Wachile and Negele

between ethnic groups, so it is worth making enquiries in Yabello or Negele before travelling here. Obtaining permission to enter or camp in the forest has also sometimes posed problems.

Key birds Prince Ruspoli's and White-cheeked Turacos, White-breasted Cuck-ooshrike, Northern Brownbul.

Key habitats Juniper woods; altitude about 1,600 m.

Access In the past, Arero could be reached either from the west (Yabello) or from the east (Negele). However, the former road was at time of writing heavily damaged, necessitating a dog-leg via Soda and Wachile (see previous site). Should the direct road in future be repaired, it can be reached from the tar road 5.0 km south of the Yabello turn-off. Arero town lies another 83 km along this road, and in the past the journey took a minimum of two-and-a-half to three hours. Birding along the first 40 km of the road is characteristic of the Yabello region (see site 40), and **Ethiopian Bush-crow** is especially common around settlements; farther east, the bush becomes denser. See sites 38 and 41 for details of birding along the alternative route via Soda and Wachile.

From Negele, the distance is 200 km and via the villages of Melka Ghuba (see site 38), Hudat and Wachile, and again the road is passable gravel. If coming from Yabello, bring a guide from the Yabello Sanctuary office (on the northern side of the main road through Yabello town); this is strongly recommended to ease official requirements. If coming from Negele, be sure to obtain permission when you reach Arero. This can be obtained from the Agricultural Ministry office (open 09h00-17h00): turn left at the first opportu-nity when entering Arero town (at the signpost in the colours of the Oromiya

A flash of red and green is sometimes the best view obtained of a Prince Ruspoli's Turaco, which can be surprisingly elusive despite its size and plumage. (Jacques Erard)

flag: orange, white and black), and go to the first building on your right, with an iron roof and wooden shutters.

Birding To reach the juniper forest from Arero, take the first left turn at the large roundabout centred on a big tree in the middle of the town (GPS104). The road enters the outskirts of the juniper forest at 1 on map (GPS105), and 6.2 km from the roundabout turn right onto another track (GPS106). Keep an eye out from this point onwards for turacos at the roadside, although they are more commonly seen farther on. Keep going through this forest, through a cleared area, until you reach a second, better-developed forest patch. Soon after this point there is an area of exposed rock on the right-hand side of the road, which provides a fine place to stand, ideally with a scope, and scan the juniper canopy for **Prince Ruspoli's Turaco**. Also walk slowly along the road on either side of this site, and watch out for crashings in the canopy, nasal, squirrel-like trilling or explosive alarm calls, or red wings gliding amongst the junipers. Beware, though, that all of these can also indicate **White-cheeked Turaco**, which also occurs here. The forest beyond the exposed rock, extending for another 2.6 km of road (beyond which the forest peters out as one approaches Bobila village), is also an excellent area to search for the turaco.

Turacos aside, the forest can appear rather birdless until one stumbles into a foraging party. Canopy species which are likely to be encountered while scanning for turacos include **Hemprich's Hornbill**, **Grey-headed Wood-pecker**, **Abyssinian Oriole**, **White-breasted Cuckooshrike**, **White-crested Helmetshrike** and perhaps **Narina Trogon**, and forest raptors such as **Great** and **Little Sparrowhawks**. Species of the tangled forest understorey include **Blue-spotted Wood Dove**, **Northern Brownbul** (relatively common here; listen for its explosive bouts of chattering) and the strikingly black-faced *omoensis* subspecies of **White-rumped Babbler**. Forested areas can also be reached by taking the left turn at the junction north of Arero (see map), in the direction of Bokuda village. The scarce **Black Scimitarbill** has been seen in thickets in the Arero area.

On the direct road between Arero and Yabello, the open area 35 km east of Yabello (53 km west of Arero) is well worth a scan for **Somali Courser** and **White-tailed Swallow**. Other species here include **White-bellied Bustard**, **Black-capped Social Weaver** and, in the adjacent *Commiphora*, **Bare-eyed Thrush**.

40. YABELLO REGION

The area of arid savanna studded with termite mounds around the town of Yabello is ornithologically remarkable. It hosts two species, **White-tailed Swallow** and **Ethiopian Bush-crow**, described fewer than seventy years ago and whose world range is confined to an area extending about 130 km south-east and 50 km east of the town (although swallows have also been sighted at Negele, see site 35, and Moyale). More generally, there is very diverse savanna and thicket birding, including a good chance of finding several Somali-Masai biome species otherwise confined to the arid zone of northern Kenya and Somalia. The rainy seasons fall during April–May and October, but the specials can readily be found at all times.

Evening over the open *Acacia*–*Commiphora* rangelands of the Yabello region. (Paul Donald)

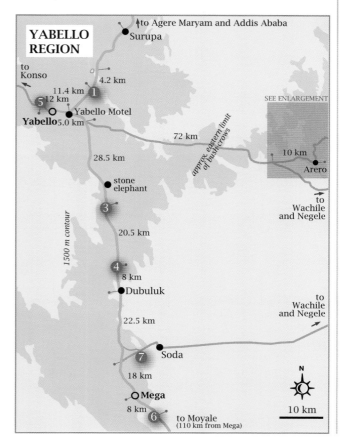

YABELLO REGION

to Agere Maryam and Addis Ababa
Surupa

to Konso

4.2 km

11.4 km **1**
5 12 km

O Yabello Motel
Yabello 5.0 km

72 km

SEE ENLARGEMENT

approx. eastern limit of bush-crows

28.5 km

10 km
Arero

stone elephant

to Wachile and Negele

3

1500 m contour

20.5 km

4

8 km

Dubuluk

to Wachile and Negele

22.5 km

7 Soda

18 km

N

O Mega

8 km **6**

to Moyale
(110 km from Mega)

10 km

The Mega hills rise up beyond the village of Dubuluk. The open, termite-studded plains in the foreground are one of the best places in the world to see White-tailed Swallow. (Claire Spottiswoode)

Key birds Vulturine Guineafowl, White-tailed Swallow, Ethiopian Bush-crow, Scaly Chatterer, Somali Crombec, Tiny Cisticola, Bare-eyed Thrush, Pygmy Batis, Pringle's Puffback, Red-naped Bush-shrike, White-crowned Starling, Grey-capped and Black-capped Social Weavers, Shelley's Rufous Sparrow, Northern Grosbeak-canary.

Key habitats Tall acacia savanna, denser, lower *Acacia–Commiphora* thicket, pure *Commiphora* bushland, open arid scrub, rocky hills, juniper woods. Altitude about 1,400–1,600 m.

Wonderfully productive *Commiphora*-dominated thornbush in the Dubuluk area (4 on map), home to many localised species including Scaly Chatterer, Somali Crombec and Northern Grosbeak-canary. The tall trees are acacias. (Claire Spottiswoode)

Access Yabello is 565 km south of Addis Ababa, and can be reached in a single long day's drive from there, although it is preferable to break up the drive by overnighting at one of the Rift Valley lakes (see sites 23, 24 and 27), or at Wondo Genet (site 26). The road is excellent broad tar as far as Awassa, after which it narrows somewhat but remains good-quality tar all the way to the Kenyan border at Moyale. Consider stopping briefly too at the roadside forest patches south of Agere Maryam (see site 42). Yabello can also be reached

from Negele (285 km to the north-east, on the most direct route, not passable at the time of writing) in a full day's drive, including birding stops. The best accommodation options in Yabello are the Yabello Motel and the Hawi Hotel, respectively just south and north of the checkpoint at the junction of the main tar road to Kenya and the access road to Yabello proper (see map). The Yabello Motel, also known as the Mobil Hotel, has a reasonable restaurant.

Birding Most of the best birding in the Yabello area is readily accessible from the easily travelled Addis–Moyale tar road. Some of the best areas of taller acacia savanna lie just to the north of Yabello town, off the main road to Addis Ababa. Just north of Yabello, the road first passes through an open agricultural area on the plains 7–10 km north of the turn-off to the town, which is particularly good for **Abyssinian Ground Hornbill** and **White-crowned Starling**. Two good acacia woodland sites are (i) a cattle ranching station, the turn-off to which is at 1 on map, signposted 'Diida Xuyyurra Ranch' (GPS107; bear left immediately on turning onto the track, obtain permission at the ranch buildings – weekdays only – and continue beyond them to an area of taller woodland), and (ii) on the southern side of a settlement called Harobake (with a livestock market on Sundays) at 2 on map (GPS108). The combination of tall acacias, little ground cover, and presence of cattle and camel enclosures is prime habitat for **Ethiopian Bush-crow**, which is especially common here. (When photographing them, do take care not to point your camera at camels.) This woodland also holds species preferring taller trees, such as **Black Cuckoo**, **Bearded Woodpecker**, **Black-billed Woodhoopoe** and **Rüppell's Starling**. A walk to the shore of the Harobake dam beyond (visible in the valley when approaching Yabello from the north) may produce various waterbirds.

White-tailed Swallows can be encountered throughout the area, and are commonly seen for example at the Diida Xuyyurra Ranch mentioned above.

Ethiopian Bush-crows, known locally as kaka, are often tame and approachable around villages, where they are often seen turning over dung in search of grubs. (Paul Donald)

Tiny Cisticola is indeed the world's smallest, and favours arid thickets in the far south. (Paul Donald)

White-tailed Swallows have an unusually rapid, bat-like flight, but quite often alight for long periods on small shrubs. (Richard Saunders)

However, probably the very best site for them is the arid, open, heavily grazed vicinity of the village of Dubuluk (GPS109), better known for the traditional Borana 'singing wells' just to the east of it. Scanning the open country immediately to the north (e.g. between 4 and Dubuluk) and south of the village is almost guaranteed to turn up one or more of these elegant swallows in their rapid, bat-like flight. See also the next site for good localities close to Mega.

In sparsely vegetated areas with grass and scrub, such as these top swallow sites, look out for **Heuglin's Courser**, **Foxy** and **Short-tailed Larks** (the latter especially just south of Dubuluk), **Plain-backed Pipit**, **Pale Prinia**, **Tiny Cisticola** and **Black-capped** and **Grey-capped Social Weavers**. White-bellied Bustard is surprisingly common at the roadside in this kind of habitat, while the most open areas hold **Kori Bustard** and (very rarely) **Somali Ostrich**. **Pygmy Falcon** is commonly perched at the roadside; other frequent raptors throughout the Yabello region include **Egyptian**, **Lappet-faced**, **Rüppell's**, **Hooded**, **White-backed** and **White-headed Vultures**, **Martial** and **Tawny Eagles**, **Black-chested Snake-eagle**, **Bateleur**, **Augur Buzzard**, **Gabar Goshawk**, **Eastern Chanting Goshawk** and occasionally **Grey Kestrel**.

Denser *Acacia–Commiphora* thornbush typically occurs in slightly lower-lying areas along much of the roads to Mega (site 41) and Arero (site 39), and can easily be birded from the roadside. Particularly good sites are the acacia-wooded drainage line in the vicinity of the small bridge 33.5 km south of the Yabello Motel (3 on map; GPS110), and the superb area of *Commiphora* bush on the western side of the road at 54 km south (4 on map and GPS111; see also next paragraph). Birding in this habitat is often concentrated around foraging parties; if the habitat seems birdless, try whistling the call of **Pearl-spotted Owlet**, which usually raises a good selection of species. Characteristic species of this habitat are **Buff-crested Bustard**, **Yellow-necked Spurfowl**, **African Orange-bellied Parrot**, **White-bellied Go-away-bird**, **Little Bee-eater**, **Von der Decken's** and **Eastern Yellow-billed Hornbills**, **Abyssinian Scimitarbill**, **Black-throated** and **Red-and-yellow Barbets** (the latter in the vicnity of termite mounds), **Black-headed Oriole**, **Northern Grey Tit**, **Banded Parisoma**, **Mouse-coloured Penduline-tit**, **Yellow-bellied Eremomela**, **Red-faced Crombec**, **Grey Wren-Warbler**, **White-browed Scrub Robin**, **Bare-eyed Thrush**, **Spotted Palm-thrush**, **African Grey Flycatcher**, **Slate-coloured Boubou**, **Grey-headed Bush-**

A male Northern Grosbeak-canary giving its repetitive song from the top of an acacia tree. (Tasso Leventis)

Shrike, Three-streaked Tchagra, White-crested Helmetshrike, Abyssinian White-eye, Golden-breasted Starling, White-headed and Red-billed Buffalo-weavers, Black-cheeked Waxbill, Purple Grenadier, White-bellied Canary and Somali Bunting. Dodson's and Common ('Dark-capped') Bulbuls appear both to occur in this area. Stands of flowering acacia or other plants can attract a remarkable diversity of sunbirds, including Hunter's, Scarlet-chested, Beautiful, Eastern Violet-backed, Marico, Shining, Variable and, with very considerable luck, Black-bellied Sunbird. Large flocks of Vulturine Guineafowl are commonly seen emerging from such thickets onto the roadside.

Purer stands of *Commiphora* bush, with rather less acacia present, are favoured by many of the arid south's more sought-after species. Several stands of this pale, deciduous, flaky-trunked tree are present south of Yabello on the road to Mega (as well as in the Dawa–Wachile region; see site 38). Try especially at that mentioned above around 54 km south of Yabello (GPS111 and 4 on map), as well as the several other patches of similar habitat between here and Dubuluk. Search here for Red-naped Bush-shrike (common), Scaly Chatterer (which can sometimes be elusive, bounding along the ground at high speed), Pygmy Batis, Somali Crombec, Tiny Cisticola, Boran Cisticola (which prefers slightly drier, denser habitat to the abundant Rattling Cisticola), Pringle's Puffback and Northern Grosbeak-canary.

Slate-coloured Boubou likes dry, denser thickets, and is found throughout much of Ethiopia's lowlands.
(Tasso Leventis)

The many small Borana villages in the area have a distinct bird community associated with livestock, bare ground and dense whistling-thorn animal enclosures. Species typical of this habitat are Blue-naped and Speckled Mousebirds, D'Arnaud's Barbet, Rufous Chatterer, Ethiopian Bush-crow, Northern White-crowned Shrike, Rosy-patched Bush-shrike, Chestnut and

Both Black-capped (pictured) and Grey-capped Social Weavers occur in the Yabello region, sometimes breeding colonially in adjacent trees.
(Dick Forsman)

A male Pygmy Batis; this localised species can be locally abundant in the dry thickets of the far south. (Tasso Leventis)

Shelley's **Rufous Sparrows**, **Cut-throat** and **Straw-tailed Whydah**. **White-tailed Swallow** also strongly favours the environs of villages, but so does **Ethiopian Swallow**, so a clear view of the tail is needed.

About 20–40 km south of Yabello, the tar road passes through an area of hills, many of which are only a short walk from the road. In particular, 29 km south of the Yabello turn-off is a large rock known locally as 'Daka Arba', meaning Stone Elephant in Borana (GPS112, or 6 km north of point 3 on map). (It does actually look like an elephant with its trunk raised, especially when seen coming from the north.) It is a short walk along livestock paths to the rock and the hillside behind it, where **Brown-tailed Rock Chat** can be found (as it can on other hills in the area). Other species associated with these hills include **Shining Sunbird** and **Fan-tailed** and (more rarely) **Dwarf Ravens**.

Immediately west of Yabello travelling to Konso, the road begins to rise into denser, moister thicket where **Bare-faced Go-away-bird** is often seen. At around 5 on map (GPS113), 5 km from the outskirts of town, taller juniper trees emerge from the thicket understorey, and **White-cheeked Turaco** is fairly

Short-tailed Lark is the only member of the genus *Pseudalaemon*, and is often seen in small parties, digging at the base of grasses with their stout bills. (Tasso Leventis)

common, often calling from near the crown of the junipers. Other species typical of juniper woods occur here, including **Northern Black Flycatcher, Olive Sunbird, Yellow-bellied Waxbill** and **African Citril**.

The Yabello Motel can attract remarkable numbers of birds to its tiny but well-watered garden. Good numbers of **Straw-tailed Whydah** are nearly always present, and **Speke's Weaver** breeds in the tree in front of the bar, or sometimes in other nearby trees. Other likely species around the motel include **Red-winged Starling, Chestnut Weaver** and **Cut-throat**. A drive of 10 km or so down the road towards Mega shortly after sunset is likely to turn up several **Donaldson Smith's Nightjars**, but check the current security situation before attempting this.

Other animals In areas of denser bush Günther's Dik-dik is common, and Gerenuk is scarce. Lesser Kudu is fairly common and often seen at the roadside, especially at night when they pose an important hazard. Common Zebra occurs in small numbers. Early in the morning one may be lucky enough to see shy predators such as Caracal and Leopard.

Foxy Lark is most easily distinguished from the similar Gillett's Lark by its rufous wing-panel. Also known as Abyssinian Lark, it has formerly been considered a subspecies of southern Africa's Fawn-coloured Lark.
(Jacques Erard)

41. MEGA AND SODA

Mega is positioned on a spur of rocky hills projecting into arid plains. Con Benson and his Mozambican collector Jali Makawa were posted here during the Second World War, when they discovered the **White-tailed Swallow** (named *Hirundo megaensis* after the town). To the south of the town lies an area where this species is frequent and reliably found, and to the north of the hills is an area of dry, stony plains excellent for arid-country specialists, again including the swallow.

Key species White-tailed Swallow, Short-tailed Lark, Somali Short-toed Lark, Somali Courser, Somali Fiscal, Magpie and Bristle-crowned Starlings, Ethiopian Bush-crow, Shelley's Rufous Sparrow.

Key habitats Arid, open plains; altitude about 1,500–1,600 m.

Open whistling-thorn (*Acacia drepanolobium*) country on the dry northern side of the Mega hills.
(Claire Spottiswoode)

A male Shelley's Rufous Sparrow perches on the characteristic swollen galls of whistling-thorn trees, dwelt in by symbiotic ants. (Jacques Erard)

Access Mega is 104 km south of Yabello, on the good tar road that leads to the Kenyan border at Moyale. East of the tar road and north of the Mega hills , the Soda plains are traversed by a good-quality gravel road, as well as a poorer but motorable sandy track (see details below).

Birding The gravel road from the main Yabello–Mega road to Soda (also known as El Sod; the turn-off is 85.8 south of the Yabello T-junction, at GPS114) is excellent for species typical of arid stony scrub. (Note that a smaller short-cut track leaving the tar road a little further north, at GPS115, and rejoining the main Soda dirt road at GPS116, is also very good for birding; you might choose to return this way). **White-tailed Swallow** is especially likely along these roads. Stop and scan in the open stony areas 3–7 km along the main Soda road (about 7 on map, p.119) for **Somali Courser**, **Kori Bustard** and **Secretarybird**, and look out for small parties of **Short-tailed Lark** on the stony road verges; both roads are excellent sites for this species. **Somali Short-toed Lark** also occurs here, and is likely to be flushed at short range or heard singing repetitively high in the sky. **Somali Fiscal** is common, although check the wing markings carefully as **Taita Fiscal** appears to occur sympatrically in the Yabello region. **Shelley's Rufous** and **Chestnut Sparrows** may be seen in scrubbier areas. **Ethiopian Bush-crow** is fairly common here, and flocks of **Magpie Starling** rarely pass through this area. **Black-faced Sandgrouse** has been seen, but is seemingly not common. Keep a look out overhead for **Egyptian Vulture** and **Dwarf Raven**.

The small town of Soda is positioned on the lip of a startlingly deep volcanic crater, concealed by some low hills. The crater and its lake far below

A male White-bellied Bustard giving its nasal, croaking call. (Paul Donald)

Ethiopian Swallow is best distinguished from White-tailed Swallow by its rufous forehead and dark patches at the sides of the breast; it also has a somewhat lazier manner of flight. (Dick Forsman)

Somali Fiscal is very common in the Soda area, but a good view of its white-edged secondaries (just visible in this photo) is needed to separate it from Taita Fiscal, which is relatively rare here. (Tasso Leventis)

are well worth a look. **Bristle-crowned Starling** occurs around the crater and adjacent buildings. The crater rim is right within Soda village and easily reached, but beware that you will need to pay a viewing fee, and will be quickly surrounded by vendors and children.

An excellent place to search for **White-tailed Swallow** is the open, largely cultivated area just to the south of Mega town, on the road to Moyale. Stop along the road 6–14 km south of the town (around 6 on Yabello Region map; GPS117), scanning especially in open areas along river valleys. Beware that **Ethiopian Swallow** also occurs here (as well as of course **Barn Swallows**); other than their dark tails and breast markings, the latter are readily distinguishable by their noticeably less agile flight. Note that **White-tailed Swallow** is also common at Dubuluk (see previous site). It is worth remembering that **Masked Lark** has been seen once in the Mega area (as well as once west of Yabello, albeit in 1941), although we are not aware of any records in the last decade.

Other animals Grant's Gazelle is common in this area, and small parties of Gerenuk are quite commonly seen on the Soda road.

42. AGERE MARYAM

A very accessible patch of juniper–*Podocarpus* forest lies at the roadside just to the south of Agere Maryam, the next major town north of Yabello on the main tar road between Addis Ababa and the Kenya border. It is a good spot for a quick stop en route. Forest lies on either side of the road around 16.0 km south of the town (GPS118); 3 km to the north is a second patch, with a grassy marsh in-between. When wet (note that it is dry in winter), this and other of the many such marshes at this altitude often hold **Woolly-necked Stork** and **Rouget's Rail** as well as other characteristic highland species such as **Wattled Ibis** and **African Stonechat**. Forest species include **Abyssinian Slaty Flycatcher** and **Abyssinian Oriole**; **Taita Falcon** (vanishingly scarce in Ethiopia), **Yellow-fronted Parrot** and **Spotted Creeper** have also been seen here. **Chestnut-naped Francolin** occurs at the roadside in this area.

Somali Courser likes the driest, most open country, and occurs regularly if not completely reliably in the Soda area. (Nik Borrow)

THE SOUTH-WEST

43. Nechisar National Park
44. Senkelle Sanctuary
45. Fejij
46. Mago National Park
47. Gambella

South-western Ethiopia is a remote and fascinating region, more often visited for its cultural diversity than for its birds. The most frequently visited site in this section is Nechisar National Park, which can readily be included in a southern Ethiopian circuit by (for example) driving from Yabello via Konso, and thus provide an opportunity to hunt for the tantalisingly little-known **Nechisar Nightjar**. The other sites mentioned here (except Senkelle Sanctuary, en route to Nechisar) are more ambitious undertakings, and each is an expedition in its own right. None is crucial to visit with respect to seeing the Horn of Africa's special birds, but each is fascinating in other respects. For example, Gambella is an outpost of the Sudan–Guinea Savanna Biome with an avifauna quite unlike the rest of the sites described in this book, but perhaps already familiar to those who have travelled in West Africa.

TOP 10 BIRDS

African Swallow-tailed Kite
Egyptian Plover
Heuglin's Bustard
Yellow-throated
    Sandgrouse
Pel's Fishing Owl
Star-spotted Nightjar
White-tailed Lark
Gambaga Flycatcher
Black-headed Gonolek
Pygmy Sunbird

43. NECHISAR NATIONAL PARK

Nechisar means 'white grass', and it is this isolated grassland on black cotton-soil which gives the Nechisar Plains their characteristic flavour, positioned between blue Lake Chamo and orange Lake Abaya and the Amaro Mountains. Nechisar is a spectacularly beautiful and remote national park, but undeniably a pain to get to. The main birding attractions are **White-tailed Lark**, which occurs nowhere else in Ethiopia, and the dream of rediscovering **Nechisar Nightjar**, described on the basis of a single wing found in 1990. Another near-mythical bird to keep at the back of one's mind here is **Fried-mann's Lark**, not seen in Ethiopia since the type specimen was collected in 1912 about 80 km to the south of the Nechisar Plains.

Key birds African Swallow-tailed Kite, Orange River ('Archer's') Francolin, Yellow-throated Sandgrouse, Black-bellied Bustard, Star-spotted Nightjar, White-tailed Lark, Northern Masked Weaver, Stripe-breasted Seedeater.

Key habitats Riparian forest, grassy plains with sparse thornbush; altitude about 1,200 m on the Nechisar Plains.

Access Nechisar National Park is just to the east of the town of Arba Minch. At the time of writing this was a full day's drive from Shashemene (the nearest town to Wondo Genet, see site 26) to the north, although the road is under reconstruction and may be improved shortly. Arba Minch can also be reached from Yabello via Konso, although the road is poor (but passable). At the park headquarters just beyond the gate, you need to pay entrance fees and collect a scout to accompany you; a high-clearance 4WD is required for access at all times of year. The main Nechisar Plains lie beyond the hilly, rocky 'Bridge of God' ('Egzer Dildiy') between the two lakes; this road can be in terrible

Zebras graze on the Nechisar Plains, with the Amaro Mountains behind. (Claire Spottiswoode)

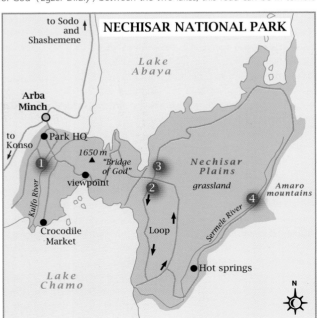

NECHISAR NATIONAL PARK

to Sodo and Shashemene

Lake Abaya

Arba Minch

to Konso

Park HQ

1650 m

"Bridge of God"

viewpoint

Nechisar Plains

grassland

Amaro mountains

Kulfo River

Sermele River

Crocodile Market

Loop

Hot springs

Lake Chamo

N

Nechisar National Park is wedged between two Rift Valley lakes, respectively Ethiopia's second- and third-largest; Lake Chamo, pictured here, is a typical blue, whereas adjacent Lake Abaya is an odd orange colour resulting from ferrous oxide in the water.
(Claire Spottiswoode)

condition in the rainy season and you might be forbidden to take it after particularly heavy rains. When wet, the black cotton soils of the plains themselves become treacherous, and there is a good chance of getting stuck or sliding off the road. Under such conditions, the riparian forest along the Kulfo River (1 on map) remains accessible. It is possible to camp along the Kulfo River, as well as near the hot springs in the far east of park (the latter site is, however, often noisy with people coming to sample the medicinal properties of the waters); otherwise, accommodation is only available in Arba Minch town. There are reputedly a lot of gin-traps in this national park, so take care when walking off-road.

Birding About 3km from the park headquarters (near the entrance gate) is a strip of lush riparian forest along the Kulfo River (1), where it is possible to camp. A walk here is well worthwhile for species such as **Bruce's Green Pigeon, Narina Trogon, Double-toothed Barbet, Scaly-throated Honeyguide, Red-capped Robin-chat, Brown-throated Wattle-eye** and **Green-backed Twinspot**. It could be worth keeping an ear open for the bizarre call of **Yellowbill**, which does occur here. With tremendous luck you might spot a day-roosting **Pel's Fishing Owl**, which you might well hear – as well as Lions – if you camp here. Scarcer forest raptors such as **African Cuckoo-hawk** and **Bat Hawk** can also be encountered.

Just south of here, along the north-western shore of Lake Chamo, is the so-called 'Crocodile Market' where large numbers of Nile Crocodiles gather to sun themselves. To reach it, take the track 9 km south from just past the bridge over the Kulfo River, near the campsites. From the Crocodile Market it may be possible to rent a little boat to take you along the lake shore. **Northern Masked Weaver**, a localised bird in Ethiopia, may be seen here, and general waterbirding is good: common species include **Goliath Heron, Glossy Ibis, Southern Pochard, Black Crake** and migrants including **Marsh Sandpiper**.

The 'Bridge of God' between the two lakes is covered in thornbush; look out here for parties of **Stripe-breasted Seedeater**, a localised bird in Ethiopia. At the eastern end of the 'Bridge of God', the road drops down onto the grass of the Nechisar Plains, about 30 km from the park entrance. For a relatively short and manageable circuit giving a good taste of the grassland, turn right at a crossroads (2; GPS119) and follow the loop marked on the map. **White-**

Double-toothed Barbet is a characteristic bird of riparian forest at Nechisar, as elsewhere.
(Tasso Leventis)

tailed Larks occur throughout the grassland but, unless they are singing, are typically seen only when flushed from the long grass. They may sometimes be flushed by the vehicle, but failing that your best bet is simply to walk; beware though that ticks are especially pestilential here, particularly during the dry season. The Nechisar population is rumoured, intriguingly, to have song and display unlike those elsewhere in East Africa.

The plains are also a good site for **Hartlaub's** and **Black-bellied Bustards**, the latter especially favouring lightly wooded grassland; **Kori Bustard** is abundant, and you may see up to hundred in a day. Look out for noisy flights of **Yellow-throated Sandgrouse**, a typical species of black cotton soils. The Nechisar plains are also one of the better sites in Ethiopia for migrant **African Swallow-tailed Kites** (Nov–Apr), **Steppe** and **Lesser Spotted Eagles**, **Lesser Kestrel** and **Pallid** and **Montagu's Harriers** all occur, sometimes commonly, during winter. Passerines include **Taita Fiscal** and **Boran** and **Desert Cisticolas**. Herds of Common Zebra and Grant's Gazelle are likely to be seen grazing below the dramatic backdrop of the Amaro Mountains, and with a little luck some of the park's small population of Korkay (also called Swayne's Hartebeest).

It is worth making a small detour north to the hilly area (3) 1–2 km north of the crossroads at the plain's edge, as this is one of the very few places in Ethiopia where one has a good chance of seeing 'Archer's' Francolin, a putative split from the otherwise South African endemic **Orange River Francolin**. The best way to search for it is to stop and walk through grassed hilly areas, hoping to flush a covey; you may also be lucky enough to hear them calling in the late afternoon, or (if you can get there in time) in the early morning.

If you have more time, consider going all the way to the hot springs and Sermele River area in the far east of the park, but do check the security situation and road conditions beforehand. This area allows access also to the riparian forest along the Sermele River and to some wonderful scenery; this is a full day's excursion. Riparian forest near the road from the hot springs northwards (4) provides similar species to the Kulfo River area, with perhaps a better chance of **Bat Hawk** and **African Cuckoo-hawk** (the former especially at dusk). Mountain species such as **Lammergeier** and **Scarce Swift** (a rare bird

Fewer than 600 individuals of the Korkay or Swayne's Hartebeest now exist, confined to just four localities including Nechisar; this subspecies of Hartebeest was rendered endemic to Ethiopia after being exterminated in adjacent Somalia. (Lajos Németh)

Throughout its range in Africa, Yellow-throated Sandgrouse particularly seeks out areas with black cotton soils, such as on the Nechisar Plains; these soils are famously impassable after rains. (Jacques Erard)

Nechisar is a very good place to search for the scarce Star-spotted Nightjar, confined to north-eastern Africa. (Claire Spottiswoode)

in Ethiopia) touch this eastern part of the park, as well as occasionally the Arba Minch escarpment on its western flank.

If you stay on the plains until dusk, you can drive back to the campsite or Arba Minch after dark and look for nightjars. Nightars can be remarkably abundant on the plains, each one giving one's heart a little leap before it turns out to be yet another **Slender-tailed Nightjar** rather than Nechisar. Ideally, any suspect nightjar should be captured to allow close examination. The plains are a very good site for the scarce and diminutive **Star-spotted Nightjar**, the occasional **Donaldson Smith's Nightjar** and **Marsh Owl**, and perhaps even a Leopard. Crossing the Bridge of God after dark, keep an eye out also for **Montane** and **Freckled Nightjars**, which favour rocky areas, and owls including **Verreaux's** and **Greyish Eagle-owls**. **Standard-winged Nightjar** has been seen a number of times between Arba Minch town and the park entrance, and is well worth looking out for if returning after dark to a hotel in town. Considering that there have also been rare records of **Dusky** and **Nubian Nightjars** in the park, the nightjar species list here is an astonishing nine in all.

Nechisar also falls within the southern fragment of **White-fronted Black Chat**'s tiny and disjunct Ethiopian range, and it has been recorded in the south-western corner of Lake Abaya. We are not aware of any recent records from Nechisar, but it is surely worth keeping in mind when crossing the 'Bridge of God'.

Other animals Lion, Grant's Gazelle, Korkay and Common Zebra, with Hippopotamus and Nile Crocodiles in Lakes Chamo and Abaya.

44. SENKELLE SANCTUARY

Black-bellied Bustard likes taller grassland, such as that at Senkelle Sanctuary. (Tasso Leventis)

This is a small highland grassland sanctuary west of Shashemene, and lies just to the south of the main road from Shashemene to Arba Minch. It would make a pleasant stop on the way to or from Arba Minch, were there time to stop; this may yet become possible as the road improves. The turn-off south to the sanctuary is 7 km west of Aje (a town 35 km west of Shashemene), and the park gate is 11 km farther on. Here, you will need to pick up a scout to accompany you. The sanctuary was established to conserve the Korkay, and remains one of the last strongholds for this endangered subspecies of

African Swallow-tailed
Kite, a dry season migrant
to several parts of the
Rift Valley, including the
Nechisar Plains.
(Dick Forsman)

Hartebeest. It is easily seen from the circular drive through the sanctuary, as is Oribi. Senkelle is a good site for **Black-bellied Bustard**. It can be difficult to see when the grass is tall, but much easier after the grass is burnt by the park authorities every January. General grassland birding is also good, including **Long-billed Pipit, African Quailfinch** and raptors of open country such as **African Swallow-tailed Kite, Bateleur, Black-chested Snake-eagle,** and **Pallid** and **Montagu's Harriers**.

45. FEJIJ

This arid, far-flung and somewhat volatile corner of Ethiopia, just north of Lake Turkana and to the west of Lake Chew Bahir (Stephanie), is a relatively reliable site for the magnificent **Heuglin's Bustard** (but see also Bogol Manyo region, site 37). However, going there is a far from trivial exercise. The nearest large town (98 km to the north of Fejij) is Turmi, where there are two lodges and a campsite. However, the journey between the two can take up to a full

Like several other species,
Somali Bee-eater's range in
Ethiopia is largely the inaccessible Ogaden, as well as
a small patch in the south-
west such as Fejij.
(Claire Spottiswoode)

day including birding stops, and may occasionally become impassable after heavy rains. At a push it might be done as a round-trip in a single day, but this would be a gamble (otherwise, permission needs to be sought to camp near Fejij). Be sure to check on the security situation before visiting. To reach Fejij, travel from Arba Minch south to Konso and west to Weito (51 km), then turn south to Erbore (also known as Arbore, and 50 km beyond Weito). In Erbore you will need to contact the local police station to arrange for a policeman to accompany you as guide and escort. The turn-off south to Fejij is another 49 km from Erbore on the road to Turmi (if coming from the other direction, this is 21 km from Turmi); see next site for roadside birding. Fejij is another 77 km south from this turn-off. **Heuglin's Bustard** has been seen on both sides of Fejij village: along the last few kilometres of road before reaching the village, and also along minor tracks 1–2 km beyond the village. Other species here include **African Swallow-tailed Kite**, **Star-spotted Nightjar** (relatively common here), **Somali Bee-eater** and **Chestnut-headed Sparrow-lark**; **Pink-breasted Lark** and **Northern Grosbeak-canary** have also been reported.

46. MAGO NATIONAL PARK

The wild hills of the South Omo valley. (Lajos Németh)

The Mago National Park lies alongside the culturally diverse and fascinating South Omo region of Ethiopia, inhabited by a remarkable mix of small but highly distinctive pastoralist tribes (including the Mursi, Hamer, Karo and Surma) about whom much has been written and many photographs taken. Cultural tourism to this region is now well developed, and for very good reason, but the birding is not well known, and might appear less interesting. The vast and wild Mago National Park is dominated by dense bushland and savanna, with swamps and riparian forest along the major rivers such as the Mago. It is the only place in Ethiopia where African Buffalo still occur, albeit in small numbers, and one of the few where African Elephant still do (see also site 19). It is not easily accessible: a letter of permission to visit the region and a high clearance vehicle are necessary at all times of year (and 4WD in the rains, if the park is accessible at all). The park is reached from Jinka, which is usually accessed by air from Addis Ababa or Arba Minch, although the gruelling drive is possible: roadside birding may compensate, and species en route from Konso to Turmi to Jinka have included **Bat Hawk**, **Grey Kestrel**, **Bateleur**, **Vulturine Guineafowl**, **Spotted Palm-thrush**, **White-shouldered Black Tit**, **Golden-breasted Starling**, **Black Bishop** (confined in Ethiopia to the west) and even **Red-billed Pytilia**.

The park's headquarters and campsite are near the entrance gate, and here riparian forest along the Neri River might just yield **Pel's Fishing Owl**, **Narina Trogon**, **White-crowned Robin-chat** and reputedly **Blue-breasted Kingfisher**. **Egyptian Plover** occurs along the Omo River, and **Dusky Babbler** has been recorded from riparian thicket at Lake Dipa. **Donaldson Smith's Sparrow-weaver** has been recorded from the acacia woodland, and if records are confirmed this would be the only place in Ethiopia where **Violet Wood-hoopoe** occurs. Commoner savanna species of Mago National Park include **Star-spotted** and **Donaldson Smith's Nightjars**, **Black Cuckoo**, **Swallow-tailed Bee-eater** (localised in Ethiopia), **Broad-billed Roller**, **Steel-blue** and **Eastern Paradise Whydahs**, **White-winged Widow** and **Little Weaver**.

47. GAMBELLA

The low-lying Gambella area has a fascinatingly different birding and cultural atmosphere compared to the rest of Ethiopia. A strong Southern Sudanese feel is provided by the Nuer and Anuak peoples, and the presence of many more typically West African or Sahelian bird species of the Sudan–Guinea Savanna Biome creates an avifauna quite different from the other sites described in this book. Gambella town is the main point of access, and is situated on the banks of the Baro River, a tributary of the Blue Nile. It was a British colonial enclave in the early twentieth century, when ships used regularly to sail the 1,366 km to Khartoum. It remained an important trading hub until the Derg coup, but today the Baro River is no longer navigable and habitat destruction in the area is rife. The humanitarian situation in the region is unfortunately fraught, with a large Sudanese refugee population, and domestic ethnic conflicts continue to occur. It is a good idea to check the current security situation before planning a visit, especially if intending to venture much outside of Gambella town.

Key birds Egyptian Plover, Black-billed Wood Dove, Little Green Bee-eater, Snowy-headed Robin-chat, Brown Babbler, Foxy Cisticola, Green-backed Eremomela, Gambaga Flycatcher, Yellow-bellied Hyliota, Black-headed Gonolek, Pygmy Sunbird, Chestnut-crowned Sparrow-weaver, Black-faced Firefinch.

Key habitats Deciduous woodland, riparian floodplain; altitude about 560 m.

Access Gambella is not logistically easy to visit. An alternative to enduring the long drive from Addis Ababa (allow two days) is to fly in on Ethiopian Airlines:

Humid and low-lying Gambella has strong Sudanese affinities, both culturally and ornithologically. (Claire Spottiswoode)

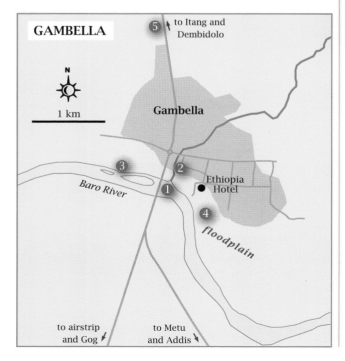

The dry broadleaved woodlands of the Gambella area are punctuated by rocky hillocks. (Claire Spottiswoode)

the airstrip (GPS120) is 13 km south of Gambella on the road to Gog, and there is no formal public transport between the two. It can prove tricky (and costly) to hire a vehicle locally, so one should consider either sending a car from Addis ahead of time, or be prepared to walk and cycle around (bicycles can be hired at the market). Travelling more widely in the area is essentially impossible during the rainy season (May–Sep), and even during the dry season it is oppressively humid. There are several hotels in Gambella town, of which the most bearable is undoubtedly the Ethiopia Hotel, which has been known to permit camping in its grounds.

Birding One of Gambella's most attractive species can be seen right within town: **Egyptian Plover** feeds along the banks of the Baro River, and roosts on protruding rocks. It can be seen from the main bridge at 1 (having first cleared your intentions with the guards on duty), and it also wanders up the small seasonal stream (crossed by a bridge at 2, GPS121) that runs through the town centre.

There are some accessible scraps of remaining taller riparian vegetation along the north bank of Baro River, west of the bridge (3). A walk along this bank could provide species localised in Ethiopia such as **Red-necked Falcon** (usually associated with palm trees), **Western Banded Snake-eagle, Lizard Buzzard, Black-billed Wood Dove, Vinaceous Dove, Swallow-tailed** and **Red-throated Bee-eaters, Green Woodhoopoe, Snowy-headed Robin-chat** and **Gambaga Flycatcher**, with **Moustached Grass Warbler** in areas of rank

The Baro River, a Nile tributary once navigable to Khartoum and fringed by now beleaguered swamps and riparian forest. (Claire Spottiswoode)

vegetation. **Bat Hawk** emerges at dusk. Areas of seeding grasses attract **Red-billed Pytilia**, **Black-rumped** and **Abyssinian Waxbills**, and **Black-faced** and **Bar-breasted Firefinches**. (The very poorly known **Barka** and **Wilson's Indigobirds** respectively parasitise the last two firefinches, and have been collected in the Gambella area; we are not aware of any sightings in the last 10 years.) South-east of town is an area of floodplain (4) where **Woolly-necked Stork** is surprisingly common, with one sighting of **Eurasian Bittern**. It is worth keeping an eye out for **White-backed Night Heron** and **Long-toed Plover**, which were both found to have bred here in the 1960s and 1970s, and might still occur on the wooded and swampy margins of the Baro, respectively.

Away from the Baro, undulating dry deciduous woodland covers much of the area, punctuated by small rocky hillocks. This habitat can be reached (for example) along the Dembidolo road (5) leading north from Gambella, between town and the Itang turn-off about 8 km to the north. Fairly commonly encountered woodland species that are localised in Ethiopia include **Brown-backed Woodpecker**, **Little Green Bee-eater**, **Brown Babbler** (especially favouring thickets on termite mounds), **Yellow-bellied Hyliota**, **Chestnut-crowned Sparrow-weaver**, **Black-headed Gonolek**, **Pygmy Sunbird** and **Brown-rumped Bunting**. Other relatively localised species in Ethiopia that do also extend to less far-flung parts of the country are **Red-necked Buzzard** (uncommon, Dec–May), **Vinaceous Dove**, **Black Scimitarbill**, **Green-backed Eremomela**, **Foxy Cisticola**, **Lesser Blue-eared Starling** and **Exclamatory Paradise Whydah**. There have been a couple of sightings of **Levant Sparrowhawk** in this habitat.

Shoebill used to be seen occasionally in papyrus swamps along the Baro well to the west of Gambella, west of Itang and in the 1960s in the Jikao region still farther west. Excitingly, a 2009 survey has confirmed that the species still occurs in this area, although only remnants of the wetlands now survive. The security situation can occasionally be precarious in this region, although trucks regularly make the journey from Gambella to Itang.

Other animals Few large mammals are likely to be seen close to Gambella town. Nile Lechwe probably still occurs in the hypothetical Gambella National Park closer to the Sudanese border, but its future in Ethiopia is highly precarious. White-eared Kob does still occur in this area, numbering in the thousands and migrating between Ethiopia and Sudan.

Foxy Cisticola is one of the suite of more characteristically central African species that are common in the Gambella area.
(Tasso Leventis)

THE NORTH

48. Bahir Dar and Lake Tana
49. The Simien Mountains
50. Lalibela and Axum

The north's rock-hewn churches, monuments and the elaborately decorated monasteries of the Ethiopian Orthodox Christian highland culture are what many foreigners most readily associate with Ethiopia. These and the magnificent Simien Mountains are all excellent reasons to visit northern Ethiopia, but most birders typically do not go there, since all the endemic species can easily be seen farther south, without necessitating internal flights to cover the vast distances of Ethiopia's northern half. These sites are briefly outlined for those birders who do, as well as the more frequently visited Lake Tana. Lake Tana is a short flight or day's drive from Addis Ababa and birding here is easy and diverse, but not essential with respect to Ethiopia's endemic species. However, it is a relatively reliable site for the endemic and sometimes elusive **White-throated Seedeater** (but also see e.g. sites 7 and 10).

TOP 10 BIRDS

Lammergeier
African Finfoot
Lesser Jacana
Yellow-fronted Parrot
Green-backed Eremomela
White-billed Starling
White-throated Seedeater
Ankober Serin
Wattled Crane
Red-billed Pytilia

48. BAHIR DAR AND LAKE TANA

Lake Tana offers very pleasant and diverse birding, interesting island monasteries, and access to the moderately spectacular Blue Nile (Tississat) Falls, but in terms of endemics it is not an essential inclusion in a time-pressed Ethiopian itinerary. It is especially good for the endemic **White-throated Seedeater**, although also making an appearance here are a number of more typically western Ethiopian species, several of which may (in Ethiopia) otherwise only be seen in the much more precarious far west (see site 47).

Key birds Black Crowned Crane, African Finfoot, Lesser Jacana, Yellow-fronted Parrot, Green-backed Eremomela, Copper Sunbird, Red-billed Pytilia, White-throated Seedeater.

Key habitats Swampy lakeshore, riparian forest; altitude about 1,850 m.

Access Bahir Dar (also known as Bahar Dar) is the better part of a day's drive from Addis; flying there from Addis is more efficient, and flights from Addis are very frequent. The Tana Hotel is much the best place to stay for birding. The Kuriftu Resort and Spa Hotel is also good for birds, but expensive.

Birding

1. Tana Hotel Most birders stay at the Tana Hotel (GPS122), just north of Bahir Dar town, owing to its fine wooded grounds and access to the lakeshore. Just within the gates to the hotel compound is a patch of marshy grassland where **African Openbill** is often present, and occasionally **Black Crowned Crane**. A stroll among the trees of the hotel's compound is likely to turn up **White-cheeked Turaco**, **Silvery-cheeked Hornbill**, **Eastern Grey Plantain-eater**, **Double-toothed Barbet**, **Black-winged Lovebird** and **Yellow-fronted Parrot** (occasionally), and several more typically western Ethiopian species including **Green-backed Eremomela**, **Copper Sunbird** (check flowering plants) and **Yellow White-eye**. You may find a **Greyish Eagle-owl** perched on the hotel roof before dawn. In the daytime, have a look in the *Euphorbia* tree in the middle of the carpark for a resident colony of Wahlberg's Epauletted Fruit

The shy and delicate Lemon Dove is common in the forest understorey at Lake Tana, as elsewhere.
(Tasso Leventis)

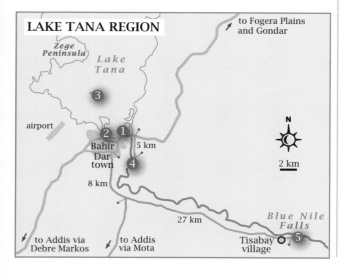

LAKE TANA REGION

Zege Peninsula

Lake Tana

to Fogera Plains and Gondar

airport

Bahir Dar town

5 km

8 km

27 km

N

2 km

to Addis via Debre Markos

to Addis via Mota

Tisabay village

Blue Nile Falls

Lake Tana's Zege Peninsula is one of the better places in Ethiopia to see the endemic Yellow-fronted Parrot. (János Oláh)

Bats, with conspicuous pale spots at the base of their ears. Species likely to be seen along the lakeshore adjoining the hotel include **Giant**, **Grey-headed**, **Woodland** and **Malachite Kingfishers**, **Whiskered**, **White-winged Black** and **Gull-billed Terns** (common), **Grey-headed Gull** year-round and in winter **Lesser Black-backed**, **Black-headed**, **Pallas's** and (more rarely) **Heuglin's Gulls**. **African Finfoot** has even been seen here a few times, although it is better searched for at Kibran Gebrial island (below).

2. Kuriftu Resort and Spa This rather expensive hotel (GPS123) offers access to a stretch of lakeshore especially good for **Lesser Jacana**, **Allen's Gallinule** and **Black Crowned Crane**. Walk out the back of the hotel and scan west and north over the shallow, vegetated areas along the lakeshore; **Lesser Jacana** is especially easy to see in the late afternoon.

3. Kibran Gebriel island From the hotel it is possible to arrange boat transport to the tiny Kibran Gebriel (GPS124) and Entos Eyesus (GPS125) islands, which is about a half-hour journey. Gulls, terns and **Pink-backed** and **Eastern White Pelicans** are all likely to be seen en route; **African Fish Eagles** are abundant, **Ospreys** scarcer. Ask the boatman to circle the islands slowly (especially Kibran Gebriel, but if you draw a blank here, try Entos Eyesus) and scan under patches of overhanging vegetation at the water's edge for **Half-collared** and

Half-collared Kingfisher occurs along the wooded fringes of Lake Tana's islands; it is most characteristically a bird of forested streams, such as at Wondo Genet (see site 26). (Dick Forman)

Giant Kingfishers; this used to be a good site for **African Finfoot**, but in recent years a low wall built around the water's edge appears to have caused them to move on. You might want to land on Kibran Gebriel to have a look at the monastery at the top of the island, but note that women are forbidden to approach it. **Lemon Dove** is particularly common and tame in the surrounding forest patches and coffee plantations. **Yellow-fronted Parrots** are occasionally seen here, and **White-cheeked Turaco, Black-winged Lovebird** and **Brown-throated Wattle-eye** are common. From Kibran Gebriel it is possible to continue north-west by boat, and land on the forested Zege Peninsula (also accessible by road from Bahir Dar). Here, **African Finfoot** still occurs where vegetation overhangs the water's edge, and **Yellow-fronted Parrot** is especially numerous in the mix of forest trees and coffee plantations. There are several interesting monasteries to visit here (permitted to women!).

4. Viewpoint over the Blue Nile There is good birding along a road that follows the eastern bank of the Blue Nile, leading to a viewpoint over the town and river. To reach it, travel east out of town, and cross the Blue Nile bridge. Immediately beyond the bridge, at GPS126, turn right (south) along a beautiful jacaranda-lined avenue. As you travel down this road, passing a civil war monument on your left, keep an eye on the reed-lined banks of the Blue Nile for **Black Crowned Crane**. Birding is good all along this road, and especially on the last stretch up a hill to the viewpoint (GPS127). Also stop particularly where the road crosses the Angodgud River (GPS128), 3 km from the turn-off, where birds come to drink in the heat of the day; this is a good spot for **Red-billed Pytilia** and occasionally **White-throated Seedeater**. All along the road, species include **Black-winged Lovebird, Vinaceous Dove, White-rumped Babbler, Bush Petronia, Black-winged Red** and **Yellow-crowned Bishops, Yellow-mantled** and **Fan-tailed Widowbird** and **Copper Sunbird**. The view-point itself, just north of an old palace (which one may not approach), is a good place to scan for scarce raptors including **Ayres's** and **African Hawk-eagles**, and has potential for migrants; **Beaudouin's Snake-eagle** has been reported from here more than once, although its occurrence in Ethiopia still requires formal confirmation. **Gambaga Flycatcher** has been reported from denser vegetation around the viewpoint, and **White-throated Seedeater** and **Chestnut-crowned Sparrow-weaver** have also been seen here.

The Blue Nile Falls have suffered from the creation of a hydro-electric scheme, but are still impressive. (Richard McManus)

5. Blue Nile (Tississat) Falls The falls are well worth a look (particularly for **White-throated Seedeater**), although they are sadly no longer as spectacular as they once were prior to the construction of a hydroelectric plant that has much reduced the water flow. The access road follows the south bank of the Blue Nile for 35 km, which is a journey of perhaps an hour. During and after the rains, areas of flooded grassland along this road liven up the journey with **Black-winged Red** and **Yellow-crowned Bishops**; **Lesser Moorhen** has also been seen here. From the parking area a little beyond Tississat village, a footpath leads one a few hundred metres to the falls, passing through secondary growth and under a few scattered big trees. This is an excellent site for **White-throated Seedeater**, which may be seen in parties anywhere along this path, as well as **White-cheeked Turaco**, **Abyssinian Oriole** and various more characteristically western Ethiopian species such as **Vinaceous Dove**, **Bush Petronia** and **Yellow White-eye**. Before reaching a final viewpoint over the falls, the path crosses the Blue Nile over a stone bridge built by the Portuguese in the seventeenth century, where **White-collared Pigeon**, **Mocking Cliff Chat**, **Red-winged** and **Slender-billed Starlings** may be seen. The path between the bridge and the first viewpoint over the falls is a good area to search for **White-throated Seedeater**. **Nyanza Swift** sometimes forage around the falls themselves, and there has been at least one report from here of the still-mysterious 'Ethiopian' Cliff Swallow (see also site 15).

6. Fogera Plains The Fogera Plains are an area of seasonally flooded grassland crossed by the main road from Bahir Dar to Gondar. They are an excellent site for **Wattled Crane**, as well as being one of the most important wintering grounds in Ethiopia for migratory ducks, herons, gulls and waders. The plains cover the last 15 km or so before the town of Woreta (50 km from Bahir Dar; GPS129), and can be birded from the roadside. This is also a key site for **Black Crowned Crane**, wintering **Common Crane** and migrant raptors including **Lesser Kestrel** and **Pallid**, **Montagu's** and **Western Marsh Harriers**. **Sooty Falcon** has been sighted here once.

African Jacana, noisy, poly-androus and ubiquitous, is a common bird of vegetated lake fringes in most of Ethiopia. (Jacques Erard)

49. THE SIMIEN MOUNTAINS

These magnificent mountains near Gondar are wonderful for hiking, and the birding is excellent. Birdlife is similar to that in the less rugged (and in many respects more accessible) southern Bale Mountains (see sites 28 and 29), where all the key montane species can be seen with less effort. However, this would perhaps miss the point of a visit to the Simiens, which are truly spectacular and well worth a week's hiking if you have the time. Montane species shared with the southern highlands include **Lammergeier, Eastern Imperial Eagle** (rare), **Chestnut-naped Francolin, Spot-breasted Plover, Rouget's Rail, White-cheeked Turaco, Abyssinian Owl** (around the park headquarters at Debark), **Abyssinian Woodpecker, Red-billed Chough** (confined to the Geech Plateau), **White-backed Black Tit, Moorland Chat, Abyssinian Long-claw, Abyssinian Catbird** and **Black-headed Siskin**. Additionally, a number of northern highland species absent at Bale join the montane assemblage, including **Erckel's Francolin, Rüppell's Black Chat, White-billed Starling** and **Ankober Serin**, the last-mentioned particularly around Chenek Camp and on Bhawit Pass. **Somali Starling** is now also well known at this site. There is a good chance of sighting a Walia Ibex, a subspecies endemic to the Simien Mountains, and Gelada is very common. Ethiopian Wolves are present, but much more elusive than in the Bale Mountains.

The endangered Walia Ibex is endemic to the Simien Mountains, and is sometimes regarded as a full species. Although only about 500 individuals exist, there is quite a good chance of seeing one, even on a short visit.
(Anup Shah/naturepl.com).

50. LALIBELA AND AXUM

Dusky Turtle Dove is fairly common in wooded areas throughout the Ethiopian highlands. (Jacques Erard)

These historical sites are the main objective of many tourist visits to Ethiopia, but are not especially distinctive for birds, although many endemics occur. The birding is typical of the northern highlands, and endemic species seen around and en route to the famous sites include **Wattled Ibis**, **White-collared Pigeon**, **White-winged Cliff Chat**, **Rüppell's Black Chat** and **White-billed Starling**, as well as the familiar panoply of highland species such as **Nyanza Swift**, **Dusky Turtle Dove**, **Brown-rumped Seedeater**, **Streaky Seedeater** and **Tacazze Sunbird**. At Lalibela, **Lammergeier** is especially common, and the poorly known endemic **Yellow-throated Seedeater** has even been seen along the road to the airport. At Axum, look out for **White-throated Seed-eater** in gardens around the town. **Semi-collared Flycatcher**, a scarce bird in Ethiopia, has been seen here regularly in winter. The hillsides above King Ezana's Tomb, just north of the town centre, are also very good for **White-throated Seedeater**, as well as **Clapperton's** and **Erckel's Francolins** and (on autumn and spring passage) **White-throated Robin**.

A soaring Lammergeier, here an immature bird, is one of the classic sights of northern Ethiopia. (Tasso Leventis)

TOP
FIFTY BIRDS

Numbers in the text refer to the sites set out above
(see site accounts or table of contents).

Photographs by Hadoram Shirihai are contributed from the forthcoming projects:
The Birds of East Africa: A Photographic Guide by Hadoram Shirihai, and *Birds of the World:
A Photographic Handbook* by Hans Jornvall and Hadoram Shirihai (A&C Black, London).

Wattled Ibis (Hadoram Shirihai)

Wattled Ibis

Endemic to Ethiopia and Eritrea. Of all Ethiopia's endemics this is the most conspicuously abundant, and most permanently dishevelled-looking. It is a bird of highland grassland moorland and open woodland near cliffs, but has readily adapted to human cultivation and habitation, and now breeds colonially on buildings as well. It is often heard giving deep, harsh, reverberating calls and showing its white wing patches as it flies to its cliff roost-sites in the evenings. It is common even in central Addis Ababa, feeding on scrawny road verges oblivious to the adjacent gridlocked traffic.

Blue-winged Goose

Endemic to Ethiopia. This is still a relatively common bird of highland ponds, marshes and streams, above about 2,100 m. It breeds at high altitudes, for example around the bitterly cold alpine tarns of the Bale Mountains, and disperses to lower altitudes during the rainy season. It is easily seen close to Addis Ababa on the Sululta Plains (8); Gefersa Reservoir (3), just west of Addis, once a classic site, is no longer reliable for it. It is common around Dinsho (28) and on the Sanetti Plateau (29) in the Bale Mountains. It remains a phylogenetic oddity, seemingly most closely related to the equally bizarre Hartlaub's Duck *Pteronetta hartlaubii* of West and Central Africa's forests, and these two are in turn related to the *Aythya* diving ducks such as scaups. It is internationally red-listed as Vulnerable, principally owing to habitat destruction, although in recent years it has also become threatened by hunting.

Blue-winged Goose (Hadoram Shirihai)

Harwood's Francolin

Endemic to Ethiopia. The known world range of Harwood's Francolin is the Blue Nile valley and its tributaries that deeply incise the northern highlands of Ethiopia. The Jemma Valley (10) is the traditional – and still much the most accessible – place to see it, and provided an early start is made it can be found here with confidence. In the early mornings, coveys move into the open to feed and males crow from exposed positions – typically large boulders on rocky, scrubby hillsides – and are reasonably easily located; at other times of the day, with luck, it might be flushed. The upper reaches of the Jemma escarpment, just below its lip, are perhaps best, although it also exists in cultivated fields, scrub and even *Typha* reedbeds all the way down the river at the valley bottom. It is considered Vulnerable owing to the pressure of human population in the highlands, which both diminishes its habitat and intensifies hunting: it is locally prized as a delicacy, and is also believed to have medicinal properties.

Chestnut-naped Francolin

Endemic to the Horn of Africa. This species effectively replaces Erckel's Francolin in the highlands south of Addis Ababa, but is on the whole more confiding and easier to see. It occurs not only on wooded slopes but also in subalpine scrub above the treeline. It is particularly abundant in the Bale Mountains, and coveys are sure to be seen with little effort at the roadside in the Dinsho (28) and Goba (29) areas.

Erckel's Francolin

Near-endemic to the Horn of Africa, also occurring in a small part of southern Sudan. This handsome francolin lives on vegetated hillsides at medium altitudes (up to 3,000 m) in the highlands north of Addis Ababa. It is typically first heard crowing, or glimpsed gliding across a woodland clearing. Early mornings are the best time to search for it, when males call from exposed places, but it is worth keeping an eye out for it at the roadside anywhere in the northern highlands. Some of the best places to search for it are the slopes beneath the Ethio-German Hotel at Debre Libanos (9), the upper reaches of the Jemma Valley escarpment (10, where it occurs alongside Harwood's Francolin), and the steeply winding road down the wooded escarpment below Ankober (12). This species has, improbably, been introduced to Hawaii, where it is more readily seen than in Ethiopia.

White-winged Flufftail

Endemic to Ethiopia and South Africa (and probably Zimbabwe), so far as is known. Three tiny ephemeral marshes around the Sululta Plains (8), in Ethiopia's highlands just north of Addis Ababa, are the only known breeding sites in the world for this miniature, Endangered and supremely enigmatic rail, which in flight more closely resembles a large locust than a bird. Where Ethiopia's breeding population might take refuge during the dry season remains unknown: it has been speculated that they migrate to known sites in South Africa, although various lines of evidence suggest this is unlikely. It is critically sensitive to disturbance and no attempt should be made to visit the marshes where it is known to breed, which are closely protected and far from the main road north across the Sululta Plains. On the other hand, any records from new sites would be of tremendous

Chestnut-naped Francolin (Dick Forsman)

Erckel's Francolin (Hadoram Shirihai)

Rouget's Rail (Hadoram Shirihai)

Heuglin's Bustard (Hadoram Shirihai)

Little Brown Bustard (Callan Cohen & Michael Mills)

Rouget's Rail

Endemic to Ethiopia and Eritrea. This is a wonderfully characterful and unusually confiding rallid, strutting alertly along
marsh fringes and road verges with tail constantly flicking to
the vertical. Although it still occurs in central Addis Ababa, its
few remaining pockets of marshy habitat within the city are
rapidly being lost to drainage and construction. It is also now
scarce at nearby wet grassland sites such as Gefersa Reservoir (3) and the Sululta Plains (8). Happily, it remains common
in the northern highlands and (particularly) the Bale Mountains (28–29), where it is easily seen in tussocky marshland,
meadows and wet scrub at all but the highest altitudes. It
occasionally perches on an exposed vantage point (especially in the mornings and evenings) to vent a series of loud
cackles. It is listed as Near-Threatened owing to the vulnera-
bility of its highland habitat to agricultural conversion, overgrazing and grass harvesting for building, and hints that it
may have declined in the last couple of decades.

Heuglin's Bustard

Not endemic to the Horn of Africa, but difficult to see elsewhere. We include this beautiful and wary bustard here on
the grounds that it is highly peripheral in Kenya, and largely
inaccessible in Somalia. It is by no means an easy target
even in Ethiopia; its range is spread along the country's
eastern and southern borders, and no site can be absolutely
depended upon to yield a sighting. Several birders have
sought it, with some success, in the far-flung south-western
Fejij area (45). Not much less of a logistical pain to visit is
the Dolo Odo area (37) in the equally far-flung south-east;
both sites require permission from local authorities and
potentially an armed escort. It is thought to be nomadic and
there have been old records in more accessible places such
as the edge of the Liben Plain (35) and north of Awash (17),
so it is worth keeping an eye out anywhere on Ethiopia's
arid fringes. It favours lightly wooded arid country, and is
undoubtedly shy; morning and evenings are best, since it is
likely to be standing quietly in the shade during the day.

Little Brown Bustard

Endemic to the Horn of Africa. Until the 1970s this species
was thought to be endemic to Somalia, but has since been
found to be relatively widespread in the vast and unfortunately now almost wholly inaccessible Ogaden region. It is
one of the many related species groups straddling north-
east and south-west Africa, since it is related to the Karoo
Bustard Eupodotis vigorsii of South Africa. These are prob-
able relics of an hypothesised ancient arid corridor between

he two regions. The only real chance of encountering it in thiopia is east of Sof Omar in the Imi region (32) and north of Dolo Odo (37); both of these areas are precarious and visiting hem involves extensive consultation with local authorities o maximise safety. We cannot in good conscience advise going there at all. The Little Brown Bustard favours arid rocky plains, with or without vegetation, and especially prefers reas where soft sandy soil and gravel are interspersed; ingles or pairs have been seen from the road.

rabian Bustard

lot endemic to the Horn of Africa, but difficult to see elsewhere within its large range. There is a good chance of seeing his elegant bustard in the Awash region, typically alone or n pairs, although it may demand a bit of searching. Excellent areas to scan for it are on the road from Melka Ghebdu outh to the Awash National Park (14), and the Bilen Lodge rea (17) to the north-east of the park. Keep an eye out for anywhere along the Djibouti road from Awash to Bilen. rabian and Kori Bustards can occur almost side-by-side, lthough on average Arabian prefers more arid country.

Arabian Bustard (Jacques Erard)

pot-breasted Plover

ndemic to Ethiopia. This is a curiously broad-shouldered nd chunky plover, rather apt-looking for its inhospitable lpine habitat of highland marshes and wet grassland. It ccurs from about 2,400 m to over 4,000 m on the Sanetti lateau. It can be seen a short way from Addis Ababa at the ululta Plains (8), or in the Muka Turi area shortly beyond, but erhaps most reliably around Dinsho (28) and the Sanetti lateau (29) in the Bale Mountains. Pairs, small parties or ccasionally large flocks (in the non-breeding season) are host easily found simply by scanning marshy habitat at high ltitude. Although relatively tame and confiding, they can lso be detected by their high-pitched and often maddenngly persistent alarm calls.

Spot-breasted Plover (Hadoram Shirihai)

White-collared Pigeon

ndemic to Ethiopia and Eritrea. This is a common but remendously attractive bird of the highlands, and might e one of the first species seen on arrival in Addis Ababa. especially favours cliffs and other rocky areas (and their ubstitutes: towns, bridges, monasteries and road cuttings) or roosting and breeding, but commonly feeds some istance away in fields and pastures, sometimes in large ocks mixed with Speckled Pigeons. It has a curious manner f flight, with erratically flapping wing-beats interspersed

White-collared Pigeon (Hadoram Shirihai)

African White-winged Dove (Hadoram Shirihai)

African White-winged Dove

Endemic to the Horn of Africa and (marginally) northern Kenya. This species is confined to the great south-eastern Ethiopian drainages of the Wabe Shebelle and Genale (and its tributary the Dawa) Rivers, which run from the Ethiopian mountains down to the coast of Somalia. In Ethiopia it is confined to the far south, and can be locally quite common in riparian acacia, palms and other tall trees, and occasionally up to a kilometre or two away from water. The most accessible site to see it is Melka Ghuba and environs along the Dawa River (38), including within the nearby village of Hudat. It is also easily seen along the lower reaches of the Genale drainage, for example along small acacia-lined tributaries of the Genale in the vicinity of Bogol Manyo (37), and even within Bogol Manyo village itself. Closer to the Somali border, it is common at Dolo Bay (37). It often perches conspicuously, and if not can be located by its distinctively rapid cooing. It is considered Near-Threatened, as its riparian habitat is highly sought-after for fuelwood collection.

Yellow-fronted Parrot (Hadoram Shirihai)

Yellow-fronted Parrot

Endemic to Ethiopia. This is not a rare bird, but can be awkward to find with certainty during a short visit. It occurs in a range of wooded habitats, from denser stands within acacia bush at medium altitudes to montane forest with juniper and *Hagenia* trees at over 3,000 m. It is often easiest to see in the early mornings and late afternoons, when birds move to and from roosts, giving typically parrot-like loud, metallic calls as they fly swiftly over the tree canopy, and often resting on exposed branches. Wondo Genet (26) is a reliable place to find it: look around hotel grounds and adjacent hills especially in the early mornings and evenings. Two other excellent but slightly less rapidly accessible sites are Bishangari Lodge (24) on the southern shore of Lake Langano and the Zege Peninsula of Lake Tana (48). It can however be encountered in any evergreen forest, especially in the highlands, and is not thought to be threatened.

Black-winged Lovebird (Hadoram Shirihai)

Black-winged Lovebird

Endemic to Ethiopia and Eritrea. This is a common and loud parrot of medium altitudes up to about 2,600 m, occurring unfussily in a range of habitats including mixed bush, forest edge, and towns. It particularly favours the large trees of hotel gardens, such as those in Addis Ababa (1), Langano (23–24) and Awassa (27), where groups may sometimes gather when trees are in fruit.

White-cheeked Turaco

Nearly endemic to Ethiopia and Eritrea, marginally occurring in eastern Sudan. This is the common turaco of Ethiopia's escarpment and montane forests and denser juniper woods, and is easily seen at many sites including the outskirts of Addis Ababa (at the Entoto Natural Park, 2), Menagesha Forest (4), Debre Libanos (9), Bishangari Lodge (24), the Bale Mountains (28–30, subspecies *donaldsoni*, see below) and even Yabello (40). Confusion with the next species is possible in the Wadera–Kebre Mengist region (34) and Arero Forest (39), where they co-occur and where hybrids are worryingly widespread. The two species share a purring alarm call and both bound through the canopy showing red wings, so care needs to be taken to separate them. The eastern *donald-soni* subspecies of White-cheeked Turaco, sometimes called Donaldson Smith's Turaco, has a partially red rather than blue nape patch, but so far as is known is otherwise identical to the nominate subspecies. The two are thought to occur alongside one another in the Bale Mountains (28–30), which certainly raises questions about their taxonomic status.

White-cheeked Turaco (Hadoram Shirihai)

Prince Ruspoli's Turaco

Endemic to Ethiopia. When Prince Ruspoli was trampled to death by an elephant in south-western Ethiopia in 1893, his collecting bag – happily intact – contained the type specimen of this turaco. The skin was presumed to origi-nate from Arero Forest (39), but it is now clear that the bird occurs patchily over a wider area of southern Ethiopia, and is not confined to forest. Despite its tolerance of tall acacias and secondary growth, it is very patchily distributed and it remains heavily threatened by wood extraction and agricul-ture. There is little confidence that its distributional limits have been properly defined, and any records outside its established range (between Arero and the Genale River) are of great interest and should be reported to EWNHS and BirdLife International. The three sites where it may perhaps most reliably be searched for are Negele (35), Arero (39) and the Genale River (33), but it is worth keeping an eye out for it at the roadside in any denser vegetation throughout the wooded highland foothills (especially perched on exposed branches early in the morning), particularly along the road from Negele to Kebre Mengist (see Wadera, 34).

Prince Ruspoli's Turaco (Hadoram Shirihai)

Abyssinian Owl

Not endemic to the Horn of Africa, but perhaps least diffi-cult to see in Ethiopia. This montane owl is poorly known, but seems to favour highland woods, particularly juniper, although it readily haunts alien trees such as eucalyptus and *Casuarina*. For many years, a pair could reliably be seen in an

Abyssinian Owl (Tasso Leventis)

Nechisar Nightjar (Roger Stafford)

Banded Barbet (Hadoram Shirihai)

Abyssinian Woodpecker (Andy Swash)

isolated grove of eucalyptus trees near Kofele, on the road to the Bale Mountains, but sadly they are no longer present. With luck, its drawn-out, disyllabic hoot might be heard at night at Dinsho (28) or Goba (29) in the Bale Mountains, Debre Libranos (9), Ankober Palace Lodge (12), or in the Simien Mountains (49). Much the most likely way of seeing it is to ask the lodge staff at these places if they happen to know of a current day roost; in particular, ask for Abdela Husa at Dinsho.

Nechisar Nightjar

Endemic to Ethiopia (presumably). To date, this species is known with certainty only from the type specimen, a single and distinctive wing rescued from a decomposing roadkill in 1990. Many attempts have been made to rediscover this species around the type locality on the Nechisar Plains (43), and in 2009 there was a tantalising report of a sighting, which has not yet been documented in any journal. In the absence of further evidence the Nechisar Nightjar still remains veiled in mystery, almost two decades after its discovery. Ideally, any suspect nightjar should be captured, and its wing pattern carefully examined: Nechisar Nightjar has its white wing-patch exceptionally far up the wing, near the carpal joint. At the time of writing the agonisingly poor road from Shashemene to Arba Minch was being rebuilt, which will hopefully simplify future searches and a long overdue rediscovery.

Banded Barbet

Endemic to Ethiopia and Eritrea. This is a widespread and fairly common species, occurring in big trees at a wide range of altitudes, from the Rift Valley to the highlands. Look in big fig trees, for example in lodge or hotel gardens. Reliable sites are the monastery at Debre Libanos (9), and the grounds of the Bekele Molla Hotel (23) or Bishangari Lodge (24) at Lake Langano. White-headed individuals of the subspecies *leucogenys* are particularly often seen at Wondo Genet (26).

Abyssinian Woodpecker

Endemic to Ethiopia and Eritrea. This beautiful endemic woodpecker can be tricky to find, owing to being small, often silent and commonly choosing to forage low in the vegetation (even sometimes on flowerheads of red-hot pokers *Kniphofia*). It especially favours open forest, parkland and forest edge. The best site for it close to Addis Ababa is the Meta Brewery (5), although it is also possible (more rarely) in Entoto Natural Park (2). Wondo Genet (26) is very good, and so are the open juniper woods above Goba (29). Perhaps the most dependable place of all is on the margins of the Harenna Forest (30) on the southern slopes of the Bale Mountains, especially around Katcha Campsite, or at the forest's upper limit around Rira village.

Gillett's Lark

Endemic to the Horn of Africa. This is a lark of acacia thorn-bush, preferring rocky, broken ground, and appears to be very vocal at most times of year. The most straightforward place to find it is probably the southern portion of Awash National Park (15), where it is not uncommon in open acacia thicket above the rocky north bank of the Awash River. Also but less accessibly at Awash it can also be seen in the Kudu Valley and the slopes of Mount Fantale (16). Its southern population *degodiensis* was until recently considered a full species, **'Degodi Lark'**. This form is common and easily located in the low-lying thornbush country around Bogol Manyo and Cole (37), while the nominate form occurs at slightly higher altitudes along the same road, closer to Filtu (36).

Gillett's Lark (Hadoram Shirihai)

Liben (or Sidamo) Lark

Endemic to Ethiopia. The Liben Lark is a perilously threat-ened bird, and in the absence of urgent conservation action is likely to become mainland Africa's first modern bird extinction. It is confined to the arid grassland of the Liben Plain near Negele (35), and recent surveys indicate that fewer – probably far fewer – than 250 individuals are likely to hold out within its tiny range, which continues to be rapidly squeezed by habitat loss through crop planting, scrub encroachment and, of most immediate concern, overgrazing. By 2009, it was confined to fewer than 3,000 hectares of heavily degraded habitat. It is a member of a uniformly threatened genus of highland grassland larks that includes the Critically Endangered Archer's Lark *H. archeri* of Somaliland, not seen with certainty since its discovery in 1922. At the time of writing, Liben Lark was still relatively easy to find for a species so near to extinction: early in the morning, males make short vertical songflights, giving a skylark-like song that is audible at several hundred metres.

Liben Lark (Hadoram Shirihai)

Erlanger's Lark

Endemic to Ethiopia. This is an Ethiopian highland outpost of the taxonomic morass that is Red-capped Lark *Calandrella cinerea*. It is sometimes regarded as conspecific with 'Blan-ford's' Lark of northern Ethiopia, Eritrea and Arabia, or indeed with all of sub-Saharan Africa's 'Red-capped' Larks. It is a bird of high-altitude short grasslands and fallow croplands, where it can be very common. Within and close to Addis, it occurs on the dry margins of the Imperial Hotel marsh (1), and at the roadside on the Sululta Plain (8). It is common en route to the Jemma Valley (10, whether approaching from Muka Turi or Debre Birhan), en route to the Gibe Gorge (7) via Sebeta, or on the northern approach to the Bale Mountains (28).

Erlanger's Lark (Hadoram Shirihai)

Somali Short-toed Lark (Hadoram Shirihai)

Somali Short-toed Lark

Endemic to the Horn of Africa and northern Kenya. Ethiopia is perhaps the easiest place to see this bird, localised in Kenya and out of reach in Somalia. It occurs patchily and often in small parties in the far south on arid, short-grass plains. It is particularly abundant on the Liben Plain (35), where it will distract you from pursuing Liben Larks by flushing at your feet with a short nasal flight call, or wittering on repetitively overhead on protracted song-flights quite unlike the Liben's. A slightly more accessible but perhaps less absolutely dependable site is the road to Soda (41), south of Yabello. When flushed from the ground at close quarters it usually only flies a short distance and is readily relocated.

White-tailed Swallow (Hadoram Shirihai)

White-tailed Swallow

Endemic to Ethiopia. The range of this species overlaps almost perfectly with that of the Ethiopian Bush-crow in the Yabello–Moyale–Arero triangle (40–41); this coincidence is not at all understood, since the birds have quite different ecologies. White-tailed Swallows have an extremely agile bat-like flight, and are typically seen speeding gracefully over open savanna and scrubland, and occasionally perching on low bushes. They especially favour places with sparser vegetation cover, such as open valleys, but sometimes occur over woodland. Con Benson, who first described the species in the 1940s, suspected that they bred in hollows in termite mounds, and this has recently been confirmed; they have also recently been found to nest against the interior beams of Borana houses, as does the sympatric Ethiopian Swallow. Any breeding records are of interest and should be submitted to EWNHS and BirdLife International. The perched bird is presumably immature.

Abyssinian Longclaw

Endemic to Ethiopia. This is a bird of highland grassland, especially favouring short moist grass at marsh edges, as well as tussocky moorlands at high altitude. It forages on the ground, occasionally perching on vantage points such as rocks, low bushes or clods of earth. Although far from abundant, it is readily seen at a number of sites: it occurs in relict pockets of grassland even within central Addis Ababa, as well as the nearby Gefersa Reservoir (3), Sululta Plains (8) and the roads to the Jemma Valley (10, approaching from either the east or the west). The Gaysay Valley at Dinsho (28) is also particularly good. Abyssinian Longclaw is considered Near-Threatened owing to the ongoing degradation of its highland grassland habitat by cultivation and grazing.

Somali Wheatear

Endemic to the Horn of Africa. This is really a Somali endemic, marginal in Ethiopia, but we include it owing to it being out of reach over the border. Although it might be widespread in the inaccessible Ogaden of far eastern Ethiopia, nearly all recent Ethiopian records are from near Cole in the Bogol Manyo region (37), where it has bred; rarely, it has been seen closer to Bogol Manyo itself. It perches on low bushes and small trees, often associated with rocky hills, and is typically quite tame and approachable.

Abyssinian Black Wheatear

Endemic to the Horn of Africa. This is a bird of vegetated rocky areas (often escarpments) and unusually occurs both in the highlands and the Rift Valley, and has variable plumage morphs. Taxonomically, it has a slightly chequered history, having at various points been considered conspecific with Mourning Wheatear *Oenanthe lugens* of North Africa and the Middle East, and Schalow's Wheatear *O. chalowi* of East Africa. It is readily seen perched confidingly on rocks, often at the roadside, for example in the Jemma Valley (10) or on the escarpment below Ankober (12). It is common throughout much of the northern tourist circuit of historical sites. In the Rift Valley, it is especially easily seen on the low cliffs above the Bekele Molla Hotel (23) on the western shore of Lake Langano.

Sombre Rock Chat

Endemic to the Horn of Africa. This is an enigmatic bird, and remains very poorly known over a century after its discovery. Better understanding may have been hampered by confusion over its identification: it can be surprisingly difficult to separate from Brown-tailed Rock Chat and even Blackstart, and a good look at its undertail-coverts is crucial. It is also slightly larger than these species and has a somewhat leggier jizz. It favours very arid, rocky hillsides, and is particularly partial to lava flows. The first specimen was collected on Mount Fantale (16; a dormant volcano) at Awash, and the mountain and its adjacent lava flows remain the most reliable places to see it. Although the road up to the crater rim is bad, Sombre Rock Chat also occurs at the bottom of the mountain, in the lava flow that has created Lake Beseka (16). Here it can be seen metres from a tar road. It is considered a 'Data Deficient' potentially threatened species, and any records away from Fantale/Beseka are of great interest; please report any such records to EWNHS and BirdLife

Somali Wheatear (Hadoram Shirihai)

Abyssinian Black Wheatear (Hadoram Shirihai

White-winged Cliff Chat (Hadoram Shirihai)

Rüppell's Black Chat (Hadoram Shirihai)

White-winged Cliff Chat

Endemic to Ethiopia and Eritrea. This is a bird of rocky areas at medium altitudes (1,500–2,500 m), and especially favours road cuttings and streamsides, as well as around bridges and even buildings. It is perhaps commonest in the northern highlands, but also extends to the far south. Debre Libanos (9) and the Jemma Valley (10) are both excellent sites to search for it, but it can be seen at the roadside even on the outskirts of Addis Ababa, especially along the Jimma road (i.e. en route to Menagesha, 4, and the Gibe Gorge, 7). This species and the much more widely-distributed Mocking Cliff Chat commonly occur in the same habitat, within a stone's throw of one another.

Rüppell's Black Chat

Endemic to Ethiopia and Eritrea. Like White-billed Starling, this species is confined to rocky areas of the highlands north of Addis Ababa, always in the vicinity of cliffs, gorges or rocky road cuttings, and often near water. It is a poorly known but very characterful bird, strutting upright among the rocks and cocking its tail, and showing its striking white wing-patches as it glides from rock to rock. It is not especially common, but can reliably be found at the top of the Jemma Valley escarpment (10; keep an eye at the roadside) and along the cliff-tops of the Portuguese Bridge area a Debre Libanos (9), and at the Muger Gorge (6).

Philippa's Crombec

Endemic to the Horn of Africa. This species was described as recently as the 1950s and remains very poorly known since most of its range is inaccessible in Somalia. It appears to favour dense scrub or thicket (especially *Commiphora*) at low altitudes (300–900 m). In Ethiopia it is known to occur in the Bogol Manyo–Cole–Melka Suftu area (37), where it may still need some effort to locate. There are also reports from Melka Ghuba (38, and from there to Wachile) and *Commiphora* scrub between Dubuluk and Yabello (40), but more information is needed. Especially given that it is considered a 'Data Deficient' potentially threatened species, it would be interesting to establish whether it is more widespread in this area than is currently known. Single birds, pairs or parties are typically seen moving rapidly through scrub and a good look is needed to separate it with confidence from the two eremomelas with yellow underparts, since these too can at first glance appear to show a dusky face mask.

Abyssinian Slaty Flycatcher

Endemic to Ethiopia and Eritrea. This confiding and star- lingly pale-eyed flycatcher quietly sallies from the forest canopy and mid-strata, and is easily seen along forest edges and in dense woods at most of the highland forest sites in this book. It even occurs in stands of alien plantation, and larger gardens in Addis (such as that of the Ghion Hotel, 1).

Abyssinian Catbird

Endemic to Ethiopia. This species's alternative name, Juniper Babbler, describes it perfectly. It belongs to one of Ethio- pia's four endemic genera (the others being *Zavattariornis*, Ethiopian Bush-crow, *Cyanochen*, Blue-winged Goose, and *Rougetius*, Rouget's Rail) and does indeed seem to be a babbler; certainly, it has no common ground with the North American catbird other than its general colour-scheme. It is a forest species particularly favouring open juniper and *Hagenia* woods, and is easily located by its explosive, fluting call, often given as a duet. It often calls from a concealed position, but will readily emerge into the open and provide good views. It is especially abundant at Dinsho (28), Goba (29) and the Harenna Forest (30) in the Bale Mountains, and closer to Addis is best seen at Menagesha Forest (4). It also occurs on the outskirts of Addis proper, in the Entoto Hills (2) and the grounds of the British Embassy (1), but is harder to locate here.

Abyssinian Slaty Flycatcher (Hadoram Shirihai)

White-backed Black Tit

Endemic to Ethiopia and Eritrea. This species is widespread in montane woodland and bush, especially *Hagenia* and juniper woods, although it occurs right up to giant heath forest at 3,400 m. It also ventures into wooded gardens in Addis Ababa, such as those of the Ghion Hotel (1). Pairs or parties move through open woods, giving harsh, typically tit-like calls. However, it is not necessarily easy to find; good places to focus on searching it for it are Debre Libanos (9), and in the Bale Mountains, the juniper woods at Dinsho (28) and Goba (29), and the more stunted upper margins of Harenna Forest (30).

Abyssinian Catbird (Hadoram Shirihai)

White-backed Black Tit (Hadoram Shirihai)

Abyssinian Oriole (Hadoram Shirihai)

Ethiopian Bush-crow (Hadoram Shirihai)

Thick-billed Raven (Hadoram Shirihai)

Abyssinian Oriole

Endemic to Ethiopia and Eritrea. This is a widespread montane forest endemic that is typically common and easily located in the canopy by means of its typically oriole-like, liquid songs and mewing alarm calls. Field (and even museum) identification can be problematic, and habitat is the most pragmatic feature to separate it with certainty from Black-headed Oriole, which is unknown from montane forests. It can be seen within Addis Ababa's outskirts at the Entoto Natural Park (2), and is also common and readily seen at Menagesha Forest (4), Debre Libanos (9), Wondo Genet (26) and the Harenna Forest (30).

Ethiopian (or Stresemann's) Bush-crow

Endemic to Ethiopia. Ethiopia's star endemic is also an evolutionary and ecological enigma: its closest relatives are the ground-jays *Podoces* of Central Asia, and the west and central African Piapiac *Ptilostomus*, which appears to be a scarce visitor to south-west Ethiopia. Like the White-tailed Swallow it is bafflingly confined to a small scrap of arid savanna within the triangle formed by Yabello (40), Arero (39) and Moyale, but happily is patchily common in this area, and very easily seen. The first sign of its presence is often its nest, sitting on the flat top of an acacia: a large spiny mass of sticks with an upward-facing entrance tunnel. Bush-crows are highly social, confiding, wonderfully characterful, and especially common and tame in the vicinity of villages and livestock enclosures, where they turn over pieces of dry dung in search of food, and even perch on cattle. Flocks are noisy and mobile, frequently giving metallic, jackdaw-like calls. While they are still relatively numerous, there is much concern that they are currently declining owing to the whittling away of their habitat of mature acacia savanna by commercial cultivation, charcoal production, and bush encroachment probably caused by overgrazing and fire suppression.

Thick-billed Raven

Endemic to Ethiopia and Eritrea. This extraordinary endemic is widespread and occurs in a wide range of habitats, from forests to cities to alpine moorlands. It is especially common around towns, where it feeds on rodents, carrion and scraps, and may become somewhat menacingly tame. It is especially common in larger Rift Valley towns such as Shashemene (26), Awassa (27) and Dilla, and is likely to wake you with its gurglingly cacophonous dawn (or even pre-dawn) chorus at Wondo Genet (26). In mountainous areas it reputedly kleptoparasitises bone-dropping Lammergeiers.

White-billed Starling

Endemic to Ethiopia and Eritrea. This is one of the handful of Ethiopian endemics to be confined to the highlands only north of Addis Ababa. Here it is fairly common and easy to find in any rocky habitat at altitudes of 2,400 m and above, especially in the vicinity of cliff-faces; it even reaches alpine moorland at over 4,000 m in the Simien Mountains (49). Closest to Addis Ababa, it is readily seen at Debre Libanos (9) or the Muger Gorge (6), and is also common throughout the northern tourist circuit of historical sites (50). It may wander to lower altitudes outside of the breeding season, when flocks may gather to feed on fruiting trees.

White-billed Starling (Hadoram Shirihai)

Somali Starling

Endemic to the Horn of Africa. The Somali Starling's status in Ethiopia remains poorly understood. Its stronghold in Ethiopia and Eritrea is in the Eritrean highlands, and it is well-established as occuring regularly in the Simien Mountains (49) and patchily along the Rift Valley's north-eastern escarpments (e.g. there are recent reports from Melka Ghebdu, 13). Its status in the southern highlands is less clear: records from the Bale Mountains (at Dinsho, 28, and the Sanetti Plateau, 29) have been variously questioned, but certainly it is well worth checking any suspicious-looking Slender-billed Starlings for Somali's characteristic diamond-shaped tail with its widest point relatively near to the base, and the unmarked ash-grey head and bespectacled eyes of females.

Somali Starling (János Oláh)

Juba Weaver

Endemic to the Horn of Africa and northern Kenya. Like African White-winged Dove, Juba Weaver is endemic to riverine bush along the major drainage lines leading from Ethiopia down into Somalia: the Dawa, Genale and Wabe Shebelle Rivers. It reguarly breeds at relatively accessible Melka Ghuba (38), but is not wholly reliable there, and for the best chance of seeing it you may have to venture down the rattling road to Bogol Manyo (37). Here it may be found along nearby drainage lines leading down to the Genale River (which itself is inaccessible at this point). Best of all, look for it at Dolo Bay (37) on the Genale proper; unfortunately, this area requires permission and a yet longer drive. It needs care to identify when out of breeding plumage, but no other regularly occurring species shared its bicoloured bill (pictured at right). A photo of a male in breeding plumage is shown on page 113.

Red-billed Pytilia (Mike Haley)

Red-billed Pytilia

Near-endemic to Ethiopia, also occurring marginally in southern Sudan. This is a widespread but unobtrusive and curiously awkward-to-find species of bushy lowland country, especially denser thicket in dry, broken country, and in the west in broadleaved *Combretum-Terminalia* woodland. It often perches unobtrusively in dense vegetation, but is perhaps more often seen along rivercourses and especially near pools where it alights to drink. Good places to stay alert for it are Lake Tana (48), the Jemma Valley (10, especially along the Lomi stream), the Gibe Gorge (7) and Melka Ghebdu (13), but it is quite possible to visit all these places and not encounter it. As far as we know, the photograph reproduced here is the only one in existence of this species. Its sister species, the Red-winged Pytilia, is by contrast relatively widespread across western Africa. It has a similar song and was formerly considered conspecific; however, experiments in captivity have shown that its dark bill prevents the two interbreeding, even though their natural ranges never overlap.

Northern Grosbeak-canary (Hadoram Shirihai)

Northern Grosbeak-canary

Endemic to the Horn of Africa and northern Kenya (where it is scarce and localised). This is a species of Ethiopia's arid southern lowlands, where it favours open *Commiphora*-dominated thornbush above all else (see Habitats). It is thin on the ground but ought to be encountered during a few days' thorough birding in the south, especially along the Yabello–Mega (40) and Negele–Filtu (36) roads. It also occurs more remotely in the far north-east, east of Hara (19), and in the far south-west, such as in the Fejij area (45). Both sexes are easily identified by their giant pinkish bills and often join *Commiphora* bird parties. The male's song, given from the top of a tree, can be striking: a fluty series of about ten repeated notes, dropping an octave half-way through.

Black-headed Siskin

Endemic to Ethiopia. The only strikingly coloured endemic seedeater in Ethiopia is all the more beautiful for being one of the few passerine species to endure the freezing, wind-blasted alpine moorlands of the country's high plateaus (such as the Sanetti, 29). Parties and large mobile flocks (sometimes of over a hundred birds) typically feed on or near the ground, and males sing from whatever vantage points are available. This species occurs widely and commonly in any highland grassland, typically above about 2,400 m, and can readily be

White-throated Seedeater

Endemic to Ethiopia and Eritrea. This understated endemic is inconspicuous but not uncommon in large parts of northern Ethiopia, including the northern tourist circuit of historical sites. The most accessible places to see it from Addis Ababa are the Jemma Valley (10) and Gibe Gorge (7), and it is also reliably found at several sites around Lake Tana (48). It occurs in any bushy country, and is even found on the edges of cultivation and around human habitation. Its typical seedeater-like song and calls usually draw attention to it, but a good view of its unstreaked underparts and face are needed to separate it with confidence from the more widespread Reichenow's Seedeater.

White-throated Seedeater (Hadoram Shirihai)

Salvadori's Seedeater

Endemic to Ethiopia. This is one of Ethiopia's marginally more distinctive endemic seedeaters, with a diagnostic although variably conspicuous black throat-bar. It is most reliably to be encountered at Sof Omar (31), in the dry lowlands east of the Bale Mountains, but it is not crucial to make this long and bumpy trek just for this species: it is more widespread in the arid south, and can also be found without too much difficulty in the Negele–Filtu region (35–36), particularly nearer to Filtu. It occurs in *Acacia–Commiphora* bushland – within a rock gorge at Sof Omar – and has even been recorded in gardens within the town of Negele. It often joins bird parties, and sings loudly from conspicuous perches atop acacia trees; it is also worth keeping an eye out for foraging parties flushed from the roadside. It is currently considered as Vulnerable, but more information is needed to assess just how large its range is, and how it might be affected by the land-use changes that are

Salvadori's Seedeater (Hadoram Shirihai)

Brown-rumped Seedeater (Hadoram Shirihai)

Brown-rumped Seedeater

Endemic to the Horn of Africa. Finding this handsome and understated species will not pose any problems: it is abundant in the highlands in any open country with bushes o trees, and along forest edges. It even occurs commonly ir gardens and road verges within Addis Ababa, and is readily identifiable as Ethiopia's only unstreaked seedeater, with a striking white chin and eyebrow stripe.

Ankober Serin

Endemic to Ethiopia. This high-mountain endemic occurs only at altitudes of over 2,600 m, and was described to science as recently as 1976. The type locality of Ankober (12) itself remains an excellent place to look for it, and it car even be seen in a day trip from Addis Ababa at Gemessa Gedel (11). It is also now known in the Simien Mountain (49), where it can survive at altitudes of well over 4,000 m Recent surveys suggest that it may be considerably more widespread in the remote and largely inaccessible northern highlands. It is a bird of steep and wind-blasted rocky slopes and cliff-faces with little cover other than grass tussocks and lichens. It usually occurs in small parties, which need to be scanned for with care as they shelter alongside crevices and tussocks, or dangle precariously while feeding on cliff-faces They also feed in ploughed fields and closely grazed pasture near cliffs (sometimes in association with other seedeaters such as Brown-rumped and Streaky), and flocks can be seen flying between the two habitats. It is considered as Vulnerable owing to the relentless human pressure on Ethiopia's highlands, whether through grazing, cultivatio plantatio

Ankober Serin (11)

APPENDICES

Appendix A: List of GPS coordinates
(available electronically from CS – see p.20)

GPS001	Addis Ababa: Ghion Hotel	09° 00'49.22"N	38° 45'36.88"E
GPS002	Addis Ababa: Imperial Hotel marsh	08° 59'49.11"N	38° 47'46.63"E
GPS003	Addis Ababa: Entoto turn-off	09° 05'04.31"N	38° 43'22.58"E
GPS004	Entoto church and view	09° 05'22.24"N	38° 45'49.05"E
GPS005	Gefersa Reservoir view	09° 04'18.66"N	38° 37'20.37"E
GPS006	Menagesha Forest Office	08° 57'49.84"N	38° 32'34.11"E
GPS007	Meta Brewery	08° 54'41.40"N	38° 35'42.87"E
GPS008	Derba turn-off at Chancho	09° 18'07.88"N	38° 45'06.75"E
GPS009	Derba cement factory turn-off	09° 26'13.27"N	38° 38'52.53"E
GPS010	Gibe Gorge bridge	08° 13'46.76"N	37° 34'41.16"E
GPS011	Duber River	09° 12'02.00"N	38° 45'35.00"E
GPS012	Debre Libanos fig tree	09° 43'15.60"N	38° 50'08.27"E
GPS013	Stream crossing on Lemi road	09° 38'36.35"N	38° 59'01.25"E
GPS014	Stream crossing 1 near Mendida	09° 37'20.03"N	39° 21'28.12"E
GPS015	Stream crossing 2 near Mendida	09° 38'43.48"N	39° 26'00.85"E
GPS016	Lemi T-junction	09° 47'20.54"N	38° 59'32.78"E
GPS017	Jemma Valley: church	09° 49'54.16"N	38° 53'09.96"E
GPS018	Jemma Valley: cliffs	09° 50'34.94"N	38° 54'20.81"E
GPS019	Jemma Valley: bridge	09° 54'39.74"N	38° 55'29.24"E
GPS020	Jemma Valley: Lomi River	09° 57'16.74"N	38° 53'54.89"E
GPS021	Jemma Valley: Awar Wuha	09° 58'32.90"N	38° 53'30.60"E
GPS022	Gemessa Gedel	09° 49'46.00"N	39° 43'52.00"E
GPS023	Ankober plantation	09° 40'58.30"N	39° 43'10.60"E
GPS024	Ankober cliffs, north (2 on map)	09° 40'54.98"N	39° 44'13.56"E
GPS025	Ankober cliffs, south (3 on map)	09° 40'26.47"N	39° 44'47.98"E
GPS026	Ankober Palace Lodge	09° 35'02.87"N	39° 44'27.85"E
GPS027	Aliyu Amba	09° 33'52.81"N	39° 47'34.22"E
GPS028	Melka Ghebdu	09° 34'04.80"N	39° 49'45.05"E
GPS029	Dulesa	09° 32'52.22"N	39° 57'11.20"E
GPS030	Confusion point	09° 24'14.17"N	40° 05'30.18"E
GPS031	Riverbed N of Boloyta	09° 13'45.05"N	40° 00'51.01"E
GPS032	Boloyta	09° 12'43.20"N	40° 00'10.22"E
GPS033	Awash NP: waterhole	08° 53'49.81"N	40° 04'36.59"E
GPS034	Awash NP: Gillett's Lark	08° 52'01.81"N	40° 03'48.85"E
GPS035	Awash NP: Kereyou Lodge	08° 52'41.34"N	40° 05'44.77"E
GPS036	Awash NP: Awash Falls	08° 50'34.84"N	40° 00'43.60"E
GPS037	Awash NP: microwave tower	08° 56'11.11"N	40° 04'41.27"E
GPS038	Turn-off north from Metahara	08° 55'04.33"N	39° 50'20.00"E
GPS039	Turn-off to Fantale	09° 01'05.41"N	39° 50'58.56"E
GPS040	Beseka lava flow	08° 54'21.28"N	39° 53'43.98"E
GPS041	Garibaldi	08° 50'00.03"N	39° 42'39.04"E
GPS042	Andido	09° 24'06.91"N	40° 19'47.42"E
GPS043	Bilen Lodge	09° 28'23.84"N	40° 18'36.76"E
GPS044	Awash Arba	09° 07'53.36"N	40° 09'56.70"E

GPS045	Mileage post NE of Andido	09° 24′36.70″N	40° 20′42.40″E
GPS046	Turn-off to Ali Dege	09° 18′56.09″N	40° 15′45.40″E
GPS047	Lake Alemaya	09° 23′59.28″N	41° 59′55.96″E
GPS048	Turn-off to Lake Cheleleka (east)	08° 45′02.39″N	38° 58′04.50″E
GPS049	Turn-off to Lake Cheleleka (west)	08° 45′05.71″N	38° 57′25.98″E
GPS050	Green Lake	08° 41′52.92″N	38° 58′31.33″E
GPS051	Lake Koka wetlands north	08° 24′28.15″N	39° 01′16.38″E
GPS052	Lake Koka wetlands south	08° 22′48.07″N	39° 00′23.11″E
GPS053	Alem Tena plains	08° 12′28.50″N	38° 52′13.30″E
GPS054	Langano Bekele Molla turn-off	07° 31′42.24″N	38° 40′08.94″E
GPS055	Langano Wabe Shabelle turn-off	07° 39′20.15″N	38° 40′31.88″E
GPS056	Bishangari/Wenney turn-off	07° 30′28.62″N	38° 40′37.81″E
GPS057	Bishangari next turn-off	07° 29′05.28″N	38° 45′01.01″E
GPS058	Bishangari container bridge	07° 31′22.76″N	38° 46′15.67″E
GPS059	Abiata–Shalla viewpoint	07° 29′50.16″N	38° 38′16.46″E
GPS060	Wondo Genet stream	07° 04′36.17″N	38° 38′30.94″E
GPS061	St Mary's church N of Awassa	07° 06′03.02″N	38° 29′07.08″E
GPS062	Tikur Wuha bridge	07° 05′29.23″N	38° 28′55.71″E
GPS063	Awassa fish market woodland	07° 02′40.22″N	38° 27′29.68″E
GPS064	Mountain acacias W of Dodola	06° 59′37.95″N	39° 09′21.91″E
GPS065	Mountain acacias E of Dodola	06° 59′37.64″N	39° 14′54.61″E
GPS066	Ashiro stream	07° 02′23.50″N	39° 29′43.37″E
GPS067	Cape Eagle-owl near Dinsho	07° 06′14.90″N	39° 41′23.80″E
GPS068	Pond in Gaysay Valley	07° 07′15.86″N	39° 43′12.57″E
GPS069	Web River crossing in Gaysay Valley	07° 06′33.73″N	39° 45′41.51″E
GPS070	Bale National Park signboard	07° 07′15.74″N	39° 44′07.51″E
GPS071	Turn-off to Bale HQ at Dinsho	07° 06′19.08″N	39° 47′29.00″E
GPS072	*Hagenia* woods above Goba	06° 56′05.14″N	39° 56′53.59″E
GPS073	*Hypericum* terraces above Goba	06° 55′36.05″N	39° 56′24.00″E
GPS074	Sanetti: Wattled Crane valley	06° 51′09.12″N	39° 53′22.49″E
GPS075	Sanetti: turn-off to Garba Guracha	06° 50′54.39″N	39° 53′19.60″E
GPS076	Katcha Camp	06° 42′54.97″N	39° 43′26.87″E
GPS077	Woods above Rira	06° 46′34.82″N	39° 43′54.08″E
GPS078	Katcha signboard	06° 42′45.65″N	39° 43′08.15″E
GPS079	Sof Omar footpath	06° 54′14.65″N	40° 51′08.78″E
GPS080	Imi	06° 27′24.67″N	42° 08′19.20″E
GPS081	Dolo Odo	04° 10′41.88″N	42° 03′24.62″E
GPS082	Genale drift	05° 41′06.00″N	39° 31′50.99″E
GPS083	Wadera forest patch 1	05° 47′35.15″N	39° 16′54.47″E
GPS084	Wadera forest patch 2	05° 53′36.90″N	39° 12′02.58″E
GPS085	Wadera forest patch 3	05° 52′43.49″N	39° 08′53.76″E
GPS086	Liben Lark turn-off	05° 16′27.07″N	39° 40′52.23″E
GPS087	Negele Prince Ruspoli's Turaco	05° 18′26.18″N	39° 38′02.29″E
GPS088	Filtu *Commiphora*	04° 52′21.06″N	40° 51′01.91″E
GPS089	Bur Amino	04° 18′07.13″N	41° 56′02.29″E
GPS090	Bogol Manyo village	04° 31′02.08″N	41° 32′13.58″E
GPS091	Cole village	04° 25′38.27″N	41° 48′46.23″E
GPS092	River 3 km beyond Bogol Manyo	04° 31′26.64″N	41° 33′50.59″E
GPS093	River 32 km beyond Bogol Manyo	04° 28′01.74″N	41° 46′37.20″E

GPS094	'Degodi Lark' type locality	04° 31'44.33"N	41° 37'07.61"E
GPS095	Turn-off to track near Cole	04° 26'12.12"N	41° 47'43.69"E
GPS096	Watercourse S of Cole	04° 22'13.55"N	41° 50'16.08"E
GPS097	Turn-off to Melka Suftu	04° 18'10.93"N	41° 53'54.99"E
GPS098	Open area on Melka Suftu road	04° 16'51.46"N	41° 53'44.23"E
GPS099	Dolo Bay	04° 16'21.61"N	42° 03'49.32"E
GPS100	River crossing 72 km from Negele	04° 55'51.71"N	39° 27'07.63"E
GPS101	Melka Ghuba track	04° 51'52.38"N	39° 19'03.50"E
GPS102	Wachile village	04° 32'39.37"N	39° 03'41.08"E
GPS103	Hudat village	04° 45'38.81"N	39° 14'21.44"E
GPS104	Arero village roundabout	04° 44'29.08"N	38° 49'44.18"E
GPS105	Arero Forest edge	04° 46'18.73"N	38° 49'33.46"E
GPS106	Arero Forest junction	04° 47'27.13"N	38° 49'28.02"E
GPS107	Turn-off to Diida Xuyyurra ranch	04° 57'44.42"N	38° 11'59.32"E
GPS108	Harobake market & woodland	04° 59'33.80"N	38° 12'35.53"E
GPS109	Dubuluk village	04° 21'41.40"N	38° 16'52.26"E
GPS110	Culvert S of Yabello	04° 37'13.80"N	38° 14'27.42"E
GPS111	Commiphora patch S of Yabello	04° 26'15.29"N	38° 16'27.12"E
GPS112	Stone elephant	04° 40'28.50"N	38° 13'58.00"E
GPS113	Junipers NW of Yabello	04° 55'08.94"N	38° 03'13.64"E
GPS114	Turn-off to Soda	04° 09'33.62"N	38° 16'49.55"E
GPS115	Short-cut turn-off to Soda	04° 12'31.43"N	38° 16'51.96"E
GPS116	Junction of short-cut to Soda road	04° 11'30.34"N	38° 20'35.09"E
GPS117	Valley S of Mega	04° 01'02.68"N	38° 22'00.88"E
GPS118	Agere Maryam forest patch	05° 31'00.00"N	38° 15'32.00"E
GPS119	Nechisar Plains crossroads	05° 57'59.15"N	37° 39'15.05"E
GPS120	Gambella airport	08° 07'58.24"N	34° 33'56.02"E
GPS121	Gambella small stream	08° 15'00.20"N	34° 35'20.02"E
GPS122	Bahir Dar: Lake Tana Hotel	11° 36'13.43"N	37° 23'40.44"E
GPS123	Bahir Dar: Kuriftu Resort	11° 36'13.33"N	37° 22'47.30"E
GPS124	Kibran Gebriel Island	11° 39'05.41"N	37° 21'51.63"E
GPS125	Entos Eyesus Island	11° 38'44.16"N	37° 22'05.30"E
GPS126	Bahir Dar: turn-off to jacarandas	11° 36'17.75"N	37° 24'43.01"E
GPS127	Bahir Dar: Blue Nile viewpoint	11° 34'30.94"N	37° 24'47.23"E
GPS128	Bahir Dar: Angodgud River	11° 34'48.97"N	37° 24'51.31"E
GPS129	Woreta	11° 55'27.54"N	37° 41'42.79"E

Appendix B: Mammals mentioned in the text

(taxonomy follows *The Kingdon Field Guide to African Mammals*; see p.18)

Species	Site numbers
Guereza Colobus *Colobus guereza*	4, 24, 26, 30
Sacred Baboon *Papio hamadryas*	14, 16, 19, 31
Olive Baboon *Papio anubis*	10, 15
Gelada *Theropithecus gelada*	6, 9, 10, 11, 12, 49
Grivet Monkey *Cercopithecus (aethiops) aethiops*	15
Bale Monkey *Cercopithecus (aethiops) djamdjamensis*	30
Wahlberg's Epauletted Fruit Bat *Epomophorus wahlbergi*	48
Harenna Shrew *Crocidura harenna*	30
Starck's Hare *Lepus starcki*	12, 29
Unstriped Ground Squirrel *Xerus rutilus*	17, 37
Naked Mole-rat *Heterocephalus glaber*	17, 37
Giant Root-rat *Tachyoryctes macrocephalus*	28, 29
Ethiopian Meadow Rat *Stenocephalemys albocaudata*	29
Ethiopian Wolf *Canis simensis*	12, 28, 29, 49
Bat-eared Fox *Otocyon megalotis*	15
Wild Dog *Lycaon pictus*	30
Spotted Hyaena *Crocuta crocuta*	9, 15, 17, 19, 30,
Aardwolf *Proteles cristatus*	15
African Civet *Civettictis civetta*	30
Wild Cat *Felis sylvestris*	15, 35
Serval Cat *Felis serval*	28, 29, 30
Caracal *Felis caracal*	17, 28, 40
Leopard *Panthera pardus*	4, 14, 15, 29, 30, 40, 43
Lion *Panthera leo*	14, 15, 17, 30, 37, 43
Cheetah *Acinonyx jubatus*	37
Ethiopian Rock Hyrax *Procavia habessinica*	12, 16, 23, 29
Yellow-spotted Hyrax *Heterohyrax brucei*	4, 22
African Elephant *Loxodonta africana*	19, 46
Somali Wild Ass *Equus africanus*	page 48
Common Zebra *Equus quagga*	40, 43
Grevy's Zebra *Equus grevyi*	18
Hippopotamus *Hippopotamus amphibius*	7, 22, 24, 43
Bush Pig *Potamochoerus larvatus*	30
Giant Hog *Hylochoerus meinertzhageni*	30

Species	Site numbers
Common Warthog *Phacochoerus africanus*	4, 15, 17, 28
African Buffalo *Syncerus caffer*	46
Menelik's Bushbuck *Tragelaphus scriptus meneliki*	4, 28, 30
Lesser Kudu *Tragelaphus imberbis*	14, 15, 16, 17, 40
Mountain Nyala *Tragelaphus buxtoni*	28
Greater Kudu *Tragelaphus strepsiceros*	15, 16
Bush Duiker *Sylvicapra grimmia*	4
Oribi *Ourebia ourebi*	44
Klipspringer *Oreotragus oreotragus*	29
Salt's Dik-dik *Madoqua saltiana*	15
Günther's Dik-dik *Madoqua kirkii*	37, 38, 40
Bohor Reedbuck *Redunca redunca*	28
White-eared Kob *Kobus kob leucotis*	47
Nile Lechwe *Kobus megaceros*	47
Grant's Gazelle *Gazella granti*	25, 41, 43
Soemmerring's Gazelle *Gazella soemmerringi*	15, 18
Gerenuk *Litocranius walleri*	17, 37, 40, 41
Swayne's Hartebeest or Korkay *Alcelaphus buselaphus swaynei*	43, 44
Beisa Oryx *Oryx beisa*	15, 18
Walia Ibex *Capra ibex walie*	49

Appendix C: Complete Annotated Checklist of the Birds of Ethiopia

Since the species lists mentioned in the site accounts cannot hope to be complete, the site numbers are only intended as a guide to possible places to look for any species of particular interest. The quantity of sites listed for each species is not an indication of its abundance but often, by contrast, of its scarcity. We have tended for reasons of space to omit extremely common species or ones with widespread African ranges from the main text, and as a result many such species will have no further information given about them in the list below.

English names and taxonomy largely follow Redman *et al.*'s *Birds of the Horn of Africa* (see Introduction, p.20, for exceptions). Very distinctive subspecies are highlighted by giving them distinct common names in inverted commas (e.g. 'Archer's' Francolin), and listing their trinomial scientific names.

In the 'Endemism' column, ET stands for Ethiopia, ER for Eritrea and HoA for Horn of Africa. Square brackets indicate that the species is a near-endemic to the stated region.

In the 'Status' column, R stands for resident, AM for Afrotropical migrant, PM for Palearctic migrant, V for vagrant, S for scarce, M for marginal (along borders and off the main birding routes, typically in the far west or north), U for unconfirmed (reported from Ethiopia, but still awaits formal substantiation), and ? for uncertainty about its suggested status.

Species	Endemism	Status	Site numbers	✓
Ostriches STRUTHIONIDAE				
Common Ostrich *Struthio camelus*		R		
Somali Ostrich *Struthio molybdophanes*		R	18, 40, 17	
Grebes PODICIPEDIDAE				
Little Grebe *Tachybaptus ruficollis*		R		
Great Crested Grebe *Podiceps cristatus*		R		
Black-necked Grebe *Podiceps nigricollis*		R?		
Cormorants PHALACROCORACIDAE				
Great Cormorant *Phalacrocorax carbo*		R	27	
Long-tailed Cormorant *Phalacrocorax africanus*		R	22	
Darters ANHINGIDAE				
African Darter *Anhinga rufa*		R	22	
Pelicans PELECANIDAE				
Great White Pelican *Pelecanus onocrotalus*		R, PM & AM	48, 22, 25, 27	
Pink-backed Pelican *Pelecanus rufescens*		R	48	
Bitterns, herons and egrets ARDEIDAE				
Eurasian Bittern *Botaurus stellaris*		V	47	
Little Bittern *Ixobrychus minutus*		AM & PM		
Dwarf Bittern *Ixobrychus sturmii*		AM	15	
White-backed Night Heron *Gorsachius leuconotus*		M	47	
Black-crowned Night Heron *Nycticorax nycticorax*		R & PM		
Squacco Heron *Ardeola ralloides*		R & PM		
Cattle Egret *Bubulcus ibis*		R, AM & PM		
Striated Heron *Butorides striata*		R		
Black Heron *Egretta ardesiaca*		AM	22, 27	
Western Reef Egret *Egretta gularis*		AM	16	
Little Egret *Egretta garzetta*		R & PM		
Yellow-billed Egret *Egretta intermedia*		R		
Great Egret *Egretta alba*		R & PM		
Purple Heron *Ardea purpurea*		R & PM	24	
Grey Heron *Ardea cinerea*		R & PM		
Black-headed Heron *Ardea melanocephala*		R		
Goliath Heron *Ardea goliath*		R	10, 15, 21, 27, 43	
Hamerkop SCOPIDAE				
Hamerkop *Scopus umbretta*		R	22, 10	
Storks CICONIIDAE				
Yellow-billed Stork *Mycteria ibis*		R	21	
African Openbill *Anastomus lamelligerus*		R & AM	48	
Black Stork *Ciconia nigra*		PM		
Abdim's Stork *Ciconia abdimii*		R & AM	21, 23	
Woolly-necked Stork *Ciconia episcopus*		R & AM	10, 24, 42, 47	
White Stork *Ciconia ciconia*		PM	21	
Saddle-billed Stork *Ephippiorhynchus senegalensis*		R	21, 22, 24	
Marabou Stork *Leptoptilos crumeniferus*		R	22, 27	

Species	Endemism	Status	Site numbers	✓
Shoebill BALAENICIPITIDAE				
Shoebill *Balaeniceps rex*		M	47	
Ibises and spoonbills THRESKIORNITHIDAE				
Glossy Ibis *Plegadis falcinellus*		AM&PM	43	
Hadada Ibis *Bostrychia hagedash*		R		
Wattled Ibis *Bostrychia carunculata*	ET & ER	R	1, 3, 8, 24, 28, 42, 50	
Sacred Ibis *Threskiornis aethiopicus*		R	25	
Northern Bald Ibis *Geronticus eremita*		S	8	
Eurasian Spoonbill *Platalea leucorodia*		S		
African Spoonbill *Platalea alba*		R		
Flamingos PHOENICOPTERIDAE				
Greater Flamingo *Phoenicopterus ruber*		AM&PM	21, 24, 25	
Lesser Flamingo *Phoeniconaias minor*		AM	20, 25	
Ducks and geese ANATIDAE				
Fulvous Whistling Duck *Dendrocygna bicolor*		AM	22, 27	
White-faced Whistling Duck *Dendrocygna viduata*		R & AM	22	
White-backed Duck *Thalassornis leuconotus*		R	20, 22, 27	
Blue-winged Goose *Cyanochen cyanoptera*	ET	R	3, 8, 10, 28, 29	
Egyptian Goose *Alopochen aegyptiaca*		R		
Ruddy Shelduck *Tadorna ferruginea*		R	29	
Common Shelduck *Tadorna tadorna*		V		
Spur-winged Goose *Plectropterus gambensis*		R & AM		
Knob-billed Duck *Sarkidiornis melanotos*		AM	20	
African Pygmy-goose *Nettapus auritus*		AM	20, 22, 27	
Eurasian Wigeon *Anas penelope*		PM	29	
Gadwall *Anas strepera*		PM		
Eurasian Teal *Anas crecca*		PM		
Cape Teal *Anas capensis*		R	20	
Mallard *Anas platyrhynchos*		V		
Yellow-billed Duck *Anas undulata*		R	3, 29	
African Black Duck *Anas sparsa*		R	3, 29	
Northern Pintail *Anas acuta*		PM	3, 20, 29	
Red-billed Duck *Anas erythrorhyncha*		R & AM	3, 20, 21	
Hottentot Teal *Anas hottentota*		AM	21, 22, 27	
Garganey *Anas querquedula*		PM	3, 20, 21	
Northern Shoveler *Anas clypeata*		PM	3, 20, 25, 29	
Southern Pochard *Netta erythrophthalma*		AM	3, 20, 21, 43	
Common Pochard *Aythya ferina*		PM		
Ferruginous Duck *Aythya nyroca*		PM	16, 20	
Tufted Duck *Aythya fuligula*		PM	3, 20	
Maccoa Duck *Oxyura maccoa*		R		
Hawks, buzzards and eagles ACCIPITRIDAE				
Osprey *Pandion haliaetus*		R & PM	48	
African Cuckoo-hawk *Aviceda cuculoides*		R	43	
European Honey-buzzard *Pernis apivorus*		PM		
Bat Hawk *Macheiramphus alcinus*		R	15, 26, 27, 43, 46, 47	

Species	Endemism	Status	Site numbers	✓
Black-winged Kite *Elanus caeruleus*		R		
African Swallow-tailed Kite *Chelictinia riocourii*		AM	15, 17, 21, 43, 44, 45	
Black Kite *Milvus migrans*		PM		
Yellow-billed Kite *Milvus (migrans) aegyptius*		R & AM		
African Fish Eagle *Haliaeetus vocifer*		R	48	
Lammergeier *Gypaetus barbatus*		R	2, 6, 8, 9, 10, 11, 12, 16, 28, 43, 49, 50	
Egyptian Vulture *Neophron percnopterus*		R	14, 18, 36, 41	
Hooded Vulture *Necrosyrtes monachus*		R	1, 15, 40	
White-backed Vulture *Gyps africanus*		R	1, 15, 40	
Rüppell's Vulture *Gyps rueppellii*		R	15, 16, 20, 40	
Griffon Vulture *Gyps fulvus*		S & PM		
Lappet-faced Vulture *Torgos tracheliotus*		R	15, 40	
White-headed Vulture *Trigonoceps occipitalis*		R	40	
Short-toed Snake-eagle *Circaetus gallicus*		PM		
Beaudouin's Snake-eagle *Circaetus beaudouini*		AM & U	48	
Black-chested Snake-eagle *Circaetus pectoralis*		AM	35, 40, 44	
Brown Snake-eagle *Circaetus cinereus*		R	28	
Western Banded Snake-eagle *Circaetus cinerascens*		R	26, 27, 47	
Bateleur *Terathopius ecaudatus*		R	40, 44, 46	
African Harrier-hawk *Polyboroides typus*		R		
Pallid Harrier *Circus macrourus*		PM	15, 28, 43, 44, 48	
Montagu's Harrier *Circus pygargus*		PM	15, 28, 43, 44, 48	
African Marsh Harrier *Circus ranivorus*		S, AM		
Western Marsh Harrier *Circus aeruginosus*		PM	17, 28, 48	
Gabar Goshawk *Micronisus gabar*		R	40	
Dark Chanting Goshawk *Melierax metabates*		R		
Eastern Chanting Goshawk *Melierax poliopterus*		R	15, 38, 40	
African Goshawk *Accipiter tachiro*		R	9, 28, 30	
Shikra *Accipiter badius*		R	15	
Levant Sparrowhawk *Accipiter brevipes*		V & PM	47	
Little Sparrowhawk *Accipiter minullus*		R	15, 26, 39	
Ovambo Sparrowhawk *Accipiter ovampensis*		S, AM?	15	
Eurasian Sparrowhawk *Accipiter nisus*		S, PM		
Rufous-breasted Sparrowhawk *Accipiter rufiventris*		R	2, 9, 12	
Great Sparrowhawk *Accipiter melanoleucus*		R	2, 12, 26, 30, 39	
Grasshopper Buzzard *Butastur rufipennis*		AM	17, 28, 36	
Lizard Buzzard *Kaupifalco monogrammicus*		M	47	
Common Buzzard *Buteo buteo*		PM		
Mountain Buzzard *Buteo oreophilus*		R	2, 4, 12, 29	
Long-legged Buzzard *Buteo rufinus*		PM	28	
Red-necked Buzzard *Buteo auguralis*		AM	47	
Augur Buzzard *Buteo augur*		R	8, 28, 29, 40	
Lesser Spotted Eagle *Aquila pomarina*		PM	43	
Greater Spotted Eagle *Aquila clanga*		PM		
Tawny Eagle *Aquila rapax*		R	8, 9, 28, 35, 40	

Species	Endemism	Status	Site numbers	✔
Steppe Eagle *Aquila nipalensis*		PM	8, 9, 28, 43	
Eastern Imperial Eagle *Aquila heliaca*		S, PM	28, 29, 49	
Golden Eagle *Aquila chrysaetos*		R	28, 29	
Verreaux's Eagle *Aquila verreauxii*		R	6, 9, 10, 11, 12, 19, 29	
Wahlberg's Eagle *Aquila wahlbergi*		AM		
African Hawk-eagle *Hieraaetus spilogaster*		R	48	
Booted Eagle *Hieraaetus pennatus*		PM		
Ayres's Hawk-eagle *Hieraaetus ayresii*		R	26, 48	
Long-crested Eagle *Lophaetus occipitalis*		R		
African Crowned Eagle *Stephanoaetus coronatus*		R	4, 26, 30, 34	
Martial Eagle *Polemaetus bellicosus*		R	28, 40	
Secretarybird SAGITTARIIDAE				
Secretarybird *Sagittarius serpentarius*		R	15, 18, 41	
Falcons FALCONIDAE				
Pygmy Falcon *Polihierax semitorquatus*		R	15, 19, 40	
Lesser Kestrel *Falco naumanni*		PM	21, 28, 35, 43, 48	
Common Kestrel *Falco tinnunculus*		R & PM	10, 21, 23, 28	
Greater Kestrel *Falco rupicoloides*		M		
Fox Kestrel *Falco alopex*		R	10, 16	
Grey Kestrel *Falco ardosiaceus*		R	35, 40, 46	
Red-necked Falcon *Falco chicquera*		R	47	
Red-footed Falcon *Falco vespertinus*		S & PM		
Amur Falcon *Falco amurensis*		S & PM		
Eleonora's Falcon *Falco eleonorae*		S & PM		
Sooty Falcon *Falco concolor*		S & AM	15, 48	
Eurasian Hobby *Falco subbuteo*		PM		
African Hobby *Falco cuvierii*		R	3, 6	
Lanner Falcon *Falco biarmicus*		R	6, 16, 28, 29	
Saker Falcon *Falco cherrug*		PM	18, 23	
Peregrine Falcon *Falco peregrinus*		R & PM	6	
Barbary Falcon *Falco pelegrinoides*		R?	25	
Taita Falcon *Falco fasciinucha*		R?	29, 42	
Guineafowl NUMIDIDAE				
Vulturine Guineafowl *Acryllium vulturinum*		R	38, 40, 46	
Helmeted Guineafowl *Numida meleagris*		R		
Quails and francolins PHASIANIDAE				
Common Quail *Coturnix coturnix*		PM & AM		
Blue Quail *Coturnix adansonii*		U		
Harlequin Quail *Coturnix delegorguei*		AM		
Stone Partridge *Ptilopachus petrosus*		R	10	
Coqui Francolin *Francolinus coqui*		R		
Moorland Francolin *Francolinus psilolaemus*		R	28, 29	
Orange River ('Archer's') Francolin *Francolinus levaillantoides archeri*		R	43	
Crested Francolin *Francolinus sephaena*		R		
Scaly Francolin *Francolinus squamatus*		R	24, 26, 30	

Species	Endemism	Status	Site numbers	✓
Clapperton's Francolin *Francolinus clappertoni*		R	7, 13, 23, 50	
Harwood's Francolin *Francolinus harwoodi*	ET	R	10	
Chestnut-naped Francolin *Francolinus castaneicollis*	ET & ER	R	28, 29, 30, 42, 49	
Erckel's Francolin *Francolinus erckelii*	[HoA]	R	5, 6, 9, 10, 12, 49, 50	
Yellow-necked Spurfowl *Francolinus leucoscepus*		R	40	
Buttonquails TURNICIDAE				
Quail-plover *Ortyxelos meiffrenii*		S & AM	35	
Common Buttonquail *Turnix sylvaticus*		R & AM		
Rails, crakes and gallinules RALLIDAE				
Buff-spotted Flufftail *Sarothrura elegans*		S	26	
Red-chested Flufftail *Sarothrura rufa*		R?		
White-winged Flufftail *Sarothrura ayresi*		S	8	
African Crake *Crex egregia*		S & AM		
Corncrake *Crex crex*		S & PM		
Rouget's Rail *Rougetius rougetii*	ET & ER	R	1, 3, 8, 28, 29, 34, 42, 49	
African Rail *Rallus caerulescens*		R	22	
Little Crake *Porzana parva*		S & PM		
Baillon's Crake *Porzana pusilla*		S & R		
Spotted Crake *Porzana porzana*		S & PM		
Black Crake *Amaurornis flavirostra*		R	22, 43	
Allen's Gallinule *Porphyrio alleni*		AM	48	
Purple Swamphen *Porphyrio porphyrio*		R	24	
Common Moorhen *Gallinula chloropus*		R		
Lesser Moorhen *Gallinula angulata*		AM	48	
Red-knobbed Coot *Fulica cristata*		R		
Cranes GRUIDAE				
Common Crane *Grus grus*		PM	20, 21, 25, 48	
Wattled Crane *Bugeranus carunculatus*		R	25, 28, 29, 48	
Demoiselle Crane *Anthropoides virgo*		V & PM		
Black Crowned Crane *Balearica pavonina*		R & AM	21, 25, 27, 48	
Finfoot HELIORNITHIDAE				
African Finfoot *Podica senegalensis*		R	48	
Bustards OTIDIDAE				
Denham's Bustard *Neotis denhami*		S, M		
Heuglin's Bustard *Neotis heuglinii*		S	18, 32, 35, 37, 45	
Arabian Bustard *Ardeotis arabs*		R	14, 15, 16, 17, 18	
Kori Bustard *Ardeotis kori*		R	15, 16, 18, 35, 40, 43	
Buff-crested Bustard *Lophotis gindiana*		R	14, 15, 40, 41	
Little Brown Bustard *Eupodotis humilis*		S	32, 37	
White-bellied Bustard *Eupodotis senegalensis*		R	15, 17, 35, 39, 40	
Black-bellied Bustard *Lissotis melanogaster*		R	15, 25, 43, 44	
Hartlaub's Bustard *Lissotis hartlaubii*		R	15, 35, 43	
Jacanas JACANIDAE				
African Jacana *Actophilornis africanus*		R	22, 27	
Lesser Jacana *Microparra capensis*		R	22, 27, 48	

Species	Endemism	Status	Site numbers	✓
Painted-snipe ROSTRATULIDAE				
Greater Painted-snipe *Rostratula benghalensis*		R		
Oystercatchers HAEMATOPODIDAE				
Eurasian Oystercatcher *Haematopus ostralegus*		U		
Stilts and avocets RECURVIROSTRIDAE				
Black-winged Stilt *Himantopus himantopus*		R & PM		
Pied Avocet *Recurvirostra avosetta*		AM?		
Thick-knees BURHINIDAE				
Stone-curlew *Burhinus oedicnemus*		PM	25	
Senegal Thick-knee *Burhinus senegalensis*		R	7, 10, 23, 27	
Water Thick-knee *Burhinus vermiculatus*		R	14, 37, 38	
Spotted Thick-knee *Burhinus capensis*		R	17	
Coursers and pratincoles GLAREOLIDAE				
Egyptian Plover *Pluvianus aegyptius*		AM	7, 46, 47	
Cream-coloured Courser *Cursorius cursor*		V		
Somali Courser *Cursorius somalensis*		R	35, 37, 39, 41	
Temminck's Courser *Cursorius temminckii*		R	16, 25, 35	
Double-banded Courser *Rhinoptilus africanus*		R	15, 18, 25	
Heuglin's Courser *Rhinoptilus cinctus*		R	15, 23, 24, 40	
Bronze-winged Courser *Rhinoptilus chalcopterus*		S	10	
Collared Pratincole *Glareola pratincola*		AM & PM	17	
Black-winged Pratincole *Glareola nordmanni*		S & PM		
Madagascar Pratincole *Glareola ocularis*		V & PM		
Rock Pratincole *Glareola nuchalis*		M		
Plovers CHARADRIIDAE				
Little Ringed Plover *Charadrius dubius*		PM	25	
Ringed Plover *Charadrius hiaticula*		PM	25	
Kittlitz's Plover *Charadrius pecuarius*		R	25	
Three-banded Plover *Charadrius tricollaris*		R		
Kentish Plover *Charadrius alexandrinus*		PM	25	
Lesser Sand Plover *Charadrius mongolus*		PM	25	
Greater Sand Plover *Charadrius leschenaultii*		V, PM		
Caspian Plover *Charadrius asiaticus*		PM	25	
Pacific Golden Plover *Pluvialis fulva*		S & PM	25	
Grey Plover *Pluvialis squatarola*		PM	25	
African Wattled Plover *Vanellus senegallus*		R		
Spot-breasted Plover *Vanellus melanocephalus*	ET	R	8, 28, 29, 49	
Black-headed Plover *Vanellus tectus*		R	15, 19	
Spur-winged Plover *Vanellus spinosus*		R	22	
Black-winged Plover *Vanellus melanopterus*		R	8, 28, 35	
Crowned Plover *Vanellus coronatus*		R	35, 37	
Sociable Plover *Vanellus gregarius*		V & PM		
White-tailed Plover *Vanellus leucurus*		V & PM		
Long-toed Plover *Vanellus crassirostris*		M	47	
Sandpipers and allies SCOLOPACIDAE				
Sanderling *Calidris alba*		S & PM		

Species	Endemism	Status	Site numbers	✓
Little Stint *Calidris minuta*		PM	25	
Temminck's Stint *Calidris temminckii*		PM		
Long-toed Stint *Calidris subminuta*		V & PM		
Pectoral Sandpiper *Calidris melanotos*		V		
Curlew Sandpiper *Calidris ferruginea*		PM	25	
Dunlin *Calidris alpina*		S & PM		
Broad-billed Sandpiper *Limicola falcinellus*		V & PM		
Ruff *Philomachus pugnax*		PM	20, 25	
Jack Snipe *Lymnocryptes minimus*		S & PM		
Common Snipe *Gallinago gallinago*		PM		
African Snipe *Gallinago nigripennis*		R	3, 8, 28	
Great Snipe *Gallinago media*		PM	8	
Black-tailed Godwit *Limosa limosa*		PM	20, 21	
Bar-tailed Godwit *Limosa lapponica*		U & PM		
Whimbrel *Numenius phaeopus*		S & PM		
Eurasian Curlew *Numenius arquata*		PM		
Spotted Redshank *Tringa erythropus*		PM		
Common Redshank *Tringa totanus*		PM		
Marsh Sandpiper *Tringa stagnatilis*		PM	43	
Common Greenshank *Tringa nebularia*		PM		
Green Sandpiper *Tringa ochropus*		PM	21, 29	
Wood Sandpiper *Tringa glareola*		PM	21	
Terek Sandpiper *Xenus cinereus*		PM		
Common Sandpiper *Actitis hypoleucos*		PM		
Ruddy Turnstone *Arenaria interpres*		S & PM		
Red-necked Phalarope *Phalaropus lobatus*		S & PM	25	
Grey Phalarope *Phalaropus fulicarius*		V & PM		
Skuas STERCORARIIDAE				
Arctic Skua *Stercorarius parasiticus*		V & PM		
Gulls LARIDAE				
Pallas's Gull *Larus ichthyaetus*		PM	22, 23, 25, 48	
Grey-headed Gull *Larus cirrocephalus*		AM	22, 27, 48	
Black-headed Gull *Larus ridibundus*		PM	22, 23, 25, 48	
Slender-billed Gull *Larus genei*		S & PM	22	
Lesser Black-backed Gull *Larus fuscus*		PM	22, 23, 25, 48	
Heuglin's Gull *Larus heuglini*		PM	22, 23, 25, 48	
Terns STERNIDAE				
Gull-billed Tern *Sterna nilotica*		PM	20, 22, 23, 48	
Caspian Tern *Sterna caspia*		AM&PM		
Sandwich Tern *Sterna sandvicensis*		V		
Common Tern *Sterna hirundo*		S & PM		
Sooty Tern *Sterna fuscata*		V		
Little Stern *Sterna albifrons*		U		
Saunders's Tern *Sterna saundersi*		S		
Whiskered Tern *Chlidonias hybrida*		PM	21, 48	
Black Tern *Chlidonias niger*		S & PM		

Species	Endemism	Status	Site numbers	✓
White-winged Black Tern *Chlidonias leucopterus*		PM	21, 48	
Skimmers RYNCHOPIDAE				
African Skimmer *Rynchops flavirostris*		AM		
Sandgrouse PTEROCLIDAE				
Chestnut-bellied Sandgrouse *Pterocles exustus*		R	14, 15, 21, 37	
Spotted Sandgrouse *Pterocles senegallus*		M		
Black-faced Sandgrouse *Pterocles decoratus*		R	37, 41	
Lichtenstein's Sandgrouse *Pterocles lichtensteinii*		R	14, 15, 17, 37	
Four-banded Sandgrouse *Pterocles quadricinctus*		R	7, 17, 21, 23	
Yellow-throated Sandgrouse *Pterocles gutturalis*		R	7, 18, 43	
Pigeons and doves COLUMBIDAE				
African Green Pigeon *Treron calvus*		R		
Bruce's Green Pigeon *Treron waalia*		R	10, 15, 20, 33, 43	
Tambourine Dove *Turtur tympanistria*		R		
Blue-spotted Wood Dove *Turtur afer*		R	39	
Black-billed Wood Dove *Turtur abyssinicus*		M	47	
Emerald-spotted Wood Dove *Turtur chalcospilos*		R		
Namaqua Dove *Oena capensis*		R		
Eastern Bronze-naped Pigeon *Columba delegorguei*		M		
Lemon Dove *Columba larvata*		R	9, 24, 48	
African Olive Pigeon *Columba arquatrix*		R	4	
Speckled Pigeon *Columba guinea*		R		
White-collared Pigeon *Columba albitorques*	ET & ER	R	1, 8, 10, 28, 48, 50	
Rock Dove/Feral Pigeon *Columba livia*		R		
Red-eyed Dove *Streptopelia semitorquata*		R		
African Mourning Dove *Streptopelia decipiens*		R	14, 37	
Vinaceous Dove *Streptopelia vinacea*		R	7, 10, 47, 48	
Ring-necked Dove *Streptopelia capicola*		R		
African Collared Dove *Streptopelia roseogrisea*		R	14, 17	
African White-winged Dove *Streptopelia reichenowi*	[HoA]	R	32, 37, 38	
European Turtle Dove *Streptopelia turtur*		PM		
Dusky Turtle Dove *Streptopelia lugens*		R	1, 50	
Laughing Dove *Streptopelia senegalensis*		R	37	
Parrots and lovebirds PSITTACIDAE				
Meyer's Parrot *Poicephalus meyeri*		M		
African Orange-bellied Parrot *Poicephalus rufiventris*		R	40	
Yellow-fronted Parrot *Poicephalus flavifrons*	ET	R	2, 4, 24, 26, 28, 30, 34, 42, 48	
Red-headed Lovebird *Agapornis pullarius*		M		
Black-winged Lovebird *Agapornis taranta*	ET & ER	R	1, 2, 5, 10, 20, 23, 24, 26, 27, 28, 30, 48, 49	
Rose-ringed Parakeet *Psittacula krameri*		M		
Turacos MUSOPHAGIDAE				
White-cheeked Turaco *Tauraco leucotis*	[ET & ER]	R	2, 4, 9, 26, 29, 30, 35, 39, 40, 48	
Prince Ruspoli's Turaco *Tauraco ruspolii*	ET	R	33, 34, 35, 39	
Bare-faced Go-away-bird *Corythaixoides personatus*		R	13, 19, 24, 40	
White-bellied Go-away-bird *Corythaixoides leucogaster*		R	13, 15, 40	

Species	Endemism	Status	Site numbers	✓
Eastern Grey Plantain-eater *Crinifer zonurus*		R	13, 14, 15, 48	
Cuckoos and coucals CUCULIDAE				
Jacobin Cuckoo *Clamator jacobinus*		AM		
Levaillant's Cuckoo *Clamator levaillantii*		R		
Great Spotted Cuckoo *Clamator glandarius*		PM&AM?		
Red-chested Cuckoo *Cuculus solitarius*		AM?		
Black Cuckoo *Cuculus clamosus*		AM	40, 46	
Common Cuckoo *Cuculus canorus*		PM		
African Cuckoo *Cuculus gularis*		AM		
African Emerald Cuckoo *Chrysococcyx cupreus*		R	26, 30	
Klaas's Cuckoo *Chrysococcyx klaas*		R & AM		
Diederik Cuckoo *Chrysococcyx caprius*		AM		
Yellowbill *Ceuthmochares aereus*		R	24, 43	
White-browed Coucal *Centropus superciliosus*		R		
Black Coucal *Centropus grillii*		S & AM?		
Senegal Coucal *Centropus senegalensis*		R		
Blue-headed Coucal *Centropus monachus*		R	27	
Barn owls TYTONIDAE				
African Grass Owl *Tyto capensis*		V		
Barn Owl *Tyto alba*		R	23	
Typical owls STRIGIDAE				
Eurasian Scops Owl *Otus scops*		PM?		
African Scops Owl *Otus senegalensis*		R	15, 17	
Northern White-faced Owl *Ptilopsis leucotis*		R	15, 17, 23, 27	
Cape Eagle-owl *Bubo capensis*		R	9, 28, 29	
Greyish Eagle-owl *Bubo cinerascens*		R	15, 16, 17, 23, 25, 43, 48	
Verreaux's Eagle-owl *Bubo lacteus*		R	15, 17, 23, 25, 27, 43	
Pel's Fishing Owl *Scotopelia peli*		R	43, 46	
Pearl-spotted Owlet *Glaucidium perlatum*		R	40	
Little Owl *Athene noctua*		R		
African Wood Owl *Strix woodfordii*		R	9, 12, 26, 28, 30	
Abyssinian Owl *Asio abyssinicus*		R	9, 12, 28, 29, 49	
Short-eared Owl *Asio flammeus*		PM		
Marsh Owl *Asio capensis*		R?	43	
Nightjars CAPRIMULGIDAE				
Swamp Nightjar *Caprimulgus natalensis*		S, AM		
Long-tailed Nightjar *Caprimulgus climacurus*		M		
Slender-tailed Nightjar *Caprimulgus clarus*		R	15, 17, 23, 37, 43	
Montane Nightjar *Caprimulgus poliocephalus*		R	26, 28, 29, 43	
Donaldson Smith's Nightjar *Caprimulgus donaldsoni*		R	37, 40, 43, 46	
Plain Nightjar *Caprimulgus inornatus*		R	15, 26	
Star-spotted Nightjar *Caprimulgus stellatus*		R	15, 17, 43, 45, 46	
Nubian Nightjar *Caprimulgus nubicus*		AM	15, 43	
Freckled Nightjar *Caprimulgus tristigma*		R	23, 43	
Egyptian Nightjar *Caprimulgus aegyptius*		S & PM	17	
Dusky Nightjar *Caprimulgus fraenatus*		R&AM?	15, 37, 43	

Species	Endemism	Status	Site numbers	✓
European Nightjar *Caprimulgus europaeus*		PM		
Nechisar Nightjar Caprimulgus solala	ET	R?	43	
Standard-winged Nightjar *Macrodipteryx longipennis*		AM	43	
Swifts APODIDAE				
Scarce Swift *Schoutedenapus myoptilus*		S, AM	43	
African Palm Swift *Cypsiurus parvus*		R		
African Black Swift *Apus barbatus*		U		
Nyanza Swift *Apus niansae*		R	6, 9, 10, 24, 26, 48, 50	
Common Swift *Apus apus*		PM		
White-rumped Swift *Apus caffer*		R		
Horus Swift *Apus horus*		R		
Little Swift *Apus affinis*		R		
Mottled Swift *Tachymarptis aequatorialis*		R	24	
Alpine Swift *Tachymarptis melba*		R, AM & PM?		
Mousebirds COLIIDAE				
Blue-naped Mousebird *Urocolius macrourus*		R	15, 17, 23, 40	
Speckled Mousebird *Colius striatus*		R	1	
Trogons TROGONIDAE				
Narina Trogon *Apaloderma narina*		R	4, 24, 26, 30, 34, 39, 43, 46	
Kingfishers ALCEDINIDAE				
Grey-headed Kingfisher *Halcyon leucocephala*		R	13, 48	
Blue-breasted Kingfisher *Halcyon malimbica*		S, R?	46	
Woodland Kingfisher *Halcyon senegalensis*		R	27, 48	
Striped Kingfisher *Halcyon chelicuti*		R	13	
African Pygmy Kingfisher *Ceyx pictus*		R	27	
Malachite Kingfisher *Alcedo cristata*		R	27, 48	
Half-collared Kingfisher *Alcedo semitorquata*		R	13, 26, 48	
Giant Kingfisher *Megaceryle maxima*		R	10, 26, 27, 48	
Pied Kingfisher *Ceryle rudis*		R	27	
Bee-eaters MEROPIDAE				
Little Bee-eater *Merops pusillus*		R	40	
Blue-breasted Bee-eater *Merops (variegatus) lafresnayii*		R	1, 10, 23	
Swallow-tailed Bee-eater *Merops hirundineus*		M & R	46, 47	
Red-throated Bee-eater *Merops bulocki*		M&AM?	47	
Somali Bee-eater *Merops revoilii*		R	32, 37, 45	
White-throated Bee-eater *Merops albicollis*		AM	15, 17	
Little Green Bee-eater *Merops orientalis*		M, AM?	47	
Blue-cheeked Bee-eater *Merops persicus*		PM		
Madagascar Bee-eater *Merops superciliosus*		AM	15	
European Bee-eater *Merops apiaster*		PM		
Northern Carmine Bee-eater *Merops nubicus*		R&AM?	15, 17	
Rollers CORACIIDAE				
Rufous-crowned Roller *Coracias naevius*		R		
Abyssinian Roller *Coracias abyssinicus*		R	15, 17	
European Roller *Coracias garrulus*		PM		

Species	Endemism	Status	Site numbers	✓
Lilac-breasted Roller *Coracias caudatus*		R & AM		
Broad-billed Roller *Eurystomus glaucurus*		AM	46	
Woodhoopoes and scimitarbills PHOENICULIDAE				
Green Woodhoopoe *Phoeniculus purpureus*		M	47	
Black-billed Woodhoopoe *Phoeniculus somaliensis*		R	15, 23, 25, 40	
Violet Woodhoopoe *Phoeniculus damarensis*		U	46	
Black Scimitarbill *Rhinopomastus aterrimus*		R	25, 39, 47	
Abyssinian Scimitarbill *Rhinopomastus minor*		R	15, 40	
Hoopoes UPUPIDAE				
Eurasian Hoopoe *Upupa epops*		PM		
African Hoopoe *Upupa (epops) africana*		AM & R?		
Hornbills BUCEROTIDAE				
Abyssinian Ground Hornbill *Bucorvus abyssinicus*		R	15, 21, 25, 30, 40	
Red-billed Hornbill *Tockus erythrorhynchus*		R	23	
Eastern Yellow-billed Hornbill *Tockus flavirostris*		R	17, 40	
Von der Decken's Hornbill *Tockus deckeni*		R	23, 30, 31, 40	
Jackson's Hornbill *Tockus jacksoni*		S & M		
Hemprich's Hornbill *Tockus hemprichii*		R	9, 10, 23, 39	
Crowned Hornbill *Tockus alboterminatus*		R		
African Grey Hornbill *Tockus nasutus*		R	17	
Silvery-cheeked Hornbill *Bycanistes brevis*		R	26, 27, 30, 48	
Barbets and tinkerbirds CAPITONIDAE				
Red-fronted Tinkerbird *Pogoniulus pusillus*		R		
Yellow-fronted Tinkerbird *Pogoniulus chrysoconus*		R		
Red-fronted Barbet *Tricholaema diademata*		R	15, 17, 23, 24	
Black-throated Barbet *Tricholaema melanocephala*		R	40	
Banded Barbet *Lybius undatus*	ET & ER	R	2, 4, 5, 9, 13, 20, 23, 24, 26, 27	
Vieillot's Barbet *Lybius vieilloti*		V & M		
Black-billed Barbet *Lybius guifsobalito*		R	15, 20, 23, 24, 33	
Double-toothed Barbet *Lybius bidentatus*		R	24, 26, 27, 43, 48	
Red-and-yellow Barbet *Trachyphonus erythrocephalus*		R	15, 30, 40	
Yellow-breasted Barbet *Trachyphonus margaritatus*		R	13, 15, 16, 17	
d'Arnaud's Barbet *Trachyphonus darnaudii*		R	40	
Honeyguides INDICATORIDAE				
Green-backed Honeybird *Prodotiscus zambesiae*		S & R		
Wahlberg's Honeybird *Prodotiscus regulus*		R	26	
Scaly-throated Honeyguide *Indicator variegatus*		R	24, 43	
Greater Honeyguide *Indicator indicator*		R		
Lesser Honeyguide *Indicator minor*		R	26	
Woodpeckers and wrynecks PICIDAE				
Eurasian Wryneck *Jynx torquilla*		PM	25, 27	
Red-throated Wryneck *Jynx ruficollis*		R	23, 24, 25, 27	
Nubian Woodpecker *Campethera nubica*		R	23, 25, 27	
Green-backed Woodpecker *Campethera cailliautii*		S & M		
Abyssinian Woodpecker *Dendropicos abyssinicus*	ET & ER	R	1, 2, 4, 5, 9, 24, 26, 28, 29, 30, 49	

Species	Endemism	Status	Site numbers	✓
Cardinal Woodpecker *Dendropicos fuscescens*		R	25	
Bearded Woodpecker *Dendropicos namaquus*		R	23, 25, 40	
Grey Woodpecker *Dendropicos goertae*		R		
Grey-headed Woodpecker *Dendropicos spodocephalus*	[HoA]	R	23, 24, 26, 27, 28, 30, 39	
Brown-backed Woodpecker *Picoides obsoletus*		R & M	47	
Pittas PITTIDAE				
African Pitta *Pitta angolensis*		V & AM		
Larks ALAUDIDAE				
Singing Bush Lark *Mirafra cantillans*		R	15	
White-tailed Lark *Mirafra albicauda*		S & R	43	
Friedmann's Lark *Mirafra pulpa*		V?	43	
Rufous-naped Lark *Mirafra africana*		M & V?		
Red-winged Lark *Mirafra hypermetra*		R	15	
Flappet Lark *Mirafra rufocinnamomea*		R	35	
Collared Lark *Mirafra collaris*		S & M		
Foxy Lark *Mirafra (africanoides) alopex*		R	25, 40	
Gillett's Lark *Mirafra gilletti*	HoA	R	15, 16, 36, 37	
Pink-breasted Lark *Mirafra poecilosterna*		R & M	45	
Archer's Lark *Heteromirafra archeri*		U	19	
Liben (Sidamo) Lark *Heteromirafra sidamoensis*	ET	R	35	
Greater Hoopoe-lark *Alaemon alaudipes*		R & M		
Bimaculated Lark *Melanocorypha bimaculata*		S & PM	16, 18	
Desert Lark *Ammomanes deserti*		R	16	
Greater Short-toed Lark *Calandrella brachydactyla*		PM		
Blanford's Lark *Calandrella blanfordi*		R & M		
Erlanger's Lark *Calandrella erlangeri*	ET	R	1, 8, 10, 28	
Somali Short-toed Lark *Calandrella somalica*		R	35, 41	
Masked Lark *Spizocorys personata*		S	41	
Short-tailed Lark *Pseudalaemon fremantlii*		R	37, 40, 41	
Crested Lark *Galerida cristata*		R & M		
Thekla Lark *Galerida theklae*		R	8, 9, 10, 12, 28, 29	
Chestnut-backed Sparrow-lark *Eremopterix leucotis*		R	15, 18, 21	
Black-crowned Sparrow-lark *Eremopterix nigriceps*		R		
Chestnut-headed Sparrow-lark *Eremopterix signatus*		R	15, 18, 37, 45	
Swallows and martins HIRUNDINIDAE				
Black Saw-wing *Psalidoprocne pristoptera*		R	24, 26	
White-headed Saw-wing *Psalidoprocne albiceps*		U		
Plain Martin *Riparia paludicola*		R	30	
Sand Martin *Riparia riparia*		PM		
Banded Martin *Riparia cincta*		R&AM?	8, 10	
Grey-rumped Swallow *Pseudhirundo griseopyga*		AM	3	
Mosque Swallow *Cecropis senegalensis*		R&AM?		
Lesser Striped Swallow *Cecropis abyssinica*		R		
Red-rumped Swallow *Cecropis daurica*		R & PM	1	
'Ethiopian' Cliff Swallow *Petrochelidon* sp.		U	15, 23, 48	
Rock Martin *Ptyonoprogne fuligula*		R	9, 11	

Species	Endemism	Status	Site numbers	✓
Eurasian Crag Martin *Ptyonoprogne rupestris*		PM		
Wire-tailed Swallow *Hirundo smithii*		R		
White-tailed Swallow *Hirundo megaensis*	ET	R	35, 39, 40, 41	
Ethiopian Swallow *Hirundo aethiopica*		R	17, 36, 40, 41	
Red-chested Swallow *Hirundo lucida*		R	8	
Barn Swallow *Hirundo rustica*		PM	25, 41	
Common House Martin *Delichon urbicum*		PM		
Wagtails, pipits and longclaws MOTACILLIDAE				
Yellow Wagtail *Motacilla flava*		PM	25	
Citrine Wagtail *Motacilla citreola*		V & PM		
Grey Wagtail *Motacilla cinerea*		PM		
Mountain Wagtail *Motacilla clara*		R	26	
White Wagtail *Motacilla alba*		PM		
African Pied Wagtail *Motacilla aguimp*		R		
Golden Pipit *Tmetothylacus tenellus*		R	32, 35, 36, 37	
Grassland Pipit *Anthus cinnamomeus*		R		
Tawny Pipit *Anthus campestris*		PM		
Long-billed Pipit *Anthus similis*		R	10, 16, 44	
Plain-backed Pipit *Anthus leucophrys*		R	35, 40	
Bush Pipit *Anthus caffer*		S & M		
Tree Pipit *Anthus trivialis*		PM	30	
Red-throated Pipit *Anthus cervinus*		PM	8, 28	
Abyssinian Longclaw *Macronyx flavicollis*	ET	R	1, 3, 8, 10, 28, 49	
Cuckooshrikes CAMPEPHAGIDAE				
Red-shouldered Cuckooshrike *Campephaga phoenicea*		R	24, 26	
Black Cuckooshrike *Campephaga flava*		R		
Grey Cuckooshrike *Coracina caesia*		R	24, 26, 30, 34	
White-breasted Cuckooshrike *Coracina pectoralis*		R	39	
Bulbuls PYCNONOTIDAE				
Sombre Greenbul *Andropadus importunus*		V & M		
Yellow-throated Leaflove *Chlorocichla flavicollis*		R		
Northern Brownbul *Phyllastrephus strepitans*		R	31, 39	
Common Bulbul *Pycnonotus barbatus schoanus*		R		
'Dark-capped' Bulbul *Pycnonotus (barbatus) spurius*		R	40	
Somali Bulbul *Pycnonotus (barbatus) somaliensis*		R	14, 15, 17	
Dodson's Bulbul *Pycnonotus (barbatus) dodsoni*		R	31, 40	
Thrushes and chats TURDIDAE				
Thrush Nightingale *Luscinia luscinia*		PM	15, 23, 27	
Common Nightingale *Luscinia megarhynchos*		PM	23	
Bluethroat *Luscinia svecica*		PM		
White-throated Robin *Irania gutturalis*		PM	10, 50	
Rüppell's Robin-chat *Cossypha semirufa*		R	1, 4, 9	
White-browed Robin-chat *Cossypha heuglini*		R		
Red-capped Robin-chat *Cossypha natalensis*		AM&R?	43	
Snowy-headed Robin-chat *Cossypha niveicapilla*		R	7, 47	
White-crowned Robin-chat *Cossypha albicapillus*		R & M	46	

Species	Endemism	Status	Site numbers	✓
Spotted Palm-thrush *Cichladusa guttata*		R	38, 40, 46	
White-browed Scrub Robin *Cercotrichas leucophrys*		R	40	
Rufous Scrub Robin *Cercotrichas galactotes*		R & PM		
Black Scrub Robin *Cercotrichas podobe*		R	13, 17	
Black Redstart *Phoenicurus ochruros*		S & PM		
Common Redstart *Phoenicurus phoenicurus*		PM		
Siberian Stonechat *Saxicola (torquatus) maura*		PM		
African Stonechat *Saxicola torquatus*		R	8, 28, 29, 42	
Whinchat *Saxicola rubetra*		PM		
White-crowned Black Wheatear *Oenanthe leucopyga*		R & M		
Somali Wheatear *Oenanthe phillipsi*		R	32, 37	
Northern Wheatear *Oenanthe oenanthe*		PM	8, 28	
Pied Wheatear *Oenanthe pleschanka*		PM	8, 28	
Cyprus Wheatear *Oenanthe cypriaca*		PM	28, 35	
Black-eared Wheatear *Oenanthe hispanica*		PM		
Abyssinian Black Wheatear *Oenanthe lugubris*	HoA	R	10, 11, 12, 20, 23, 25	
Red-tailed Wheatear *Oenanthe chrysopygia*		V & PM		
Desert Wheatear *Oenanthe deserti*		PM		
Red-breasted Wheatear *Oenanthe bottae*		R	1, 3, 8, 10, 28	
Heuglin's Wheatear *Oenanthe heuglini*		S & M		
Isabelline Wheatear *Oenanthe isabellina*		PM	8, 28	
Familiar Chat *Cercomela familiaris*		R		
Brown-tailed Rock Chat *Cercomela scotocerca*		R	31, 33, 40	
Sombre Rock Chat *Cercomela dubia*	HoA	R	16	
Blackstart *Cercomela melanura*		R	16, 19	
Moorland Chat *Cercomela sordida*		R	8, 11, 12, 28, 49	
Rüppell's Black Chat *Myrmecocichla melaena*	ET & ER	R	6, 9, 10, 49, 50	
White-fronted Black Chat *Myrmecocichla albifrons*		R	43	
Mocking Cliff Chat *Thamnolaea cinnamomeiventris*		R	9, 20, 23, 48	
White-winged Cliff Chat *Thamnolaea semirufa*	ET & ER	R	2, 5, 6, 8, 9, 11, 20, 26, 50	
Little Rock Thrush *Monticola rufocinereus*		R	7, 12, 19, 23, 26, 31	
Common Rock Thrush *Monticola saxatilis*		PM	19	
Blue Rock Thrush *Monticola solitarius*		PM	11	
Abyssinian Ground Thrush *Zoothera piaggiae*		R	2, 4, 24, 26, 28, 29, 30	
Groundscraper Thrush *Psophocichla litsitsirupa*		R	8, 28	
Mountain Thrush *Turdus (olivaceus) abyssinicus*		R	1, 30	
African Thrush *Turdus pelios*		R		
Bare-eyed Thrush *Turdus tephronotus*		R	36, 38, 39, 40	
Song Thrush *Turdus philomelos*		M & PM		
Warblers SYLVIIDAE				
Little Rush Warbler *Bradypterus baboecala*		R		
Bamboo Warbler *Bradypterus alfredi*		S & AM?		
Cinnamon Bracken Warbler *Bradypterus cinnamomeus*		R	11, 12, 28, 29, 30	
Moustached Grass Warbler *Melocichla mentalis*		R	7, 47	
Fan-tailed Grassbird *Schoenicola brevirostris*		S		
Grasshopper Warbler *Locustella naevia*		PM		

Species	Endemism	Status	Site numbers	✓
River Warbler *Locustella fluviatilis*		PM		
Savi's Warbler *Locustella luscinioides*		PM		
Sedge Warbler *Acrocephalus schoenobaenus*		PM	22	
Eurasian Reed Warbler *Acrocephalus scirpaceus*		PM		
African Reed Warbler *Acrocephalus (scirpaceus) baeticatus*		R		
Marsh Warbler *Acrocephalus palustris*		PM	27	
Great Reed Warbler *Acrocephalus arundinaceus*		PM		
Basra Reed Warbler *Acrocephalus griseldis*		PM		
Lesser Swamp Warbler *Acrocephalus gracilirostris*		R	22, 24	
Dark-capped Yellow Warbler *Chloropeta natalensis*		R		
Eastern Olivaceous Warbler *Hippolais pallida*		PM		
Upcher's Warbler *Hippolais languida*		PM	17, 19, 27	
Olive-tree Warbler *Hippolais olivetorum*		S & PM	27	
Icterine Warbler *Hippolais icterina*		PM		
Yellow-bellied Eremomela *Eremomela icteropygialis*		R	17, 37, 40	
Yellow-vented Eremomela *Eremomela flavicrissalis*		R	32, 37, 38	
Green-backed Eremomela *Eremomela canescens*		R	47, 48	
Northern Crombec *Sylvietta brachyura*		R	37	
Red-faced Crombec *Sylvietta whytii*		R	40	
Philippa's Crombec *Sylvietta philippae*		R	32, 37, 38	
Somali Crombec *Sylvietta isabellina*		R	32, 38, 40	
Willow Warbler *Phylloscopus trochilus*		PM		
Common Chiffchaff *Phylloscopus collybita*		PM		
Wood Warbler *Phylloscopus sibilatrix*		S & PM		
Eastern Bonelli's Warbler *Phylloscopus orientalis*		S & PM		
Brown Woodland Warbler *Phylloscopus umbrovirens*		R	4, 9, 28, 30, 34	
Barred Warbler *Sylvia nisoria*		PM	27	
Orphean Warbler *Sylvia hortensis*		M & PM		
Garden Warbler *Sylvia borin*		PM		
Blackcap *Sylvia atricapilla*		PM		
Common Whitethroat *Sylvia communis*		PM		
Lesser Whitethroat *Sylvia curruca*		PM		
Asian Desert Warbler *Sylvia nana*		S & M		
Ménétriés's Warbler *Sylvia mystacea*		PM	17	
Subalpine Warbler *Sylvia cantillans*		U		
Brown Parisoma *Parisoma lugens*		R	1, 28, 29, 30	
Banded Parisoma *Parisoma boehmi*		R	36, 38, 40	
Yellow-bellied Hyliota *Hyliota flavigaster*		R	47	
Cisticolas and allies CISTICOLIDAE				
Red-faced Cisticola *Cisticola erythrops*		R		
Singing Cisticola *Cisticola cantans*		R	9, 10, 12	
Rattling Cisticola *Cisticola chiniana*		R	23, 40	
Boran Cisticola *Cisticola bodessa*		R	16, 23, 30, 40, 43	
Ashy Cisticola *Cisticola cinereolus*		R	15, 35	
Winding Cisticola *Cisticola (galactotes) marginatus*		R		
Ethiopian Cisticola *Cisticola (galactotes) lugubris*		R	1, 28, 30	

Species	Endemism	Status	Site numbers	✓
Stout Cisticola *Cisticola robustus*		R	9	
Croaking Cisticola *Cisticola natalensis*		R		
Red-pate Cisticola *Cisticola ruficeps*		S & M		
Tiny Cisticola *Cisticola nana*		R	36, 40	
Siffling Cisticola *Cisticola brachypterus*		R		
Foxy Cisticola *Cisticola troglodytes*		R	7, 10, 47	
Zitting Cisticola *Cisticola juncidis*		R		
Desert Cisticola *Cisticola aridulus*		R	43	
Black-backed Cisticola *Cisticola eximius*		S & R		
Pectoral-patch Cisticola *Cisticola brunnescens*		R	35	
Tawny-flanked Prinia *Prinia subflava*		R		
Pale Prinia *Prinia somalica*		R	36, 38, 40	
Graceful Prinia *Prinia gracilis*		R & M		
Red-winged Warbler *Heliolais erythropterus*		R		
Red-fronted Warbler *Urorhipis rufifrons*		R	14, 19, 36, 38	
Buff-bellied Warbler *Phyllolais pulchella*		R	23, 25	
Yellow-breasted Apalis *Apalis flavida*		R		
Grey-backed Camaroptera *Camaroptera brachyura*		R		
Grey Wren-warbler *Calamonastes simplex*		R	15, 36, 40	
Flycatchers MUSCICAPIDAE				
Abyssinian Slaty Flycatcher *Melaenornis chocolatinus*	ET & ER	R	1, 3, 4, 9, 26, 29, 30, 34, 42	
Northern Black Flycatcher *Melaenornis edolioides*		R	40	
Pale Flycatcher *Bradornis pallidus*		R		
African Grey Flycatcher *Bradornis microrhynchus*		R	17, 36, 40	
Silverbird *Empidornis semipartitus*		R? & M		
Spotted Flycatcher *Muscicapa striata*		PM		
Gambaga Flycatcher *Muscicapa gambagae*		R	47, 48	
African Dusky Flycatcher *Muscicapa adusta*		R	1	
Lead-coloured Flycatcher *Myioparus plumbeus*		R	31	
Semi-collared Flycatcher *Ficedula semitorquata*		PM	50	
Monarch flycatchers MONARCHIDAE				
African Paradise Flycatcher *Terpsiphone viridis*		R		
Wattle-eyes and batises PLATYSTEIRIDAE				
Brown-throated Wattle-eye *Platysteira cyanea*		R	30, 43, 48	
Grey-headed Batis *Batis orientalis*		R	17, 23, 31	
Black-headed Batis *Batis minor*		R	23, 35	
Pygmy Batis *Batis perkeo*		R	31, 36, 38, 40	
Babblers TIMALIIDAE				
African Hill Babbler *Pseudoalcippe abyssinica*		R	4, 24, 26, 30, 34	
Brown Babbler *Turdoides plebejus*		R & M	47	
White-headed Babbler *Turdoides leucocephala*		R & M		
Dusky Babbler *Turdoides tenebrosa*		R & M	36	
White-rumped Babbler *Turdoides leucopygia*		R	15, 39, 48	
Scaly Babbler *Turdoides squamulata*		S & M		
Rufous Chatterer *Turdoides rubiginosa*		R	36, 37, 40	
Scaly Chatterer *Turdoides aylmeri*		R	36, 38, 40	

Species	Endemism	Status	Site numbers	✓
Abyssinian Catbird *Parophasma galinieri*	ET	R	1, 3, 4, 9, 12, 26, 28, 29, 30, 49	
Tits PARIDAE				
Northern Grey Tit *Parus thruppi*		R	31, 36, 40	
White-backed Black Tit *Parus leuconotus*	ET & ER	R	1, 2, 4, 5, 9, 28, 29, 30, 49	
White-winged Black Tit *Parus leucomelas*		R	25	
White-shouldered Black Tit *Parus guineensis*		R	46	
Penduline-tits REMIZIDAE				
Mouse-coloured Penduline-tit *Anthoscopus musculus*		R	23, 40	
Treecreepers CERTHIIDAE				
Spotted Creeper *Salpornis spilonotus*		R	5, 26, 27, 42	
Sunbirds NECTARINIIDAE				
Eastern Violet-backed Sunbird *Anthreptes orientalis*		R	37, 38, 40	
Olive Sunbird *Cyanomitra olivacea*		R	30, 40	
Scarlet-chested Sunbird *Chalcomitra senegalensis*		R	26, 40	
Hunter's Sunbird *Chalcomitra hunteri*		R	19, 38, 40	
Tacazze Sunbird *Nectarinia tacazze*		R	1, 26, 29, 50	
Malachite Sunbird *Nectarinia famosa*		R	28, 29	
Collared Sunbird *Hedydipna collaris*		R	38	
Pygmy Sunbird *Hedydipna platura*		R & M	47	
Nile Valley Sunbird *Hedydipna metallica*		R	14, 15, 16, 17	
Olive-bellied Sunbird *Cinnyris chloropygius*		S & M		
Beautiful Sunbird *Cinnyris pulchellus*		R	26, 40	
Marico Sunbird *Cinnyris mariquensis*		R	40	
Black-bellied Sunbird *Cinnyris nectarinioides*		R	38, 40	
Purple-banded Sunbird *Cinnyris bifasciatus*		V & M		
Shining Sunbird *Cinnyris habessinicus*		R	17, 19, 31, 36, 37, 40	
Variable Sunbird *Cinnyris venustus*		R	40	
Copper Sunbird *Cinnyris cupreus*		R	48	
White-eyes ZOSTEROPIDAE				
Yellow White-eye *Zosterops senegalensis*		R	48	
Abyssinian White-eye *Zosterops abyssinicus*		R	40	
Montane White-eye *Zosterops poliogastrus*		R	1, 4, 9, 26, 40	
Shrikes LANIIDAE				
Common Fiscal *Lanius collaris*		R		
Taita Fiscal *Lanius dorsalis*		R	35, 41, 43	
Somali Fiscal *Lanius somalicus*		R	15, 16, 19, 37, 41	
Masked Shrike *Lanius nubicus*		PM	15	
Grey-backed Fiscal *Lanius excubitoroides*		R	24	
Lesser Grey Shrike *Lanius minor*		PM		
Southern Grey Shrike *Lanius meridionalis*		R & PM	15	
Isabelline Shrike *Lanius isabellinus*		PM	27	
Red-backed Shrike *Lanius collurio*		PM		
Woodchat Shrike *Lanius senator*		PM		
Northern White-crowned Shrike *Eurocephalus rueppelli*		R	40	
Bush-shrikes MALACONOTIDAE				
Grey-headed Bush-shrike *Malacanotus blanchoti*		R	35, 40	

Species	Endemism	Status	Site numbers	✓
Sulphur-breasted Bush-shrike *Telophorus sulfureopectus*		R		
Rosy-patched Bush-shrike *Rhodophoneus cruentus*		R	15, 19, 40	
Marsh Tchagra *Tchagra minuta*		R		
Three-streaked Tchagra *Tchagra jamesi*		R	36, 40	
Black-crowned Tchagra *Tchagra senegalus*		R		
Northern Puffback *Dryoscopus gambensis*		R		
Pringle's Puffback *Dryoscopus pringlii*		R	36, 38, 40	
Slate-coloured Boubou *Laniarius funebris*		R	15, 35, 40	
Red-naped Bush-shrike *Laniarius ruficeps*		R	36, 38, 40	
Ethiopian Boubou *Laniarius aethiopicus*		R		
Black-headed Gonolek *Laniarius erythrogaster*		R & M	47	
Brubru *Nilaus afer*		R		
Helmetshrikes PRIONOPIDAE				
White-crested Helmetshrike *Prionops plumatus*		R	15, 23, 39, 40	
Orioles ORIOLIDAE				
Black-headed Oriole *Oriolus larvatus*		R	40	
Abyssinian Oriole *Oriolus monacha*	ER & ER	R	2, 4, 9, 24, 26, 30, 34, 39, 42, 48	
African Golden Oriole *Oriolus auratus*		AM		
Eurasian Golden Oriole *Oriolus oriolus*		PM	15	
Drongos DICRURIDAE				
Common Drongo *Dicrurus adsimilis*		R		
Crows CORVIDAE				
Cape Rook *Corvus capensis*		R	28, 8	
Brown-necked Raven *Corvus ruficollis*		S & M		
Dwarf Raven *Corvus edithae*		R	19, 35, 36, 38, 40, 41	
Pied Crow *Corvus albus*		R		
Fan-tailed Raven *Corvus rhipidurus*		R	15, 23, 40	
Thick-billed Raven *Corvus crassirostris*	[ET & ER]	R	1, 26, 27	
Piapiac *Ptilostomus afer*		S & M		
Red-billed Chough *Pyrrhocorax pyrrhocorax*		R	28, 29, 49	
Ethiopian (Stresemann's) Bush-crow *Zavattariornis stresemanni*	ER	R	39, 40, 41	
Starlings STURNIDAE				
Stuhlmann's Starling *Poeoptera stuhlmanni*		R		
Red-winged Starling *Onychognathus morio*		R	40, 48	
Somali Starling *Onychognathus blythii*		S & R?	12, 28, 29, 49	
Bristle-crowned Starling *Onychognathus salvadorii*		R	15, 16, 19, 31, 41	
White-billed Starling *Onychognathus albirostris*	ET & ER	R	6, 9, 10, 11, 12, 33, 49, 50	
Slender-billed Starling *Onychognathus tenuirostris*		R	9, 12, 26, 27, 28, 29, 30, 48	
Greater Blue-eared Starling *Lamprotornis chalybaeus*		R		
Lesser Blue-eared Starling *Lamprotornis chloropterus*		R	47	
Splendid Starling *Lamprotornis splendidus*		R		
Rüppell's Starling *Lamprotornis purpuroptera*		R	15, 23, 40	
Golden-breasted Starling *Lamprotornis regius*		R	17, 30, 31, 33, 38, 40, 46	
Shelley's Starling *Lamprotornis shelleyi*		R	35	
Superb Starling *Lamprotornis superbus*		R		

Species	Endemism	Status	Site numbers	✓
Chestnut-bellied Starling *Lamprotornis pulcher*		R & M		
Fischer's Starling *Spreo fischeri*		R & M	31, 37	
White-crowned Starling *Spreo albicapillus*		R	30, 35, 36, 37, 40	
Magpie Starling *Speculipastor bicolor*		R	32, 37, 38, 41	
Sharpe's Starling *Pholia sharpii*		R	4, 26, 30, 34	
Violet-backed Starling *Cinnyricinclus leucogaster*		R & AM		
Wattled Starling *Creatophora cinerea*		R	35	
Common Starling *Sturnus vulgaris*		V & PM		
Rosy Starling *Pastor roseus*		V & PM		
Yellow-billed Oxpecker *Buphagus africanus*		S & M		
Red-billed Oxpecker *Buphagus erythrorhynchus*		R	28	
Sparrows and petronias PASSERIDAE				
Northern Grey-headed Sparrow *Passer griseus*		R		
Swainson's Sparrow *Passer swainsonii*		R		
Parrot-billed Sparrow *Passer gongonensis*		R	32, 37	
Shelley's Rufous Sparrow *Passer shelleyi*		R	35, 40, 41	
Somali Sparrow *Passer castanopterus*		R	32	
Chestnut Sparrow *Passer eminibey*		R	21, 40, 41	
Sudan Golden Sparrow *Passer luteus*		R & M		
Bush Petronia *Petronia dentata*		R	7, 10, 48	
Yellow-spotted Petronia *Petronia pyrgita*		R		
Pale Rockfinch *Carpospiza brachydactyla*		PM	17, 18	
Weavers PLOCEIDAE				
White-billed Buffalo-weaver *Bubalornis albirostris*		R & M		
Red-billed Buffalo-weaver *Bubalornis niger*		R	40	
White-headed Buffalo-weaver *Dinemellia dinemelli*		R	15, 40	
White-browed Sparrow-weaver *Plocepasser mahali*		R		
Chestnut-crowned Sparrow-weaver *Plocepasser superciliosus*		R	13, 47, 48	
Donaldson Smith's Sparrow-weaver *Plocepasser donaldsoni*		R & M	32, 46	
Speckle-fronted Weaver *Sporopipes frontalis*		R	10	
Grey-capped Social Weaver *Pseudonigrita arnaudi*		R	35, 40	
Black-capped Social Weaver *Pseudonigrita cabanisi*		R	38, 39, 40	
Red-headed Weaver *Anaplectes rubriceps*		R		
Baglafecht Weaver *Ploceus baglafecht*		R	1	
Little Weaver *Ploceus luteolus*		R	23, 24, 27, 46	
Black-necked Weaver *Ploceus nigricollis*		R & M		
Spectacled Weaver *Ploceus ocularis*		R		
Golden Palm Weaver *Ploceus bojeri*		R & M		
Northern Masked Weaver *Ploceus taeniopterus*		R	43	
Lesser Masked Weaver *Ploceus intermedius*		R		
Vitelline Masked Weaver *Ploceus vitellinus*		R	22	
Rüppell's Weaver *Ploceus galbula*		R	13, 15, 20, 23, 24	
Speke's Weaver *Ploceus spekei*		R	36, 40	
Village Weaver *Ploceus cucullatus*		R		
Juba Weaver *Ploceus dichrocephalus*	[HoA]	R	37, 38	
Yellow-backed Weaver *Ploceus melanocephalus*		S & M	38	

Species	Endemism	Status	Site numbers	✓
Chestnut Weaver *Ploceus rubiginosus*		R	17, 23, 38, 40	
Compact Weaver *Ploceus superciliosus*		S		
Grosbeak Weaver *Amblyospiza albifrons*		R	27	
Cardinal Quelea *Quelea cardinalis*		S & AM		
Red-headed Quelea *Quelea erythrops*		S		
Red-billed Quelea *Quelea quelea*		R		
Northern Red Bishop *Euplectes franciscanus*		R		
Black-winged Red Bishop *Euplectes hordeaceus*		R	10, 48	
Black Bishop *Euplectes gierowii*		R	46	
Yellow-crowned Bishop *Euplectes afer*		R	8, 48	
Yellow Bishop *Euplectes capensis*		R	8, 28	
White-winged Widowbird *Euplectes albonotatus*		R	46	
Yellow-mantled Widowbird *Euplectes macrourus*		R	27, 48	
Red-collared Widowbird *Euplectes ardens*		R	10, 28, 34	
Fan-tailed Widowbird *Euplectes axillaris*		R	8, 28, 48	
Waxbills ESTRILDIDAE				
Green-backed Twinspot *Mandingoa nitidula*		R	24, 26, 30, 43	
Abyssinian Crimsonwing *Cryptospiza salvadorii*		R	4, 30	
Yellow-bellied Waxbill *Estrilda quartinia*		R	9, 26, 28, 30, 40	
Abyssinian Waxbill *Estrilda (paludicola) ochrogaster*		R	7, 27, 47	
Crimson-rumped Waxbill *Estrilda rhodopyga*		R	10, 23	
Black-rumped Waxbill *Estrilda troglodytes*		R & M	47	
Common Waxbill *Estrilda astrild*		R		
Black-cheeked Waxbill *Estrilda charmosyna*		R	40	
Red-cheeked Cordon-bleu *Uraeginthus bengalus*		R		
Blue-capped Cordon-bleu *Uraeginthus cyanocephalus*		S & M		
Purple Grenadier *Uraeginthus ianthinogaster*		R	31, 40	
Red-billed Pytilia *Pytilia lineata*	[ET]	R	7, 10, 13, 46, 47, 48	
Green-winged Pytilia *Pytilia melba*		R	19	
Orange-winged Pytilia *Pytilia afra*		S		
Red-billed Firefinch *Lagonosticta senegala*		R	10	
Bar-breasted Firefinch *Lagonosticta rufopicta*		R	7, 47	
Black-faced Firefinch *Lagonosticta larvata*		R	7, 10, 47	
African Firefinch *Lagonosticta rubricata*		R	24, 26	
Jameson's Firefinch *Lagonosticta rhodopareia*		R		
Cut-throat *Amadina fasciata*		R	40	
Black-faced Quailfinch *Ortygospiza atricollis*		S & M		
African Quailfinch *Ortygospiza fuscocrissa*		R	8, 44	
Zebra Waxbill *Amandava subflava*		R		
Grey-headed Silverbill *Lonchura griseicapilla*		R & M		
Bronze Mannikin *Lonchura cucullata*		R		
Black-and-white Mannikin *Lonchura bicolor*		R	30	
Magpie Mannikin *Lonchura fringilloides*		S & M		
African Silverbill *Lonchura cantans*		R	10	
Whydahs and indigobirds VIDUIDAE				
Cuckoo Finch *Anomalospiza imberbis*		R?		

Species	Endemism	Status	Site numbers	✓
Pin-tailed Whydah *Vidua macroura*		R		
Sahel Paradise Whydah *Vidua orientalis*		S & M		
Exclamatory Paradise Whydah *Vidua interjecta*		S	7, 47	
Eastern Paradise Whydah *Vidua paradisaea*		R	15, 46	
Steel-blue Whydah *Vidua hypocherina*		R	15, 38, 46	
Straw-tailed Whydah *Vidua fischeri*		R	40	
Village Indigobird *Vidua chalybeata*		R	10	
Wilson's Indigobird *Vidua wilsoni*		S & M	47	
Jambandu Indigobird *Vidua raricola*		S?		
Barka Indigobird *Vidua larvaticola*		S & M	47	
Canaries and seedeaters FRINGILLIDAE				
African Citril *Serinus citrinelloides*		R	10, 20, 26, 30, 34, 40	
Southern Citril *Serinus hypostictus*		V?		
White-rumped Seedeater *Serinus leucopygius*		R		
Reichenow's Seedeater *Serinus reichenowi*		R	13, 24, 31, 35, 36	
White-throated Seedeater *Serinus xanthopygius*	ET & ER	R	7, 10, 48, 50	
Yellow-fronted Canary *Serinus mozambicus*		R	7	
White-bellied Canary *Serinus dorsostriatus*		R	19, 40	
Yellow-throated Seedeater *Serinus flavigula*	ET	R	13, 16, 50	
Salvadori's Seedeater *Serinus xantholaemus*	ET	R	19, 30, 31, 35, 36	
Northern Grosbeak-canary *Serinus donaldsoni*	[HoA]	R	36, 38, 40, 45	
Streaky Seedeater *Serinus striolatus*		R	1, 12, 50	
Stripe-breasted Seedeater *Serinus reichardi*		R	7	
Brown-rumped Seedeater *Serinus tristriatus*	ET & ER	R	1, 12, 50	
Yellow-crowned Canary *Serinus canicollis*		R	28	
Black-headed Siskin *Serinus nigriceps*	ET	R	3, 8, 10, 11, 12, 28, 29, 49	
Ankober Serin *Carduelis ankoberensis*	ET	R	10, 11, 12, 49	
Buntings EMBERIZIDAE				
Golden-breasted Bunting *Emberiza flaviventris*		R & M		
Somali Bunting *Emberiza poliopleura*		R	31, 40	
Brown-rumped Bunting *Emberiza affinis*		R	47	
Cinnamon-breasted Bunting *Emberiza tahapisi*		R	10, 16	
Striolated Bunting *Emberiza striolata*		R	16	
Cinereous Bunting *Emberiza cineracea*		S & PM		
Ortolan Bunting *Emberiza hortulana*		PM	3, 8	
Cretzschmar's Bunting *Emberiza caesia*		U		

INDEX OF SITES AND LOCALITIES

Entries in **bold** refer to the page numbers of principal sites.